NATIONS OF THE MODERN WORLD

ARGENTINA	H. S. Ferns *Professor of Political Science, University of Birmingham*
AUSTRALIA	O. H. K. Spate *Director, Research School of Pacific Studies, Australian National University, Canberra*
AUSTRIA	Karl R. Stadler *Professor of Modern and Contemporary History, University of Linz*
BURMA	F. S. V. Donnison, C.B.E. *Formerly Chief Secretary to the Government of Burma Historian, Cabinet Office, Historical Section 1949–66*
CYPRUS	H. D. Purcell *Professor of English, University of Libya, Benghazi*
DENMARK	W. Glyn Jones *Professor of Scandinavian Studies, University of Newcastle-upon-Tyne*
EL SALVADOR	Alastair White *Lecturer in Sociology, University of Stirling*
EAST GERMANY	David Childs *Senior Lecturer in Politics, University of Nottingham*
WEST GERMANY	Michael Balfour, C.B.E. *Professor of European History, University of East Anglia*

MODERN GREECE	John Campbell *Fellow of St Antony's College, Oxford*
	Philip Sherrard *Lecturer in the History of the Orthodox Church, King's College, London*
HUNGARY	Paul Ignotus *Formerly Hungarian Press Counsellor, London, 1947–49, and Member, Presidential Board, Hungarian Writers' Association*
MODERN INDIA	Sir Percival Griffiths *President India, Pakistan and Burma Association*
MEXICO	Peter Calvert *Senior Lecturer in Politics, University of Southampton*
NORWAY	Ronald G. Popperwell *Fellow of Clare Hall, and Lecturer in Norwegian, Cambridge*
PAKISTAN	Ian Stephens *Formerly Editor of* The Statesman, *Calcutta and Delhi, 1942–51* *Fellow, King's College, Cambridge, 1952–58*
PERU	Sir Robert Marett *H.M. Ambassador in Lima, 1963–67*
THE PHILIPPINES	Keith Lightfoot *Naval, Military, and Air Attaché, British Embassy, Manila, 1964–67*
POLAND	Václav L. Beneš *Late Professor of Political Science, Indiana University*
	Norman J. G. Pounds *Professor of History and Geography, Indiana University*
SOUTH AFRICA	John Cope *Formerly Editor-in-Chief of* The Forum *and South Africa Correspondent of* The Guardian

THE SOVIET UNION	Elisabeth Koutaissoff *Formerly Professor of Russian, Victoria University, Wellington*
SPAIN	George Hills *Formerly Correspondent and Spanish Programme Organizer, British Broadcasting Corporation*
SWEDEN	Irene Scobbie *Senior Lecturer in Swedish, University of Aberdeen*
SYRIA	Tabitha Petran
MODERN TURKEY	Geoffrey Lewis *Senior Lecturer in Islamic Studies, Oxford*
YUGOSLAVIA	Stevan K. Pavlowitch *Lecturer in Balkan History, University of Southampton*

NATIONS OF THE MODERN WORLD

MODERN TURKEY

MODERN TURKEY

By GEOFFREY LEWIS

PRAEGER PUBLISHERS
NEW YORK · WASHINGTON

Published in the United States of America in 1974
by Praeger Publishers, Inc.
111 Fourth Avenue, New York, N.Y. 10003

Library of Congress Cataloging in Publication Data

Lewis, Geoffrey L.
Modern Turkey

(Nations of the modern world)
First-3d ed. published under title: Turkey.
Bibliography: p.
1. Turkey—History. I. Title. II. Series.
DR441.L45 1974 956.1 73-15170
ISBN 0-275-33400-7

Printed in Great Britain

FOR TUSSA

Preface to Fourth Edition

ALTHOUGH SOME SENTENCES, paragraphs, and even pages of earlier editions have been incorporated in the present work, it is virtually a new book. Every chapter has been recast, new material has been added throughout, and the narrative has been brought down to January 1974.

I ought perhaps to apologize to the majority of my readers for the fact that the book now begins with a cautionary word to the effect that Turks are not Arabs. Years of lecturing and writing about Turkey had made me suspect that not everyone was aware of the difference. My suspicion was confirmed when I wrote an article for one of the most revered of British weeklies, in which I drew a comparison between 'Turkey and the Arab countries'. Some watchful sub-editor, assuming that my pen had slipped, amended what I had written to 'Turkey and the other Arab countries'.

As in previous editions, the Turkish alphabet has been used for Turkish words and names, except for those with accepted English forms, so that 'Istanbul' has been spelled thus and not with a dotted I. 'İzmir' has now taken the place of 'Smyrna' throughout, and 'Edirne' of 'Adrianople'.

Oxford, G.L.L.
January 1974

Preface to Third Edition

THE REVOLUTION of 27 May 1960 made it desirable to carry out a major revision of the book and this has now proved possible. I was an eye witness of the revolution and my experience is similar to that of eye witnesses of earlier revolutions in Turkey: public rejoicing that tyranny was dead, followed by a long period of disillusionment because the millennium had in fact not arrived. But I have learned never to despair of the Turks; they have an almost British talent for muddling-through and a self-respect that will one day lead them to the heights of which Atatürk dreamed.

Oxford 1964 **G.L.L.**

Note to Second Edition

THIS EDITION incorporates a large amount of additional material, as well as corrections. My thanks are due to the many readers who have written to give me the benefit of their special knowledge.

It has not always been possible to make the full alterations in the text, so that extensive footnotes have been added throughout. Chapter 28, 'Economic Policy and Overseas Trade', is supplemented by the first part of the new Chapter 31, entitled 'Postscript 1959'.

Oxford 1959 G.L.L.

Preface to First Edition

WHEN I WAS invited to contribute a book on Turkey to Benn's Nations of the Modern World Series, I was offered the choice of writing a completely new work or revising the volume written by Professor A. J. Toynbee and Mr Kenneth P. Kirkwood for the same series and published in 1926.

To do justice to all that has happened in Turkey during the last quarter-century would naturally have involved a drastic recasting of the earlier work. If all that was required was the addition of new facts and the deletion of those which had diminished in importance through the perspective of the years, revision might have been the obvious choice. But revision would also have involved pruning the observations and conclusions of my predecessors and grafting on the results of my own recent visits to Turkey. A close study of the book persuaded me that one could not hope to bring it up to date without inevitably ruining the flow of its argument and distorting the carefully drawn pattern of history which it presents.

This book then is new, but it is not to be regarded as rendering obsolete its earlier namesake : Toynbee and Kirkwood's *Turkey* will always hold an honoured place on the student's shelves. On one point only do I disagree profoundly with my predecessors, and that is the quotation from Thucydides which introduces their book :

> I shall be satisfied if my narrative is favourably received by readers whose object is exact knowledge of facts which have not only actually occurred, but which are destined approximately to repeat themselves in all human probability.

For it seems unlikely that the events leading up to the foundation of the Turkish Republic and its progress along the hard road to democracy can ever be duplicated between now and Doomsday.

It is one of the oddities of scholarship that, although there is no

2

shortage of narratives written by British travellers in Turkey from the sixteenth century onwards, very few British orientalists have devoted themselves to Turkish studies. Until recent years, therefore, the field was left open to the non-specialists, who did not permit their ignorance of the language, history, and institutions of Turkey to deter them from writing books about it. This they contrived to do by the device of treating the Turks as they would a non-human Act of God, an impersonal entity which any historian was entitled to discuss, as he might discuss the Fire of London or the Krakatoa Eruption. The Turks were not a people, with a cultural tradition of their own; they were a troublesome appendix to European history, they were a thorn in the flesh, they were the Eastern Question.

During the last few years, political and military cupboard-love have helped to increase Western interest in the Turks, and this has resulted in a more realistic appraisal of the achievements and potentialities of this hitherto underrated people. Inevitably, however, the balance has swung the other way. Even a few years ago, a journalist called upon to supply a half-column about Turkey at short notice would have filled it out with a few references to the prevalence of veiled women. In like circumstances today, he will refer to the absence of veiled women. Both pictures are false.

The purpose of the present work is to convey an impression of what has been going on in Turkey of recent years, and what the Turks are like, with enough information about the past to make intelligible the present. The book is in two parts: the first and longer tells the story of the Turkish Republic down to the present day; the second describes some aspects of the modern Turkish scene.

At the end of the Preface will be found a note on the Turkish alphabet, which has been used for Turkish words and names. I have to own to some inconsistency: words familiar to English readers are left in their Anglicized form, and this principle is extended to the familiar spelling 'Istanbul', although most Turks spell it with a dotted I. The reader will notice that I also use the old name 'Constantinople': when dealing with Turkish history, sometimes the one name seems more appropriate, sometimes the other. For fluctuating between 'Smyrna' and 'İzmir' I have no real excuse. 'Smyrna' comes more naturally but the influence of NATO is giving currency to 'İzmir'; the latter will probably prevail and only figs will keep alive the memory of the old name, just as the time-honoured English names for 'Ankara' and 'Thailand' survive in the wool of the one and the twins and cat of the other.

I gratefully acknowledge my indebtedness to the works of Professor Paul Wittek, Dr Tarik Z. Tunaya, and Professor Enver Ziya Karal. I wish also to thank Dr Berna Moran and Bay Nejat Sönmez, for their prompt and helpful replies to my queries.

Oxford 1955 G. L. LEWIS

Note on the Turkish Alphabet

MOST OF THE CONSONANTS have much the same values as in English, and the vowels as in Italian, with these exceptions:

c is pronounced like *j* in 'jam'; *ç* like *ch* in 'church'; *j* is pronounced as it is in French; *ş* is like *sh* in 'shop'; *ğ* is silent in standard Turkish, serving only to lengthen a preceding vowel; *g* is always hard, as in 'get'.

Dotted *i* is like *i* in 'bit', undotted *ı* like *i* in 'cousin' (the corresponding capital letters are respectively *İ* and *I*); *ö* and *ü* are pronounced as in German. A circumflex accent over a vowel denotes a slight *y*-sound between it and a preceding *g*, *k*, or *l*; thus the British pronunciation of 'lurid' would be written *lûrid* in Turkish letters, the American pronunciation *lurid.* After any other consonant, a vowel bearing a circumflex is pronounced long.

Contents

List of Illustrations

(*All are inserted between pages* 128 *and* 129)

Map

Acknowledgements

Acknowledgement for kind permission to reproduce illustrations is made to the following, to whom the copyright of the illustrations belongs:

Camera Press Limited:	4, 19
Freeman Fox and Partners, London:	23
Paul Popper Limited:	1, 12
The Turkish Embassy, London:	5, 6, 7, 8, 9, 10, 11, 14, 15, 16, 17, 20, 21, 22

CHAPTER I

Turks and Ottomans

WHO ARE THE TURKS? The question must be answered because it is sometimes supposed that they are akin to the Arabs. This impression is due to the fact that a thousand years ago the ancestors of the present-day Turks adopted Islam, the religion of the Arabs, at the same time adopting the Arabic alphabet, as being that of the language in which God revealed the Koran to the Prophet Muhammad. But in its basic structure the Turkish language is as different from Arabic as English is from Chinese. It is likewise sometimes supposed that the Turks are related to the Finns and the Hungarians, because of the nineteenth-century 'Ural-Altaic' theory, which claimed that the languages of all three peoples belonged to the same family. But most modern scholars are agreed that this is not so and that the resemblances among these languages, structural similarities aside, arose from mutual borrowings, some in historic times, others in the remote past. The only people for whom a kinship with the Turks may plausibly be claimed are the Mongols; even here some scholars deny the antiquity of the relationship and ascribe it to comparatively recent times when the two peoples campaigned together. Thus the Golden Horde, which in the first half of the thirteenth century swept out of Central Asia to occupy much of eastern Europe and the Volga basin, included both Turks and Mongols in its ranks. So did the armies of Babur (1483–1530), the founder of the empire which ruled Afghanistan and the north of the Indian subcontinent until 1858. That empire was called 'Moghul', that is, Mongol, but Babur called himself a Turk and wrote in Turkish.

The earliest Turks were a pastoral people of the steppes. The Orkhon Inscriptions, found in what is now Outer Mongolia, show that they had a powerful state there in the seventh and eighth centuries of our era. But we know from the Chinese chroniclers that the Turks had menaced and harried the Chinese empire for at least 1,000 years before. It is worth remembering that the purpose of the Great Wall of China, a purpose not consistently achieved, was to keep the Turks out.

After the fall of their empire in 744 they migrated south-westward. Over the next two centuries an ever-growing number of them took service as mercenary soldiers with the rulers of the Arab empire, the Caliphs of Baghdad, and gradually usurped their power. It was during this time that they became Muslims, like the Arabs among whom they were living. In the course of their wanderings across Asia they had come under the influence of several other faiths: Buddhism, Manichaeism, Judaism, and Christianity. All these had at various times and in various places seduced them from their original worship of Sky, Earth, and Water, though it is perhaps not too fanciful to see an ancestral memory lurking in a line of one of the modern Turkish army's favourite marching-songs: 'Let earth, sky, water listen to our voice!' But no creed had for them the lasting appeal of Islam. Its intrinsic suitability as a faith for warriors is obvious: the demands which it makes are few; the rewards which it promises are great, particularly to those who die fighting 'in the Path of Allah'. But what must have had at least as much weight with the Turks who came over to Islam in such numbers during the tenth century was that acceptance of Islam automatically conferred citizen-rights in a vast and flourishing civilization. A passage from the Iranian polymath al-Biruni (970–1050) is worth quoting in this context:

> In his *Geography*, Ptolemy fixed the latitude of places remote from Greece solely by hearsay, for in his day those lands were ruled by mutually warring peoples, so that to travel unmolested was impossible. But now the world has changed: the domain of Islam has spread over all the regions, from the borders of China in the far east to the Spanish frontier in the far west; from Abyssinia in the south and from India, to the Turks and Slavs in the north. In all these broad lands, the various peoples who formerly nurtured feelings of enmity to one another have now united in God-given amity.

The 'amity', however, was at best a participation in a common religion and culture; politically, the world of Islam in the tenth century was rent by faction and beset by external enemies.

The Turks found the situation well suited to the exercise of their warlike gifts. There is an Arabic tradition, put into the mouth of the Prophet, which runs thus: 'God Almighty says, "I have an army which I have named the Turks. Whenever I am wroth with a people, I unleash the Turks upon them"'. Enthusiastically they became Ghazis, warriors for the Faith. In 1055 Baghdad was seized by the Turkish horde known as the Seljuks, after a famous chief who was the ancestor of their ruling family. This produced a somewhat paradoxical position because, as Muslims, they owed allegiance to the Caliph who was head of the Muslim community. They manipulated the Caliphate but did not overthrow it, a situation accepted by the classical Muslim legal authorities, on the principle that the leadership of the community belongs to him who is best able to exercise it. The Seljuks advanced westward into Asia Minor, then part of the territories of the Byzantine emperor, whose seat was at Constantinople. In 1071 the Byzantine armies suffered a heavy defeat in the east, at Malazgirt, where the emperor, Romanus IV Diogenes, fell prisoner to the Seljuk Sultan Alparslan. Within the next few years virtually the whole of Anatolia became a Seljuk province, with its capital at Nicaea (now İznik).

By the thirteenth century, however, the Seljuk dynasty was in decline, but an endless stream of fresher, unspoilt Turkish warriors was coming out of the East, ready to take up the fight against the infidel. The origins of the Ottoman dynasty, which was to replace the Seljuks and create the greatest of all Islamic empires, are partially veiled by the mists of legend; the received view may be summed up as follows.

By 1230 the Seljuk Sultan's power had shrunk to a small area round Konya. A number of little Turkish principalities were casting covetous eyes at his throne, but none was sufficiently stronger than the others to seize it. In that year, among the nomadic Turks who were being driven westward by pressure on the available grazing-lands in the east, a perennial problem lately aggravated by the advance of Genghis Khan and his Mongols, was a leader named Ertuğrul, whose followers consisted of 'four hundred tents', that is, at most 4,000 souls. They happened to be passing a place not far from Erzincan where a battle was in progress between the forces of the Seljuk Sultan Ala'eddin Kaykobad and a numerically superior Mongol army. Ertuğrul came to the aid of the weaker side and won the day for the Sultan. In gratitude, he gave Ertuğrul a grant of land in the north-west of Anatolia, up against the boundaries of the diminished Byzantine empire, the one place where Muslim religious zeal and Turkish martial ardour could find a satisfactory outlet. Ghazis came flocking to join Ertuğrul from all over western Asia and, as the word spread, from further east, all led on by the vision of what was by now a rarity, a rich land unplundered by Mongols. By the time of Ertuğrul's death in 1281 he had increased his territories at the expense of the Byzantines from a conjectural 500 or so square miles to some 2,000.

But Ertuğrul was not an independent sovereign, nor at first was his son Osman, who succeeded him. They were subordinate to the Çobanoğlu of Kastamonu, one of the great houses of Wardens of the Marches who were subject to the Seljuk Sultan in Konya, himself a vassal of the Mongol Ilkhan of Tabriz, who in turn owed allegiance to the Great Khan who ruled from Pekin. The traditional date of Osman's achieving his independence is 1299, from which time it is proper to speak of the Ottoman Sultanate. The name 'Ottoman' is conventionally explained as a Western corruption of the name Osman, itself the Turkish form of the Arabic 'Uthman. It is more likely, however, that what underlies it is a purely Turkish name, Toman, which was piously but incorrectly assimilated to the Arabic name of the third Successor of the Prophet.

In 1326 the Ottomans made their capital at Bursa, south of the Sea of Marmara at the foot of the Mysian Olympus, now Uludağ. In 1365 Sultan Murad I shifted the capital to Adrianople (Edirne), from where, year after year, was mounted a campaign against Christian Europe. It was in 1365 that Ragusa (Dubrovnik) became an Ottoman protectorate. Nish was conquered in 1375, Sofia in 1386, the whole of Bulgaria and Bosnia in 1389. Wallachia became an Ottoman vassal-state in 1391. Albania was conquered in 1396. The eastern frontier had reached the Euphrates three years later. Salonika fell in 1430 and the Serbian capital in 1439. In 1453 the last great Byzantine stronghold, 'East Rome which is Constantinople', fell to Sultan Mehmed II the Conqueror.

A word must be said against the assumption that the capture of Constantinople was the work of barbarians from the steppes of Central Asia whose victory over the Byzantines was a victory of darkness over light. It was no such thing; it marked the end of a struggle between two different lights, one of which had long been fading. The Turks were far from being barbarians before the conquest, as anyone can see who visits that jewel of a city, their old capital at Bursa. Nor were they fresh from Central Asia; they had been near neighbours of the Byzantines for over a century before the conquest, and the cultural exchanges had been considerable. And not only the cultural exchanges; many an Anatolian Greek had a Ghazi for a son-in-law. The second Sultan, Orhan, married a

Byzantine princess and betrothed his son to another, though it is not certain that they ever married. The empire of the Comneni at Trebizond (Trabzon) managed to survive the greater Greek empire by eight years till 1461 because of the matrimonial alliance between the ruling family and Uzun Hasan, the Turkish ruler of Persia and eastern Anatolia. His wife was Theodora, daughter of the Emperor John IV (1429–58). But at least seven princesses of Trebizond before her had married Turks, the first in 1352. The friendship between Andronicus, son of John V Palaeologus, and Savcı, son of Murad I, had been close enough for them to conspire (unsuccessfully) to murder their respective fathers and seize their thrones. The barrier between Greek and paynim in the fourteenth and fifteenth centuries was not so impassable as it may now seem to us.

At their greatest extent, in the seventeenth century, the Ottoman dominions included the Balkan peninsula, the Crimea, Iraq and the western shores of the Persian Gulf, Syria, Palestine, west and south Arabia, Egypt, Libya, Tunisia, and Algeria. This is how Süleyman, known to Europe as 'The Magnificent' (1520–66), introduced himself to lesser kings:

> I who am Sultan of the sultans of East and West, touchstone of emperors, bestower of crowns on the kings of the world, God's shadow on earth, well-starred lord of the domains of the Romans, Persians and Arabs, hero of creation, champion of the earth and time, Padishah and Sultan of the Mediterranean and the Black Sea, of Mecca the extolled and Medina the illustrious and Jerusalem the noble, of the throne of Egypt and the province of Yemen, Aden and San'a, of Baghdad and Basra and Hasa and Ctesiphon, of the lands of Algiers and Azerbayjan, of the steppes of the Kipchaks and the lands of the Tartars, of Kurdistan and Luristan and all Rumelia, Anatolia and Karaman, of Wallachia and Moldavia and Hungary and many kingdoms and lands besides, which I have conquered by my sword; the Sultan Süleyman Khan, son of the Sultan Selim Khan.

Although the details of the acquisition, administration, and eventual loss of these vast territories are not essential to our present purpose, certain features of the Ottoman past need a word or two of description if the Turkish present is to be fully understood. They are: (a) the Caliphate, (b) the Ulema, (c) the Sublime Porte, (d) the *Millet* system, (e) the *Devşirme*, and (f) the Capitulations.

The Caliphate

'Caliph' is the English form of the Arabic *khalīfa*, 'successor', the title assumed by the Prophet's devoted follower Abu Bakr (d. A.D. 634), who succeeded Muhammad as civil and military chief of the new Muslim community. He inherited also the Imamate, the privilege of leading the people in prayer. The prophetic function he did not inherit, for that was personal to Muhammad, 'the Seal of the Prophets', and could not be passed on. Later Islamic theory makes the Caliph the Defender of the Faith, responsible for giving effect to the *Sharī'a*, the sacred law. It was a common European fallacy to regard him as the spiritual head of Islam, which he never was; certainly the possession of the Imamate did not make him so, for that office is not sacerdotal. The truth was better apprehended by John Speed in the seventeenth century, if we may judge from the *Description of the Turkish Empire* on the back of his 1626 map:

> The Ministers of State are (1) Muffti, who interpret their law, and lay open their Alcoran, with the like authority, as the *Pope* among the *Roman-Catholicks* . . .

For practical purposes the Caliphate came to an end in 1258, when the Mongols under Hulagu sacked Baghdad, the seat of the Abbasid dynasty. But for three centuries before that date the Caliphs had been for the most part puppets in the hands of their Turkish generals. In 1261 the Mamluke Sultan of Egypt, Baybars, who was also a Turk, installed a scion of the Abbasid house as Caliph in Cairo, in order to legitimize his own rule by appearing as the protector of the titular head of the Muslim community, the living symbol of the unity of the Faith. The shadow-Caliphs continued to grace parades through the streets of Cairo and to confer diplomas on new Sultans until the Ottoman conquest of Egypt in 1517. From that time on the Ottomans were the only dynasty who could have put up any serious claim to the Caliphate. None of the Sultans, however, made much play with the title (the reader may have noticed that it is not included in the list of Süleyman's designations) until Abdülhamid II. Later we shall see how Mustafa Kemal abolished the Caliphate, putting an end *de jure* to an institution which had been deprived of its power by other Turkish commanders 1,000 years before him.

The Ulema

This anglicized word represents the Turkish pronunciation of the Arabic '*ulamā*', 'sages'. As a technical term, it was applied collectively to the religious functionaries of every grade, who were the custodians, teachers, and interpreters of the sacred law. At the head of the hierarchy there formerly stood the *Kazasker*, the Judge of the Army, but in 1480 Sultan Mehmed II, probably because of jealousy on the part of the Grand Vizier, curtailed the powers of the *Kazasker* by restricting his authority to the European provinces and appointing a second *Kazasker* to be chief of the Ulema in Asia. By the end of the sixteenth century the *Şeyhülislâm*, the chief mufti (jurisconsult) of the empire, had become head of the hierarchy, above the two *Kazaskers.*[1] The power of the office varied according to the character of the incumbent; often the interpretation of a point of law was dictated by a knowledge of the sovereign's requirements, but there is no lack of examples of a courageous stand by a *Şeyhülislâm* against a Sultan desirous of riding roughshod over the sacred law.

The Sublime Porte

The term *Babıâli*, 'High Gate', was originally applied to the house of the Sultan's chief minister, the Grand Vizier (*Sadrazam*), wherever it might be. In 1654 the name was transferred to the official residence which was then assigned to him, adjacent to the Palace. As the administrative work of most departments of state was carried out there, the rather grandiloquent translation 'Sublime Porte' came to be synonymous, for Europeans, with the Ottoman government. In the closing years of the empire the building housed not only the Grand Vizierate but also the Ministries of the Interior and of Foreign Affairs, as well as the offices of the Council of State and some smaller departments.

The Millet System

To nineteenth-century Europe, the Ottoman empire sometimes appeared as the persecutor of Christians, but such repressive action as was taken was aimed at their nationalist aspirations, not at their religious beliefs. The Prophet Muhammad regarded himself as the messenger chosen to bring God's Word to the Arabs, as others before him had brought it to other peoples; by his mission the work of his predecessors was completed and confirmed, not invalidated. Hence the principle that non-Muslim monotheists are not to be molested, so long as they behave themselves and pay their poll-tax.

Like the Arabs before them, the Ottomans generally had the wisdom to let well enough alone. The various religious communities (*millet*) among the subject peoples suffered little interference, with the notable exception of the *devşirme*, being left under the supervision of their religious leaders, who were responsible to the government for their good behaviour, the settling of their disputes, and the collection of their taxes. Arnold Toynbee saw in this a relic of the Ottomans' nomadic origins, a tendency to classify everyone as either shepherds, watch-dogs, or cattle.[2] This view is hard to maintain in face of the fact that the Byzantines practised the same sort of system. Rabbi Benjamin of Tudela, who visited Constantinople about 1170, records that every Jewish community was under the supervision of an *ephor* appointed by the government. Jewish tribunals administered Rabbinic law, and the civil power gave effect to their judgements. The Ottoman conquest extended this state of affairs to the Christians. The Ecumenical Patriarch was recognized as head of the *Millet-i Rum*, the Community of the Greeks, while the Armenians, who had not previously had one supreme religious leader, were declared a *millet* under a Patriarch of their own.

Tolerance was not only a religious duty. As the commerce of the empire was largely in the hands of non-Muslims, who also had a near-monopoly of medical knowledge, the authorities found it expedient not to make their lives a misery. Sometimes, indeed, they would remind them of their subordinate status, but the frequency with which such reminders were issued shows that the regulations were not too rigorously enforced. Here is a typical decree of Murad IV, dated 1631:

> Whereas it is a matter of religious importance that the infidel community should not ride on horseback or wear sable coats or Frankish brocade but should be humble and lowly in their style of dress, and whereas it has come to my august hearing that for a long time this has been neglected and that the infidel and Jewish communities[3] have, with the connivance of the authorities, been going about the streets on horseback and in fine clothes, and that they and their women are more imposingly dressed than the true believers, I hereby order that this practice must cease.

Eminent infidels might be dispensed from the requirements of the sumptuary laws, as shown in this decree issued by Mustafa II in 1695:

> The physician Moshe son of Nesim has petitioned for my imperial decree to confirm the order issued in the reign of my illustrious

uncle Sultan Ahmed, as follows: 'While the petitioner serves the sick among the Muslims of the capital and commits no violation of the sacred law and interferes with no one, certain people have been vexing him, saying "You wear a fur cap and ride on horseback". Let none vex him henceforth in defiance of the sacred law by interfering with the fur hat or his other garments, or by saying "You ride on horseback"'. This order has consequently been written so that action may be taken as stated.

Towards the end of the seventeenth century we find a large number of decrees relating to complaints from the Armenian and Orthodox Churches about Roman Catholic missionary activity: an Armenian priest was sentenced to the galleys for 'corrupting the Armenian community and trying to win them over to the Frankish religion', and a number of people were arrested for 'causing a mischief by altering the text of certain books and printing the altered versions and circulating them among the Armenians'. It is easy to see why the government was opposed to Catholic missionaries: a *millet* with its head out of reach of the Ottoman power was not to be encouraged. There is a modern survival of this attitude in the Republican law whereby the head of each religious community must be a Turkish citizen. Athenagoras I, who was elected archbishop of Constantinople and Ecumenical Patriarch of the Orthodox Church in November 1948, was obliged to renounce his American citizenship before taking office. Dimitrios I, who succeeded him in July 1972, was a Turkish subject by birth. In modern Turkish *millet* means 'nation', but the word has not quite lost its older sense. If you tell a Turk that your *millet* is *İngiliz*, he will assume not only that you have a British passport but also that you are a member of the Church of England.

The Devsirme

The word means 'collecting' and is the term applied to the compulsory recruitment of Christian boys for training and eventual employment in the civil and military service of the empire, a practice which seems to have arisen in the reign of Murad I (1360–89). At irregular intervals of from three to five years levies took place of unmarried males between the ages of eight and twenty, originally from the Christian population of Rumelia, later from other Christian communities, including those of Albania, Greece, Serbia, Croatia, Bosnia, and Hungary. A highly selective code of rules was laid down for the guidance of recruiting officers. The principle was that every recruit should be unspoilt raw material; consequently orphans who had had to fend for themselves were not taken, nor boys who had spent some time in the capital or the two former capitals, Bursa and Edirne. Boys from Salonika and Athens, however, were taken. Jewish boys were exempt because most Jews were engaged in business.

On arrival at Istanbul the boys were formally admitted into Islam: they raised their right hands and recited the Profession of Faith, the Arabic formula meaning 'I testify that there is no god but God; Muhammad is the messenger of God'. They were then circumcised. The good-looking ones who passed the scrutiny of various officers, including a physiognomist, were assigned for training to one or other of the palaces. The tough and manifestly unintellectual might be sent straight to the Bostancı corps, to serve as gardeners and policemen. The remainder were rented out to Turkish farmers for a period of four years or so, to work for them and to learn Turkish. They were then brought back and given military training before being admitted to the 'New Troops', *Yeniçeri*, anglicized as 'Janissary'.

The inhumanity of this systematic kidnapping of children from their parents (although it was forbidden to take an only son) is too obvious to need underlining. Yet there is ample evidence to show that while many who were eligible for the *devşirme* wished that they were not, others, who were ineligible, tried hard to be included among the levies. An exception to the rule that only Christian boys were liable to the *devşirme* was constituted by the Poturs, Muslim Bosniaks descended from certain Christians who had accepted Islam when Mehmed II conquered Bosnia, and had been permitted by him to volunteer for the service of the Imperial palaces. When drafts of Potur boys were on the march to Istanbul, especially rigorous precautions were taken to prevent other Muslim boys from adding themselves to the convoy. Again, Süleyman I is reported to have said, after listing the peoples – Russians, Persians, Gypsies, and Turks – from whom boys were not to be levied,

> If any officer recruits any of these, either for a bribe or at someone's request or because of the intervention of people in high places, and adds them to the number of my loyal slaves, may the curse of God and the hundred and twenty-four thousand prophets be upon him.

For the *devşirme*-boy was starting out on a road at the end of which lay the highest offices of state, promotion to which was by a combination of seniority and merit. The free-born Muslim could aspire to a position of greatness in the religious hierarchy of the Ulema, but if he sought high military or civil rank he would find the scales weighted against him and in favour of the Sultan's Christian-born slaves. Of the six Grand Viziers who held office between 1368 and 1453, four belonged to one Turkish family, the Çandarlı. Sultan Mehmed II seems to have become mistrustful of their great and continuing power, and in 1453 he appointed Mahmud Pasha, who was either a Greek or a Croat. Over the next 200 years, the non-Turkish Grand Viziers outnumbered the Turks by seven to one. It was in the middle of the seventeenth century that public opinion brought about the breakdown of the system and opened the doors of the Imperial service to free-born Muslim Turks, although the *devşirme* continued sporadically till the early eighteenth century.

The Capitulations

The idea of absolute national sovereignty is of even more recent growth than the idea of nationhood. Over fifty years before the Ottoman conquest there was a Turkish community in Constantinople, with its own Muslim judge administering Muslim law. The Byzantine emperors had also granted privileges to the Venetian and Genoese merchants resident in the city, which Mehmed the Conqueror confirmed. For in those days it was not regarded as a derogation of sovereignty to let foreigners be ruled by their own laws. Consular authorities were responsible for the good behaviour of their nationals.

The first capitulations, to use the term in its general modern acceptance, were those granted by Süleyman to the French in 1535, when he concluded that offensive and defensive alliance with François I which scandalized Christendom. The autonomy which the French merchants in Turkey thereby obtained, together with the respect shown them by the Turks as representatives of the Sultan's new ally, soon caused other European powers to forget their distaste and to seek similar concessions for themselves: Austria in 1567, England in 1592.

Under the capitulations, foreigners were not subject to Turkish law; they paid no taxes, their houses and business premises were inviolable, and they could be arrested or deported only by order of their own ambassadors. Disputes involving foreigners were settled by the consular court of the defendant, according to the law of his own land. Non-Muslim Turkish subjects in foreign employ could also be given this privileged status, by a diploma conferred by a consular authority.

In the old days, when Turkey was still a power to be reckoned with, and the foreign communities were small and almost exclusively mercantile, abuse of these great privileges was rare. By the mid-nineteenth century, however, Pera, the European quarter of Istanbul, had become the refuse-pit of Europe. All manner of undesirables were sheltering under the capitulations, confident that their own countrymen would back them against the Turkish authorities any day. The fact that the capitulations had been originally granted by a Turkey at the zenith of her power, as a gesture of goodwill and to encourage trade, was forgotten; they were regarded as an acknowledgement by the Ottoman empire of its own decrepitude, of the foreigner's right to laugh at its laws. In this attitude to the capitulations we have the clearest indication of the depths to which the empire had sunk.

NOTES

[1] See Richard Repp, 'Some observations on the development of the Ottoman learned hierarchy', in Nikki R. Keddie (ed.), *Scholars, Saints, and Sufis* (Berkeley, Calif., 1972).

[2] Arnold J. Toynbee and Kenneth P. Kirkwood, *Turkey* (London: Ernest Benn Limited, 1926), pp. 26–7.

[3] The Christians, being more numerous than the Jews, were the infidels *par excellence*.

CHAPTER 2

The Decline of the Empire and the Beginnings of Modernization

RICHARD KNOLLES, in his *A Generall Historie of the Turkes*, first published in 1603, tells of 'the glorious Empire of the Turkes, the present Terror of the World'. The difference brought about by the passage of a century and a half is strikingly shown by Dr Samuel Johnson's attitude to the book. He thought it 'incomparable' (which it isn't) but chided Knolles for wasting his talents on so dull a theme:

> Nothing could have sunk this author in obscurity, but the remoteness and barbarity of the people whose story he relates. . . . The nation which produced this great historian, has the grief of seeing his genius employed upon a foreign and uninteresting subject; and that writer, who might have secured perpetuity to his name, by a history of his own country, has exposed himself to the danger of oblivion, by recounting enterprizes and revolutions, of which none desire to be informed.[1]

The causes of the decline of the empire are still a topic of learned controversy. Some put the blame on the opening-up of the Americas, which is said to have ruined the Ottoman economy by the introduction of cheap silver. But certainly we must assign a major share of the blame to the complacency induced in the Ottoman rulers by two factors: long years of unchallenged military superiority, and the conviction that God's will, manifested in history, was that the Muslims should continue to be the dominant power in the world. Thus they blinded themselves, until it was too late, to the swift rise of Christian Europe, whose technological advances they dismissed as a lot of infidel monkey-tricks representing no danger to the divinely-guarded domains of the Faith. Some portion of the blame attaches to Süleyman the Magnificent in person, for he sat so securely on his throne that he forgot how that throne had been won; he became an emperor and ceased to be a Ghazi, ceased to take the field at the head of his armies. The empire's doom was sealed the moment that its leaders lost sight of their *raison d'être.* For a time they enjoyed the fruits of their ancestors' conquests and then suddenly they found themselves on the defensive. In 1683 they were forced to abandon their siege of Vienna. Three years later they lost Budapest to the Austrians. Thereafter an almost unbroken succession of defeats revealed to the Sultans a glimmering of the truth, but as yet they saw no further than the superficial fact that somehow they had lost their ancient military supremacy; the only remedy they envisaged consisted in superficial military reforms.

Mustafa III (1757–73) laid all the Turkish misfortunes at the door of the Janissaries, corrupt, pampered, and undisciplined, zealous only in guarding their privileges. He saw no hope of reforming them, but his pessimism did not prevent him from doing his best to check the decline. At his request, the Hungarian baron de Tott, who had entered the Ottoman service as an artillery instructor, founded an Imperial School of Naval Engineering and taught in it himself. Yet nothing better illustrates the Turks' complete lack of understanding of the real sources of Western superiority than the fact that this same Sultan attributed the Prussian victory in the Seven Years' War to efficient staff-work on the part of Frederick the Great's astrologers.

The Russo-Turkish War of 1768–74 did nothing to awaken the Ottoman government to a sense of reality; a year or so after the humiliating Treaty of Küçük Kaynarca which ended the war, the 600-strong artillery unit which de Tott had created and trained was disbanded on grounds of expense. But the French had perceived the serious implications of the Ottoman inability to check the Russian advance, and sent military experts to help reorganize the Turkish army. Their efforts, however, were frustrated and the Grand Vizier Halil Hâmid Pasha, who had welcomed them, was dismissed, as Sultan Abdülhamid I (1773–89) suspected him of plotting against the throne.

Selim III, who became Sultan in 1789, during the ruinous war that had been provoked by Russia's seizing the Crimea, was one of the most enlightened members of the House of Osman. Although it is his military reforms that have attracted most attention, he was not so narrow-minded as his father, Mustafa III, who had regarded the Janissaries as the root of all evil. For Selim was not blind to the anarchy that reigned among the Ulema, the hierarchy whose leaders had the power to veto any measure which they regarded as contravening the sacred law. The *medreses*, their training-schools, were without discipline, and the teaching in them was antiquated. High office could be bought; only in the great cities were learning and ability necessary qualifications for judgeships. There were exceptions, of course, but the majority of the Ulema were, by training and instinct, opposed to change. Even at best, however much the graduates of *medreses* might know of the theoretical bases of Muslim law, they tended to be ignorant of the world about them. In the first year of the new reign, during discussion of a proposed treaty with Prussia, the *Kazasker* of Rumelia, the second in rank in the hierarchy, asked, 'What's this place Prussia they're talking about?' Another of the great men present enlightened him: 'It's what they call Brandabork. It was once an Austrian duchy but it has gradually grown in strength, so that now it's the equal of Austria and Moscow'.

As soon as the Treaty of Jassy gave the Turks a breathing-space, Selim consulted various Ottoman statesmen about means to restore the empire to its former greatness. Some were in favour of reforming the army on Western lines. Others suggested a return to the code of laws promulgated by Süleyman, over 250 years before, which would surely bring back the glories of his reign. The former counsel accorded more with the Sultan's ideas, and experts were invited from England, France, Prussia, and Sweden. A small force of soldiers was raised and not only trained but also dressed in European style. Some of the Ulema, horrified, declared, 'God will begrudge His aid to a Sultan who dresses the Army in frock-coat and trousers and sets Franks at the head of them'.

Selim was not impressed by the disapproval of the Ulema. During the war, he had written on the margin of a memorandum in which he was asked to sanction further payments for the reciting of prayers for victory:

> I should think the prayers are not being read with devotion, or else we haven't hit on the right people for the job, otherwise some result might be visible. Very well, let the payments continue for another six months. What can one expect from prayers said for money?

But he would have been wiser not to underrate the religious opposition.

The new order which he planned embraced the whole administration of the empire. The details of it are now of academic interest only; Selim and his handful of supporters were not strong enough to fight against the entrenched forces of the old order. Incited by the Ulema, the people of Istanbul rose against him in 1806. The new troops were defeated by the Janissaries, and the *Şeyhülislâm* pronounced it lawful to depose him. He could have summoned the loyal troops of the Danube garrison to aid him, but would not risk opening the door to the Russians. It is fitting to praise the memory of Selim, a man whose worst fault was that his courage outran his prudence.

The first reformer who had anything to show for his pains was Mahmud II (1808–39). On his accession he found that there were no bounds to the insolence of the Janissaries, triumphant at having annihilated Selim's supporters. Mahmud bided his time until popular feeling turned against them, the comparatively small army of Egypt having crushed a Greek revolt which the Janissaries had totally failed to quell. He set about raising a new army, but profiting by his cousin Selim's mistake he let it be known that their officers would not be Europeans but Muslims. The Janissaries were not appeased; they revolted, and their barracks were shelled. Those who survived the resulting fire were hunted down and the corps was declared abolished, an event known in Turkish history as 'The Auspicious Incident' (15 June 1826). He then set to work to make the new army an efficient fighting force. He asked Muhammad Ali, ruler of Egypt and the Sultan's nominal vassal, for help, which was refused, since Muhammad Ali had his own plans for the future of the empire, plans in which a strong Ottoman army played no part. The Sultan would not ask help from France or England, who had supported the Greeks in their revolt. Prussia alone sent military instructors, thus laying the foundations of the friendship which has since been fostered by every German government down to our own day.

The Prussian instructors, however, could not work miracles; the Tsar took advantage of Turkey's lack of a seasoned army to continue the century-old Russian advance into the Balkans. The deliverance of Greece from Ottoman hands, through the armed intervention of England, France, and Russia, and her emergence as an independent kingdom in 1830, gave new hope to Turkey's other European subjects. Revolts broke out in Serbia and Bulgaria. The decrepitude of the empire being once again laid bare, Muhammad Ali cast off all pretence of allegiance to the Sultan and invaded Syria. His son Ibrahim led an army into Anatolia, which was turned back from its rapid advance on Istanbul only by the landing of a powerful Russian force on the Asian shores of the Bosphorus. The price was paid in the Treaty of Hünkâr İskelesi (8 July 1833), which gave Russian shipping the freedom of the Bosphorus and Dardanelles, while denying the same right to other powers except with Russian approval.

Other manifestations of Mahmud's zeal for reform were more successful. A school of medicine and a military academy were opened, as well as a number of secondary schools. Primary education was made compulsory. One hundred and fifty students were sent to Europe. A postal service was established, the foundations of a nationwide police system were laid, and pamphlets were distributed to teach the people the essential facts about cholera. The ancient practice of replenishing the Treasury by confiscating the property of officials and private citizens was abolished. It was ordained that the various types of male headdress were to be replaced by the fez, which took its name from the city in Morocco where it was invented, probably in the sixteenth century. It was introduced into Turkey in 1827, by the Grand Admiral Koca Husrev Mehmed Pasha, when he returned with the fleet from exercises in the Mediterranean. He had bought a quantity of fezzes in Tunis and he paraded his men in them before the Sultan, who, much taken with their smartness, decided to make everyone wear fezzes.

This apparently trifling innovation, which seems to have been enforced only in the case of sailors, soldiers, and officials, is of great importance: it was a manifestation of the Sultan's desire that his subjects of various faiths should be no longer distinguishable by their attire. The traditional Muslim tolerance, based, as we have indicated, on contempt for the benighted adherents of other creeds, was to be replaced by a true equality of religions. Mahmud is reported to have said, 'Henceforth I recognize Muslims only in the mosque, Christians only in the church, Jews only in the synagogue. Outside these places of worship I desire every individual to enjoy the same political rights and my fatherly protection'.

NOTE

1 'A criticism of the English historians', in *The Rambler*, III, 122 (Saturday, 18 May 1751).

CHAPTER 3

The *Tanzimat*

TANZİMAT, 'REGULATION', is the name given to the programme of reform that was inaugurated in November 1839. Its architect, Mustafa Reşid Pasha, was a well-read and farsighted statesman who had served as Ottoman ambassador in Paris[1] and was anxious to save his country from the doom that had overtaken the French monarchy. The Imperial Rescript proclaimed by Reşid in the Gülhane Court, with great pomp and ceremony, was a charter whereby the Sultan abdicated a portion of his authority in favour of the Council of Judicial Ordinances, which was henceforth to have the power to make laws, subject to the Sultan's approval. No one was to be punished without a public trial, and Muslims and non-Muslims were to receive equal treatment before the law. Legislation was to be introduced to end 'the traffic in favours and appointments, which is one of the chief causes of the decay of the Empire'.

Some historians have declared that the purpose of the *Tanzimat* was to deprive the Christian powers of an excuse to take the Sultan's Christian subjects under their protection. This view represents only a part of the truth; Reşid and his coadjutors were intelligent enough to see that if nothing were done to remove the grievances of the subject peoples, the empire might crumble into ruin even without foreign interference. But certainly Reşid was at great pains to sound foreign diplomats about the probable effect of the Charter on European public opinion, and rather envied Muhammad Ali the approbation with which liberal thinkers in Europe had hailed his Egyptian reforms.

Yet the *Tanzimat* was still-born; it 'stopped at the doorstep of the Sublime Porte'. Good intentions were not enough; however much European liberals might applaud this manifestation of a genuine desire for reform on the part of the Ottoman statesmen, public opinion in Turkey was hostile. For as yet the only educated class of any size among Muslim Turks was that of the Ulema, who in the main saw no reason for altering the *status quo*, although they deemed it prudent to pay lip-service to the ideals of the *Tanzimat*, being indeed singled out in the decree for a special threat of punishment in the event of their obstructing the reforms. To show the sort of thing the reformers had to contend with, here is the text of a memorandum presented to Sultan Abdülmecid in 1853 when the talks were going on with England and France which led to their siding with Turkey in the Crimean War:

> It is not permissible to make alliances with nations not of our religion. The sole source of a solution to such political problems is the sacred law. All truth is to be found in the Holy Koran. Worldly affairs must be resolved in the light of rulings to be drawn from the Holy Koran.

Despite the lack of a single word about education in the text of the Gülhane Decree, the years following its promulgation saw a remarkable advance in liberal thought in Turkey. Schools were built, by the generosity of enlightened individuals, although the state gave no financial help. An ever-growing number of scholars and officials visited Europe, and returned full of enthusiasm for the institutions they had seen there. True, this enthusiasm often betrayed them into a mere imitating of outward forms: factories were planned and even built with no source of skilled men to operate them; there was talk of founding a university, although there were no graduate teachers available.

The Treaty of Paris (30 March 1856), which ended the Crimean War, recorded an undertaking by Sultan Abdülmecid (1839–61) to ameliorate the condition of his subjects 'without distinction of creed or race'; the European powers, for their part, repudiated 'the right to interfere either collectively or separately' in the internal affairs of Turkey. Already on 18 February the Sultan had issued a Reform Decree confirming and extending the provisions of the Gülhane Decree. Among the reforms it embodied was 'the abolition and removal for ever from official documents of all discriminatory terms and expressions' indicating that any one community was held to be inferior to any other in respect of religion, language, or race. The use of such terms by officials or private individuals would be forbidden by law. The emphasis on religious equality did not please everyone; some Muslims deplored it, for obvious reasons, while some Christians resented being placed on the same footing as Jews. The higher clergy were not happy with the provision that they were to be given fixed stipends and were to stop levying 'offerings and contributions' from their flocks. But what above all was wrong with the 1856 Decree was that Muslims and non-Muslims alike believed it had been issued under pressure from the European powers. Probably its most important effect was to create a feeling among the Sultan's Christian subjects that their salvation lay with those powers and not with the Ottoman government.

During the reign of Abdülaziz (1861–76), whose unwisdom and extravagance brought his country to the verge of disaster, the beginnings were seen of the movement to which European writers have given the name 'Young Turks'. In June 1865 the Society of New Ottomans was formed secretly in Istanbul. Its members numbered only 245, but most of them were men of influence. The prime mover was the great writer and patriot Namık Kemal. Two princes, the future Sultans Murad V and Abdülhamid II, were among those who followed its discussions. The main aim of the Society, whose members were pledged to strive, *inter alia*, for the betterment of the Christian subjects of the empire, was to transform the government into a constitutional monarchy.

Although the Society was disbanded in 1872, its former members continued to work for a constitutional regime. They saw the reward of their efforts, short-lived though it proved to be, in 1876, when Abdülaziz was deposed. His policies had united almost the whole people in opposition: the advocates of reform who saw him as an incorrigible despot, the armed forces who were weary of the endless chain of defeats his reign had brought, even the Istanbul mob and many of the Ulema, who resented the conciliatory attitude adopted towards Russia by his favourite, the Grand Vizier, Mahmud Nedim Pasha, contemptuously nicknamed 'Nedimof'. His nephew, Murad V, reigned in his stead for only three months before his mind broke down; deposed, he was succeeded by his younger brother, Abdülhamid II.

NOTE

[1] He also served briefly in London. On 11 October 1972, Zeki Kuneralp, the Turkish ambassador, unveiled a plaque at 1, Bryanston Square, which had been the Pasha's residence in 1839.

CHAPTER 4

The Reign of Abdülhamid

ABDÜLHAMID WAS BROUGHT to the throne on 31 August 1876 by the great liberal statesman Midhat Pasha on the express condition that he would set up a constitutional administration. Shortly after his accession he appointed Midhat as his Grand Vizier, and on 10 December promulgated a constitution which had been drafted by Midhat, Namık Kemal, and Ziya Pasha, but under the eye of Abdülhamid, who saw to it that while the rights of his subjects were being safeguarded, his own rights suffered no diminution. The resulting document was described by a contemporary Turkish historian as establishing a 'constitutional despotism'. In particular, the Sultan had insisted on an addition to Article 113, which laid down the conditions under which martial law might be proclaimed. The addition read:

> It is exclusively within the competence of H.M. the Sultan in person to expel and to exile from the Guarded Domains of the Empire any persons whom reliable investigation by the police shows to be impairing the security of the Government.

Once safely enthroned, Abdülhamid invoked this provision to exile his Grand Vizier, on 5 February 1877. To quieten the well-justified fears of his subjects, the Sultan went ahead with the arrangements for the creation of a Parliament, consisting of an Upper House and a Chamber of Deputies, which he opened on 19 March.

On 24 April Russia declared war, the ostensible provocation being the atrocities committed by the Turks in crushing the Bulgarian revolt of 1876. The Sultan chose to blame this fresh disaster and the ensuing defeats on Parliament, which he closed on 13 February 1878. The constitution having thus served his purpose, he chose to ignore Article 73:

> In the event of the dissolution of the Chamber by Imperial decree, general elections must begin in time for the Chamber to

reassemble at the latest within six months of the date of dissolution.

The thirty years of absolutism which followed were without precedent in Ottoman history.

The word 'sultan' has, for Western ears, a ring of absolute and arbitrary power about it. It is nevertheless a fact that most of the Ottoman Sultans were not tyrants. True, the Sultan had the last word, but his decisions were usually reached after discussions with his ministers, his prospective ministers, and even his former ministers (though to avoid any appearance of whitewashing it should be added that at least twenty-five of the 215 Grand Viziers who served between the beginning and the end of the empire met their death at the executioner's hand). Moreover, in many later reigns it was possible to influence the Sultan's decisions by gaining the ear of his mother. But Abdülhamid made his own decisions. The deposition and subsequent death of his uncle, Sultan Abdülaziz (opinion is still divided about whether he committed suicide or was murdered; the weight of evidence is in favour of the former), had preyed on his naturally suspicious mind, arousing in it a pathological anxiety for the safety of his person and his throne. He organized a network of spies and informers who were paid to denounce those who might be conspiring against him. Kipling's *The Old Issue* might have been written with Abdülhamid in mind:

He shall break his Judges if they cross his word;
He shall rule above the Law calling on the Lord.
He shall peep and mutter; and the night shall bring
Watchers 'neath our window, lest we mock the King –
Hate and all division; hosts of hurrying spies,
Money poured in secret, carrion breeding flies.

In the last few years several books seeking to rehabilitate him have appeared in Turkey, an expression of some people's feeling that in comparison with the troubled present the old days were the good old days. There is this much truth in their thesis, that in his concern for his country and his people he was a better man than some of the Union and Progress leaders who usurped his power. Outside the political sphere he seems to have had no objection to any reform which did not threaten his own position; thus in his day secondary schools were opened in most towns of the empire, and the number of teachers' training colleges was increased from one (founded in 1848) to thirty-one. Significant is the wording of a memorandum presented to him in February 1895 by his Grand Vizier, Küçük Said Pasha, in support of a proposal to found a university: 'such an institution would greatly help the development of the State without endangering the security of the Throne'.[1] A rather endearing sidelight on his respect for education was given, after his deposition, by his former Chief Secretary:

> Abdülhamid used to confess to me the deficiencies in his education, which he put down to the fact that his father had had fifty children. 'Ah!' he would say, 'If I hadn't been surrounded by all those kids and had been given a proper education, I'd show you what reading and writing are!' Sometimes he would dictate a few sentences to me and get me to write them out legibly on a sheet of paper which he would put away in a pigeonhole of his desk. When he had to write a letter he would copy them.

But all educational institutions came under an increasingly rigorous control, particularly in the latter half of his reign, when his suspicions and anxieties had advanced to the point of mania. The publication of medical works dealing with insanity was forbidden, as was the presentation of plays concerning the murder of kings, such as *Hamlet* and *Macbeth*. School curricula were filled with Muslim jurisprudence, scholastic theology, Koran interpretation, and ethics, for Abdülhamid firmly believed that good Muslims do not make dangerous revolutionaries.

It is less clear whether he was sincere in his insistence that the decline of the empire was due to the decay of religious feeling, but certainly this view was general among Muslims in his day. The nineteenth century had already witnessed the eclipse of many Islamic dynasties, brought about by the steady advance of the Christian powers into India, Central Asia, Egypt, and North Africa. Apart from the Ottoman empire, Persia and Morocco were almost the last surviving strongholds of Islamic political power, and the position of these three states was far from secure. Among the educated Muslims who saw and bitterly resented this fact, the conviction was spreading that in order to restore the greatness of the Muslim world it was necessary for Muslims to unite and to turn back to their Faith, while at the same time taking all that the West had to teach them in the way of science and techniques. Abdülhamid was lavish in his subsidies to those who preached this thesis, for if

Islam were ever to unite it could unite only round the person of the Caliph. The title to which his ancestors had paid so little regard suddenly became a potent weapon in his armoury. In this policy he was given unbounded encouragement by Prussia, for reasons which must be explained in a brief digression.

In 1875, dismayed at the rapidity of the French recovery from the losses incurred during the Franco-Prussian War, Bismarck sounded Britain and Russia about their probable attitude in the event of a renewal of hostilities. Both countries replied in terms which left no doubt of their active opposition to the course he contemplated. With this road closed, Prussia's attentions swung eastward towards the Ottoman empire, whose dismemberment, to the advantage of a Greater Germany, had been one of von Moltke's dreams. The dream now seemed capable of realization. Bismarck professed to favour a division of the Sultan's Balkan territories into Austrian and Russian spheres of influence, with Germany mediating between the two. But he also had in mind an eventual conflict with Russia, for which it was essential that German influence should prevail in Asia Minor.

Turkey's long decline, with its well-nigh incessant wars punctuated by humiliating treaties, had impoverished her treasury. In earlier times the favourite method of coping with financial difficulties had been to debase the coinage. In the nineteenth century recourse was had to foreign loans, in exchange for which various items of state revenue were mortgaged. By 1881 the Ottoman Public Debt amounted to well over a hundred million gold pounds, and foreign banks were drawing the revenues of the salt and tobacco monopolies, stamp duties, fisheries, customs, and fixed annual sums representing the tribute of eastern Rumelia, Bulgaria, and Cyprus. Then suddenly, when it seemed that the Sultan had nothing left to pawn, he found that Germany was ready and willing to grant him as much credit as he required.

Between 1889 and 1896 a German syndicate financed the extension of the Istanbul–İzmit railway to Ankara and Konya, as a step towards fulfilling the Kaiser's pet scheme of a Berlin–Baghdad railway; another German ambition, incidentally, was to see the railway capable of transporting Turkish troops to British-held Egypt. Germany provided the equipment and the experts; all that the Sultan had to do was guarantee the yearly payment of 14,000 marks for every completed kilometre of track, a condition that explains some of the meanderings which afford the passenger in the front coach of the Ankara train such frequent glimpses of the guard's van and which the Turkish State Railways are hoping one day to eliminate.

By the end of the nineteenth century, Abdülhamid scarcely had a friend in Europe apart from the Kaiser, and a major reason for this was his treatment of the Armenians. Wicked though it was, it was dictated not by simple wickedness but by the fear that the Armenians, most of whom lived in those Ottoman provinces which bordered on Russia, might furnish an excuse for renewed Russian aggression. Some of the Bulgars had been given their autonomy in 1878, by the Treaty of Berlin, largely because of the sympathy which Ottoman repression had won for them. Armenian revolutionaries were thereby inspired to provoke incidents which would create martyrs, and with the aid of the callous and unimaginative authorities they succeeded all too well. Muslim Circassians, refugees from Russian persecution, who had been allowed to settle in eastern Anatolia, were encouraged to attack Armenian villages, as were the indigenous Kurds. In September 1895 a violent Armenian demonstration in Istanbul was bloodily suppressed, and in the following August the capital saw the 'Bank Incident', an operation which anticipated the terrorist methods of the 1970s. A number of Armenians occupied the Ottoman Bank and threatened to blow it up unless the European powers agreed to champion their cause. But the authorities had got wind of the plan, and the police and military soon overpowered them. The ringleaders, who held Russian passports, escaped and left the country on board a French ship, but thousands of Armenians were then killed in an organized massacre.

This made no discernible difference to the Kaiser's attitude towards the Sultan. In 1898 he paid a state visit to Istanbul, hailing Abdülhamid as a brother. From there he went on to Jerusalem, taking the salute on Mount Zion from a guard of German soldiers and sailors. A week later, at Damascus, he assured 'the Sultan and the 300 million Mohammedans scattered over the world who reverence him as their Caliph' of the undying love of the German emperor. The next day, Arabic and Turkish translations of the speech, in letters of gold, were distributed in the city.

Abdülhamid's extensive propaganda in favour of the Pan-Islamic ideal seemed to fall on particularly willing ears in India; it was no doubt consoling to the self-respect of Indian Muslims to think that they belonged to a great community beyond the frontiers of their own infidel-ridden country. Yet in the event, as the First World War showed, the Indian soldier's loyalty to the King-Emperor outweighed his devotion to the Sultan-Caliph.

But we are running ahead of our story. After the German financiers and railway engineers came a German military mission. Abdülhamid, encouraged by the Kaiser's sympathy and the thought that the reverence of the Muslims outside his empire could not fail to increase his prestige at home, showed no willingness at all to meet the new liberalism half-way.

In 1889 a group of students at the Army School of Medicine had formed a secret organization which they called 'The Ottoman Society for Union and Progress'. Some of the leaders were driven into exile, some were executed, but the ardour of the survivors was unimpaired. From the safety of London, Paris, Naples, and Cairo there flowed a stream of revolutionary publications in which all Turkey's misfortunes were blamed on the Sultan. His efforts to persuade the governments concerned to suppress the exiles' publications met with little success.

A sharp reminder that his view of the Caliphate was onesided came in a telegram addressed to him from Paris by one of the exiles, his own brother-in-law, Mahmud Pasha:

> Your Majesty's mode of government conforms to no law, nor does it resemble the behaviour of an upright Caliph, not even the methods of European sovereigns. You are empowered by the people to give effect to justice; you are bound to respect it.

The mainstay of the opposition consisted of young army officers, whose professional training brought them into contact with European ideas and technical development, and whose professional pride made them bitterly resentful of the debilitating influence of the Sultan's autocratic rule.

In the early years of the twentieth century revolutionary societies multiplied inside the empire, not always through any great divergence in aims but because of the difficulties of maintaining communications in face of the omnipresent spies and *agents provocateurs* of the Sultan. By 1908, however, the underground stream of revolt was running so high that the Sultan could no longer rely on the repressive activity of his secret police. It is virtually certain that some of his chief agents had been deliberately betraying his confidence in them, on the orders of their German trainers. A man of Abdülhamid's suspicious nature could not have failed to realize that German penetration of the Ottoman army was not entirely to his own advantage; the Kaiser may well have decided that the Sultan was not the complaisant simpleton he had at first appeared. At all events, when the blow fell, Germany did not lift a finger to maintain Abdülhamid in power.

On 22 July 1908, the Salonika branch of the Society for Union and Progress sent the Sultan a telegram, demanding that the constitution be given effect and imposing a time-limit for convening the Chamber of Deputies, failing which it threatened action 'which will not meet with your Majesty's approval'. This ultimatum and the simultaneous revolt in Rumelia, the strength of which was greatly exaggerated in a telegram sent to the capital by the Governor of Monastir, terrified the Sultan into accepting the Society's demands. The next day he issued an *irade*, a decree, convening 'the Chamber of Deputies whose form of organization is set forth in the Constitution established by His Majesty'. For although the event is generally termed 'the proclamation of the Second Constitution', the Constitution of 1876 had never been repealed but was printed throughout the thirty years of absolutism in the *Salname*, the official almanac of the empire.

On 24 July the Sultan's astonished subjects looked at their newspapers, to see words which had been proscribed for years: such words as 'freedom', 'nation', 'fatherland', and 'Chamber of Deputies', which formerly would have meant the ruin of any editor rash enough to print them.

Several European eyewitnesses have described the unprecedented demonstrations of popular joy which took place in the principal cities, once it was realized that the Sultan had been forced to yield. Bulgarian priests publicly shook hands with Turkish officers, Greeks embraced Armenians. In Macedonia, bands of revolutionaries, who had for years been waging war against the government, came down into the towns and announced the end of hostilities.

But the rejoicing did not extend to the majority of the Sultan's subjects. In the capital, a Muslim woman and the Greek gardener with whom she had eloped were arrested on a complaint from her father. The police-station to which they were taken, at Beşiktaş on the Bosphorus, was stormed by a mob, shouting 'The sacred law is being destroyed! The infidels are trampling on our honour! To hell with this freedom!' The gardener was killed and the woman gravely injured. In southern Anatolia and in Tripolitania, disorders broke out among the Muslim population, who saw the restoration of the constitution as a betrayal of Islam, involving as it did the granting of equal rights to non-Muslims. Even though the mass of Muslims did not resort to violence, they were far from regarding that day in July 1908 as the beginning of a wonderful new era.

The Sultan's absolutism had not affected them personally and they were totally out of sympathy with the intellectuals and officers who had felt the weight of it.

NOTE

[1] Ercümend Kuran, 'Küçük Said Paşa (1840–1914) as a Turkish modernist', in *International Journal of Middle Eastern Studies* I (1970), 124–32.

CHAPTER 5

The Constitutional Period

ALL TOO SOON it became clear that those who had congratulated one another on the proclamation of the constitution had no more in common than satisfaction at the downfall of Abdülhamid's tyranny. Their ideas about what was to succeed it were very different. Nor did the nations who had for so many years been sadly shaking their heads over the condition of the Sick Man of Europe rejoice now that he seemed to be on the road to recovery. In the first week of October 1908, Bulgaria declared her independence, Austria annexed Bosnia and Herzegovina, and Crete proclaimed her union with Greece.

Nor must it be thought that there was any unity of purpose among the Turks themselves. Three distinct political creeds vied for supremacy among them, sometimes within the same individuals: Pan-Islamism, Pan-Turkism, and Ottomanism.

The Pan-Islamic ideal, which, as we have seen, enjoyed the Kaiser's blessing, remained in the running until the First World War revealed that the Arabs preferred to become independent rather than follow a Turkish caliph. Indeed, even before the war, numerous societies and parties were formed whose aim was Arab independence.

Pan-Turkism, which aspired to unite all the Turks of Asia into one state, was the latest of the three creeds to emerge, and this fact is hardly surprising, because the Turks were the least united of all the peoples of the empire; the least self-conscious, the least advanced towards nationhood. Till quite recently 'Turk' had been almost a term of abuse in the Ottoman empire, connoting something like 'yokel'. All the best people were *Osmanlı*. The policy which seemed natural, the policy which at first dominated the Society for Union and Progress, was Ottomanism, which envisaged a modernized Ottoman empire, so well equipped with liberal institutions that all the conflicting religious and racial groups among the Sultan's subjects would be happy to belong to it. The hopes of the Ottomanists perished for ever in the Balkan Wars.

Before the general election which followed the proclamation of the constitution, the Society decided that those of its members who won seats in Parliament should be styled 'The Party of Union and Progress', and this title was subsequently extended to the whole movement. But certainly it was an anomalous sort of political party, consisting as it did of a parliamentary group with no party organization outside Parliament, and answerable to the Society alone.[1] The CUP won a huge majority, not so much because of its prestige as the vanquisher of Abdülhamid as because it controlled the army.

Parliament was opened on 17 December 1908 with a speech from the throne, read by the Clerk of the House on behalf of the Sultan, who presided. It was not wholly platitudinous. This is how it began:

> Because of difficulties arising when the Constitution which I promulgated at the time of my accession was put into effect, the Chamber of Deputies was prorogued on the advice of certain statesmen. It was then recommended to me that the Constitution should be suspended until such time as the capacities of the population should have attained the required level, with the progress of education in my Imperial dominions. The reconvening of the Chamber was therefore delayed until the envisaged time, and no effort was spared to bring about the advancement of education by establishing schools throughout my Imperial dominions. By the grace of God, that aim has been achieved, and as a result of the spread of education the level of ability of all classes of our population has risen. In consequence of the desire that has been manifested, and because I am satisfied that the fulfilment of this desire will bring about the felicity of our State and realm both now and in the future, I have without hesitation, in spite of those who hold opinions to the contrary, proclaimed the Constitution anew and have decreed that elections be held in accordance with the Constitution and that the Chamber of Deputies be summoned.

At the end of the speech as published occurs the sentence:

> I pledge my word that the country will henceforth be administered in accordance with the Constitution.

The Clerk of the House subsequently declared that this was an addition for which he himself was responsible and that the Sultan had never intended it. To avoid argument, the Sultan later took an oath to uphold the constitution.

For some months the administration remained in the hands of politicians of the old school, but in February 1909 the Chamber dismissed the Grand Vizier Kâmil Pasha, and the CUP formed a government. Two months later a mass revolt, which became known as 'The Thirty-first of March Incident' (see below, p. 105), broke out in the capital, in which units of the army joined, demanding the establishment of an administration that would conform to the sacred law of Islam. The First Army in Istanbul, which was responsible for guarding the Sultan's person, was particularly open to incitement because many of its officers were absenting themselves from their duties to engage in political discussion in the cafés. The other ranks were incensed by an order that soldiers should not be allowed to miss drills and exercises with the excuse that they were at prayer; there was no lack of agitators to tell them that the government was trying to forbid the practice of their religion. Chief among the agitators was a Cypriot named Derviş Vahdeti, who posed as a religious fanatic but was in fact a self-seeking man of no principles. On 28 November 1908, he had begun to put out a newspaper called *Volkan* ('The Volcano'), which claimed to be 'a religious and political journal in the service of humanity'. On 5 April 1909, he helped found the Muhammadan Unionist Party, his co-founders including some of the Ulema, though not of the highest rank, some civil servants, and one or two Palace officials. Thousands of people rallied to the party, whose Chairman, according to its manifesto, was the Prophet Muhammad himself. *Volkan* poured abuse on the CUP, 'those men of no honour who blindly imitate the West' and 'those ignoramuses who are so proud of their three days' education that they think they can look down on students of the sacred law'. Its habitual designation for what others called 'the second constitutional period' was 'the age of devils'.

The revolt was speedily crushed when the commander of the Third Army, Mahmud Şevket Pasha, sent troops from Salonika 'to wipe out this stain on the honour of the Ottoman army, with its six-century-long record of obedience' and 'to punish the secret agents of the Sultan and the base self-seekers who instigated the revolt'. Some sixty people were hanged, among them Derviş Vahdeti. The Sultan's complicity was never proved and seems, on balance, unlikely. He was nevertheless deposed, on 27 April 1909, and banished to Salonika. At the end of 1912 he was brought back to Istanbul, where he died on 10 February 1918 in his seventy-fifth year.

Abdülhamid having been deposed, his sixty-four-year-old brother was enthroned in his place. His given name was Reşad, and during his reign he was generally referred to as Sultan Reşad, but officially he was called Mehmed V, on the somewhat shaky grounds that the Salonika troops had conquered Istanbul, like the troops of Mehmed II in 1453. The pledge he gave on the day of his accession marked the opening of a new era in Turkish history.

> Since the nation [*millet*] wants me, I gratefully undertake this service. My chief hope is to carry on government in accordance with the sacred law and the Constitution. I shall not swerve by one iota from the will and aspirations of the nation.

The will of the nation! Never before had a sovereign of the House of Osman recognized the existence of such an entity.

But the CUP did not share the Sultan's liberal enthusiasm; the abortive revolt which had provided the excuse for getting rid of Abdülhamid also furnished them with a pretext to muzzle the opposition parties, whose strength grew as the ruling party abandoned its original Ottomanist policies and came out on the side of Turkish nationalism. For it should be noted that the Turks in the Chamber of Deputies were outnumbered by the non-Turks.

At the end of September 1911, Italy invaded Tripolitania and Cyrenaica. Great Britain proclaimed the neutrality of Egypt (still nominally part of the Ottoman empire), thus preventing the arrival of Turkish reinforcements by the overland route, while Italian naval superiority barred their coming by sea. During April and May 1912, with fighting still going on in Africa, Italy seized the Dodecanese, the 'Twelve Islands' also known as the Sporades, which at that time formed an Ottoman province with its capital at Rhodes. In July the CUP Cabinet was forced to resign. Bulgaria and Serbia snatched the opportunity to mobilize their armies and began to probe at the Ottoman frontiers. On 8 October, Montenegro declared war on Turkey, and ten days later Bulgaria, Serbia, and Greece followed suit.

On 15–18 October, the Ottoman representatives who had been engaged since July in desultory talks with the Italians at Ouchy in Switzerland signed a peace treaty : Tripolitania and Cyrenaica were recognized as autonomous under Italian suzerainty, and Italy would restore the Dodecanese to Turkey.[2] But the Ottoman armies, even thus relieved of the burden of war in Africa and the islands, while displaying their wonted courage, found the odds too great. Armistice talks began on 18 November, at the instance of the Great Powers, when the front line was less than 20 miles west of Istanbul, and an armistice agreement was signed with Bulgaria and Serbia on 3 December. Montenegro and Greece continued to fight, however, and a month later Bulgaria reopened hostilities. What the Bulgars wanted above all was the city of Edirne. Professing to believe that the Grand Vizier, once again Kâmil Pasha, was preparing to give it to them (for which there was and is no evidence), two of the most influential men in the CUP, Enver and Talat, staged a bloody *coup d'état* on 23 January 1913. As a result, a new government took office, under Mahmud Şevket Pasha, a government which, in the words of the British ambassador, had 'a distinct German colouring'.

But the new government was no more successful in prosecuting the war than its predecessor. An attempted landing behind the Bulgarian lines failed and on 26 March Edirne fell. Talks were at once resumed and a peace treaty was signed on 30 May. On 11 June Mahmud Şevket was assassinated and the CUP availed themselves of the opportunity to hang or to exile their principal opponents and to lay an iron hand on the administration.

The victorious Balkan states soon fell out over the division of the spoils; squabbling gave way to fighting at midnight on 29 June, when the Bulgars attacked the Greeks and Serbians. On 10 July the Romanians, who also wanted a share, invaded Bulgaria. On German advice, the Turks profited by the diversion to send Enver with an army to reoccupy Edirne (22 July), a fairly simple assignment as most of the Bulgarian garrison had been withdrawn. By the Treaty of Bucharest (10 August), which ended the Balkan War, Edirne was acknowledged to be part of the sorely diminished Ottoman territories. Now Ottoman Africa, the Dodecanese, and the Balkans were lost. Only one more act remained to be played out before the curtain could fall on 600 years of empire.

Insofar as any one man can be held responsible for the Ottoman entry into the First World War, that man was Enver. Born in 1881, he graduated from the War College in 1903 with the rank of staff captain and was posted to the Third Army in Macedonia, where, like so many young officers, he joined the CUP. Dashing, intelligent, and ambitious, he distinguished himself in the events leading up to the proclamation of the constitution and, in 1909, was rewarded with the plum job of Military Attaché in Berlin. His stay there reinforced his belief in the measureless superiority of German military methods, a belief which was not shaken by the ignominious defeat of the German-trained Ottoman army in the Balkan War. He went from success to success. On 15 May 1911, he married into the Imperial family; his wife was Emine Naciye, a granddaughter of Sultan Abdülmecid. With the glamour of his easy triumph at Edirne on him, he was promoted at one go from lieutenant-colonel to brigadier, which gave him the title of Pasha, and made Minister of War (3 January 1914).

As soon as war broke out in 1914, Enver proposed that Turkey throw in her lot with the Central Powers. He found himself in a minority; respect for Britain's naval might was strong in Turkey, and every responsible statesman in the country knew that the empire's one hope lay in neutrality. But the German web had been skilfully woven and the last word did not rest with the responsible statesmen. By a secret treaty signed on 2 August 1914, of which only three Turks beside himself had prior knowledge (the Grand Vizier Said Halim, the Minister of the Interior Talat, the Chairman of the Chamber of Deputies Halil), Enver irrevocably committed his country to war on the side of the Central Powers. In the first article of the treaty the parties undertook 'to maintain absolute neutrality in the dispute between Austria-Hungary and Serbia'. The second article ran: 'If Russia intervenes militarily in the dispute and thereby gives rise to a cause of war compelling and necessitating Germany's rendering practical assistance to Austria-Hungary, this will constitute grounds for war for Turkey also'. It could have been argued that as Germany soon breached the first article, Turkey was not bound by the second, but if there was anyone in Turkey who so argued, his voice had no chance of being heard.

On 2 August also, the British government commandeered two dreadnoughts which had been built in British yards for the Turkish navy and were about to set sail. This action aroused great resentment in Turkey, the more so because the money for the ships had been raised by popular subscription. Germany offered *Goeben* and *Breslau* in their place. To the dismay of those who had pointed to British naval supremacy as a reason for Turkey to keep out of hostilities, these two ships managed to dodge the Mediterranean blockade and made their way to Istanbul. There they were handed over to the Turkish navy in the person of its German Commander-in-Chief, Rear-Admiral Souchon, who on 27 October took his ships into the Black Sea. There they bombarded the ports of Odessa,

Sevastopol, Kaffa, and Novorossisk, and sank two Russian ships and one French. Talat Pasha, who made no secret of having favoured the German alliance, wrote in his memoirs:

> Contrary to the general belief, this incident had not taken place with the knowledge of the Porte. During the war I did not deny the rumour that it had; but now that the war is over, and I am not in power, I most emphatically declare that I learned, as everybody did, of this regrettable incident just after it happened, and that no one of the Cabinet members gave his consent to this sudden attack on the Russian fleet.[3]

He was not a notably truthful man, however.

The Allies demanded the expulsion of all German naval and military officers from the Turkish forces; this demand was rejected by a majority vote of the Turkish ministers, and by 1 November 1914 the Ottoman empire was engaged in its final war.

Of the course of the fighting it is unnecessary to speak. The position at the end of October 1918 is thus summarized by Hindenburg in his memoirs:

> In the East, the last resistance of the Turkish empire had been broken. Mosul and Aleppo had fallen into enemy hands almost without a struggle. The armies of Iraq and Syria had practically ceased to exist.

Every Turkish commander in the field impressed on the government the uselessness of further resistance.

On 30 October 1918, Turkish and British representatives signed an armistice agreement on board HMS *Agamemnon*, at anchor off Mudros, in the island of Lemnos. All Ottoman possessions in Arabia, Syria, Iraq, and Africa were placed under Allied military control, the Straits were to be opened, and the Dardanelles and Black Sea fortifications to be occupied by the Allies, who were also given the right (by the notorious Article 7) to occupy any strategic point in the event of a threat to Allied security. These terms were made more palatable to the Ottoman representatives by a secret undertaking given by Admiral Calthorpe, the British delegate: he would recommend to his government that no Greek troops should be sent to Istanbul or İzmir, both cities having large indigenous Greek populations, and that Greek warships bound for the Black Sea should pass through the Straits only by night.

Although not a few Turkish writers have since described 30 October 1918 as a black day in Turkish history, news of the Mudros Armistice was greeted in Istanbul with relief. In the circumstances its terms were not unduly harsh. Later criticisms are coloured by the memory of the unhappy events which followed because the Allies chose not only to ignore Admiral Calthorpe's recommendations, but even to violate the letter of the agreement.

On 2–3 November 1918, Enver, Talat, and other prominent members of the CUP fled to Berlin. Enver subsequently made his way to Moscow, where he engaged to further the Soviet cause among the Asian Turks. Once arrived in Turkestan, however, he set himself instead to carving out an independent kingdom there. This characteristically bold scheme was frustrated on 4 August 1922, when he met his death fighting the Red Army near Bukhara.

NOTES

[1] Apparently on the basis of an early mistranslation, in English works on Turkey the Society and party have always been termed 'The Committee of Union and Progress', abbreviated 'CUP'. Because of the familiarity and convenience of this abbreviation it will be used from now on, though not without some reluctance on the part of the author.

[2] In fact she never did, any more than she honoured her pledge in the Graeco-Italian Treaty of 10 August 1920 to cede the islands to Greece. They were eventually handed over to Greece in accordance with a decision taken by Britain, France, the USA, and Russia on 27 June 1946 and confirmed in the treaty signed in Paris on 10 February 1947.

[3] 'Posthumous Memoirs of Talaat Pasha', in *The New York Times Current History*, XV (November 1921), 287–95.

CHAPTER 6

The Turkish Revolution and the War of Independence

IN JULY 1918 Sultan Mehmed V died and was succeeded by his brother Vahdettin, known as Mehmed VI. The new Sultan seems to have been characterized by the same egotism as his older brother Abdülhamid. He availed himself of the political bankruptcy of the CUP, and the flight of its leaders, to seize the reins in his own hands. The CUP still commanded a majority in the Assembly; the Sultan therefore dissolved the Assembly (21 December 1918) and ruled through his brother-in-law, the Grand Vizier, Damad Ferid Pasha.

His policy was to maintain himself on the throne at any cost. To this end the Allies were to be conciliated and obeyed. No matter how much of his territories they might take from him, Vahdettin would raise no objection, so long as he could be Sultan of the remainder.

On 13 November 1918, an Allied fleet of sixty vessels, including the Greek ship *Averoff*, dropped anchor at Istanbul. Admiral Calthorpe explained to the Turks that no occupation of the capital was intended, that the purpose of the fleet was to fight the Bolsheviks in Russia. The following day Allied troops began to disembark, and buildings were commandeered for their use, but the Allies were careful to avoid using the word 'occupation'.

A Turkish writer has defined the Eastern Question as 'the problem of how to divide up the Ottoman Empire'. During the war, that problem had been solved to the satisfaction of the Allies by four secret agreements, whose main provisions were as follows.

The 'Constantinople Agreement' (18 March 1915), between Britain, France, and Russia, promised Russia Istanbul and the western coasts of the Bosphorus, Sea of Marmara, and Dardanelles; Thrace, south of a line drawn between Midye and Enez; the north-western tip of Asia Minor; the islands of Imbros and Tenedos and those in the Sea of Marmara. Arabia was to become an independent Muslim state.

By the Secret Treaty of London (26 April 1915), the same three powers assigned to Italy, as her price for entering the war, 'a just share of the Mediterranean region adjacent to the province of Adalia' (now the *vilâyet* of Antalya).

Under the Sykes-Picot Agreement (16 May 1916), between Britain and France, Russia was to be given the provinces of Erzurum, Trabzon, Van, and Bitlis. France would have Syria and the south-eastern quarter of Asia Minor. Britain's share would be the southern part of Mesopotamia with Baghdad, and the ports of Haifa and Acre. Between the French and British territories there would be an Arab state or confederation of states, divided into French and British zones of influence. These terms were never put into effect, because President Wilson persuaded the Peace Conference to reject the principle of annexation of the Arab provinces and to establish mandates instead.

The St-Jean-de-Maurienne Agreement (17 April 1917), between Britain, France, and Italy, was an attempt to reconcile the conflicting claims of France and Italy. France would have Adana, while Italy would be given the remainder of southern Asia Minor, including the province of İzmir, though the port of İzmir would be free.

The Russian revolution had rendered void the promises given to Tsar Nicholas II – indeed, the Bolsheviks formally renounced all claim to Turkish territory in 1917 – but the other Allies were eager to enter upon their new acquisitions. On 8 February 1919, French troops disembarked at Istanbul. Their commander, Franchet d'Espèrey, rode a white horse, a gift from the local Greeks, in conscious imitation of the way in which Mehmed II had entered the city on the day, long ago, when Constantinople fell. Wildly excited crowds of non-Turks cheered the new conqueror, a bitter sight to Turkish eyes and one not soon forgotten.

Many Turks had been ready to face with equanimity the loss of the Arab provinces. A favourite theme of Turkish novelists has been the sorrows of Anatolia, with the flower of its young manhood sent to die in the service of an empire from whose survival they had nothing to gain, wasting the best years of their lives amidst Arabs whose theoretical reverence for the Caliph of Islam did not inspire them with love for his tax-collectors and garrisons.

But this was something else. Here were foreigners lording it in the greatest of all Turkish cities, their path strewn with flowers by the Turks' ungrateful subjects. Spontaneously, all over the country, were seen the first stirrings of a Turkish nationalist spirit, distinct from Pan-Turkism. The latter had never been much more than an impractical dream (though it had served a useful purpose in providing a mystique which kept Turkish hopes alive, at a time when the bases of Ottoman society were crumbling), and by now it was manifestly outmoded. The Turks of the former Russian empire must look out for themselves; the Turks of Turkey would stand together.

In every part of Turkey patriotic societies sprang up. One of the earliest was the Ottoman Defence Committee of Thrace. Its avowed aim was local and regional: to keep Thrace in Turkish hands, but its real purpose went far beyond this, as was shown by the Committee's rejection of an offer of autonomy for the region, made by the Greek Prime Minister Venizelos. In Kars, a National Council actually ruled the province for half a year, latterly with the title of 'Provisional National Government of the South-western Caucasus', until it was dissolved by the British in April 1919. Weakened by years of war, despised by their former subjects, betrayed by their leaders, the Turks had suddenly begun to find themselves.

Early in February 1919 Venizelos presented to the Peace Conference at Paris a formal claim to possession of İzmir. The St-Jean-de-Maurienne Agreement, which assigned that region to Italy, had lapsed for want of Russian ratification, and Lloyd George and Clemenceau gave the Greek Prime Minister their backing. On 15 May a Greek division landed at İzmir with Allied naval support. This act was declared by the Allies to be in accordance with Article 7 of the Armistice agreement; falsely, for there was no threat to Allied security. The occupation troops were welcomed by delighted crowds of indigenous Greeks and were blessed by the Metropolitan of İzmir. They then began a systematic massacre of Turks in the city and province. The civilized world was shocked, but could do nothing; İzmir was the price the Allies had promised to pay for the Greek entry into the war.

Enormous protest-meetings took place in Istanbul. Speakers harangued vast crowds while French Senegalese machine-gunners stood guard and Allied aircraft flew overhead. But there was no violence; only bitter speeches and tears of anger and frustration.

As soon as the Greek forces had established themselves in İzmir they began a drive into the interior, and a trail of hanged men and smoking rubble marked their advance. Turkish guerrillas took up the struggle and a bloody war developed, in which no quarter was shown and atrocities were the norm.

The career of one guerrilla leader may be taken as typical. Yörük Ali Efe was born in 1896 in a village of south-western Anatolia. He joined the army during the First World War, but deserted after being flogged by an NCO. For three years he lived by banditry in the hills and then gave himself up. Just at that time came the occupation of İzmir, and Yörük Ali was enabled, by the connivance of the local authorities, to reassemble his gang and resume his old way of life. In June 1920, with fifty followers, he crossed the river Menderes on rafts to wipe out a Greek detachment and take their weapons. This feat inspired a large-scale rising in the province of Aydın against the invader. With the extension of the Nationalists' authority, Yörük Ali's gang, considerably enlarged, was named 'The National Aydın Regiment', and he himself was given the rank of colonel of militia. At the end of the War of Independence he settled down to be a farmer, not far from his birthplace. His services are commemorated in the title of the 37th (Yörük Ali Efe's) Regiment of the 57th Division of the Republican Army.

But undirected, the Yörük Ali Efes of Turkey could have achieved little. The time has come to bring the hero into the story.

Mustafa, son of Ali Rıza, was born in Salonika in 1881. His father, a customs official turned timber-merchant, died when the boy was seven. The widowed mother, Zübeyde, went to live on her brother's farm, with Mustafa and his young sister Makbule. He entered a school for prospective civil servants, but was taken away from it by his family after being flogged for starting a fight in class. His own ambition, which was strongly resisted by his mother, was to become a soldier. In 1893, without consulting her, he sat and passed the entrance examination for the Salonika Military School, and Zübeyde had the good sense to bow to the inevitable. It was at this stage of his career that the name Kemal ('Perfection') was conferred on him by a master, also named Mustafa, who jocularly wished to distinguish him from himself and chose this name in recognition of the boy's mathematical ability. Mustafa liked it, not unnaturally, and continued to use it. After finishing at Salonika, he studied at the Monastir Military Academy, from which, in 1899, he went on to the War College in Istanbul. Like so many young soldiers, particularly in Salonika, he detested the tyranny of Abdülhamid. Unlike almost all of them, however, he also detested the country's growing dependence on Germany.

Graduating from the War College at the beginning of 1905, with the rank of staff captain, he plunged still deeper into political intrigue, with the result that he was denounced to the Sultan. The consequences were not so grave as one might have expected, because if the Sultan had made away with every officer suspected of plotting against him he would have had no army left. Mustafa Kemal was posted to Damascus, where he joined the 'Fatherland' (*Vatan*), the local revolutionary group, which he helped to reorganize as the 'Fatherland and Freedom Society'. His talent for undercover work is seen in the Society's constitution: each member was personally known only to the man who introduced him and to the man he introduced. Mustafa Kemal undertook the direction of propaganda and put the Society into contact with his old colleagues at the Salonika headquarters of the CUP.

In September 1907, to his great joy, he was posted to the Third Army in Salonika. He played his part in the eventful days of 1908; he was Chief of Staff of a reserve division at the time of the 'Thirty-first of March'. But things did not go as well as he had hoped. His opinions were never listened to with as much respect as he would have liked. Advancement in the CUP was for those willing to become tools of German policy, and Mustafa Kemal made no secret of his contempt for those who did not put Turkish interests first. His disappointment was channelled into dislike of Enver, whose star was then in the ascendant. To the successful and triumphant young officers who had secured the proclamation of the constitution, Kemal propounded his view that as soldiers, their end having been gained, they should henceforth not meddle in politics; from this we may judge of his spiritual loneliness.

One night in the winter of 1908, while sitting with some of his few close friends in the officers' club at Salonika, he suggested – perhaps jokingly, but *in vino veritas* – that the army should be purged of all officers above the rank of major. 'And then what?' asked one of his friends. 'That will depend on how the revolution turns out', replied Kemal, and he went on:

> Yes, we're going to have a revolution. The one we've had so far isn't enough. We're going to do more. I can't leave the country in the hands of a pack of idiots. Instead of all these bodies, I'll make do with a few brains. For instance, I'll make Kâzım Minister of War. Nuri I'll make C-in-C and head of the administration. I'll send Fethi to Europe as representative of the new revolutionary Turkey.

'And what about us?' cried those whose names had not been

mentioned. 'You'll get jobs in accordance with the merit and energy you display'. At this, one of the others burst out laughing. 'What are you laughing at?' asked Kemal. 'I'm wondering about you; among all these jobs, what are you going to be?' 'I?' said Kemal, 'I shall be the one who can give you these jobs'. A true prophecy, which had to wait barely fifteen years for its fulfilment.

Meanwhile, however, he withdrew from the CUP's activities, to the satisfaction of the innumerable people he had offended, and threw himself heart and soul into the business of soldiering. He served with distinction in the wars of 1911 and 1912. The outbreak of the First World War found him as Military Attaché in Sofia, with the rank of lieutenant-colonel. At the end of 1914 he was recalled and given command of the 19th Division, which at that time scarcely existed except on paper. He devoted all his energy to making it into a serviceable fighting force and was posted with it to Arıburnu, on the west side of Gallipoli. His leadership, more than any other single factor, frustrated the British landings and brought about the evacuation of the peninsula. This campaign, which saved Istanbul, made him a national hero, much to Enver's displeasure. Mustafa Kemal, now a brigadier and a pasha, was consequently sent to the Caucasus, where the sight of him could not affront the War Minister's vanity.

Enver had been to the eastern front himself, a year before, with a plan for driving the Russians back across the Caucasus. The plan had misfired disastrously and all but a tenth of the Turkish forces had met their death at Sarıkamiş. Since then the eastern front had been left to take care of itself, and the Russians were in occupation of Bitlis and Muş. Luck was with Mustafa Kemal, for even his tireless endeavours could have done little with the dispirited remnant of the Eastern Army, had not the first stirrings of the Russian revolution broken the back of the enemy's resistance.

The recapture of Bitlis and Muş in August 1916 was Kemal's last military achievement for many months, during which time he visited Germany with the Heir Apparent, Vahdettin. On August 1918 he was sent to the Syrian front, where Allenby's brilliant advance offered the Turks only a choice between rout and surrender. Kemal saved them from this; he organized a fighting retreat all the way to the mountains north of Aleppo, and was preparing to make a stand there, when news came of the Mudros Armistice. To the Turkish soldier in defeat, Mustafa Kemal Pasha was not just a hero, he was the only hero; the man who had hurled the British out of Gallipoli and cheated them of their prey in Syria.

For many months after the Armistice he remained inactive at Istanbul. He was there when the Allied warships anchored in the Bosphorus and when Franchet d'Espèrey rode his white horse through the cheering crowds. There was nothing for him to do in the capital; it was too well policed by the victors. At General Allenby's suggestion he was offered the command of the Sixth Army at Nusaybin, away on the Syrian border, but he refused. His dream was to get into Anatolia, to organize the local Nationalist groups into a force that the Allies would have to treat with more respect than they had yet shown to conquered Turkey. But this dream seemed wildly improbable, for he was under Allied surveillance, like other prominent Turks; he, could not quietly slip away without arousing suspicion. And then the government made the blunder of many a Turk before and since : they mistook Istanbul for Turkey.

It did not suit their purpose to have Mustafa Kemal in the capital; he was too popular and too ambitious, and his notorious outspokenness might offend the Allies. Once away from the capital he would be harmless. So in April 1919 the Minister of War sent for him and told him that the Allies were complaining of armed attacks by Turks on Greek-inhabited villages in the neighbourhood of Samsun. If the Ottoman government could not maintain order there, Allied forces would do so. Mustafa Kemal had great influence with the Turkish soldiery; further, he was known as an inveterate opponent of Enver's pro-German policy and was therefore politically acceptable to the Allies. Would he be willing to put down the disorders, first in the north and then in the rest of Anatolia? Hardly able to believe his ears, he accepted, and was appointed Inspector-General of the Third Army, based on Samsun, with command of the 3rd and 15th Army Corps. On 19 May, four days after the Greek occupation of İzmir, he reached Samsun.

Immediately, he set about acquainting himself with conditions in the area and getting into touch with the local resistance groups. On 22 June, while at Amasya, he addressed a circular letter to all military and civil authorities whom he considered trustworthy, of which the following is a summary :

> The territorial integrity of the Fatherland and our national independence are in danger. The central government is incapable of carrying out its responsibilities. A national body must be set

> up, free from all outside interference, to bring to the ears of the world the nation's cry for its rights. It has been decided to hold a national congress at Sivas in the near future, to which every province is to send delegates, who must, wherever necessary, travel incognito.

It is well established that Mustafa Kemal had confided his plans to certain of the other generals. Some writers have argued, however, that the Sultan's government as a whole were not the traitors that the consensus of Republican historians makes them out to be; that they knew perfectly well what Mustafa Kemal's intentions were and deliberately sent him to Samsun, so that he might give the nation the lead which they themselves dared not give. On 23 June the Ministry of the Interior issued a circular which is worth quoting at length, as it effectively disposes of this theory:

> Although Mustafa Kemal Pasha is a great soldier, his political sagacity is not of the same standard... He has added to his political mistakes the administrative error of sending telegrams on behalf of certain illegal bodies whose only function is to extort money from the people. To bring him back to Istanbul is the duty of the Ministry of War. The Ministry of the Interior, however, orders you to recognize that this man has been dismissed, to enter into no official dealings with him whatsoever and to see that no request of his relative to governmental affairs is complied with... In these critical moments, while our destinies are being decided on by the Peace Conference and an account is being taken of the acts of madness we have committed over the past five years, it is surely the duty of every Ottoman official and citizen to show that we have at last come to our senses, to act in a reasonable and prudent manner, and to protect the life, property, and honour of every individual, without distinction of party, creed, or race, and thus to avoid any further staining of this country in the eyes of civilization.

The Ministry of War did indeed try to recall Mustafa Kemal to Istanbul, but without effect. On 8 July 1919, as the climax to a spirited exchange of telegrams, the ministry indicated that the pasha was relieved of his post, and the pasha instantly countered by resigning his commission. From that time on, until he received a new commission from the National Congress, he wore civilian clothes. Yet the military authorities of Anatolia, with very few exceptions, continued to regard him as their lawful superior. Reports and requests for instructions did not cease to come for him, addressed to 'The 3rd Army Corps Command at Sivas'.

With politicians he had more difficulty. To them he was a man who could be useful in unseating the government but would then have served his purpose. For the moment, however, they were compelled to support him, because he was the only man the army and the common people were prepared to follow.

A congress was held at Erzurum between 23 July and 6 August, of delegates from all the eastern provinces. It was not summoned by Kemal but by the 'Eastern Provinces Society for the Defence of National Rights'. Mustafa Kemal attended, however, and was elected chairman. The decisions reached by the Erzurum Congress were reaffirmed by that held at Sivas in early September.

The Sivas Congress was dominated by the personality of Mustafa Kemal, who was chosen by secret ballot to preside over it, with only three dissentient votes. He succeeded in obtaining the rejection of a proposal for seeking an American mandate over 'all the Ottoman dominions . . . since a mandate that will assure our territorial integrity is preferable to an independence that will be confined to two or three provinces'. Mustafa Kemal wondered what the boundaries were of 'all the Ottoman dominions'. 'Our pre-war boundaries? Including Syria and Iraq? If so, have the people of Anatolia the right and the authority to ask for a mandate in the name of the Arab world?' Supporters of the 'Friends of England Association' fared no better. Mustafa Kemal would settle for nothing less than the absolute independence of Turkey, a Turkey freed from the profitless burden of the Arab provinces.

The main conclusions of the Sivas Congress were these : resistance would be offered to any occupation of any part of Turkey. No minority within the country would be given any privileges which would 'upset our political and social equilibrium'. A national assembly should meet at once to settle the nation's destiny.

A message was then sent to the capital in the name of the Congress, demanding the resignation of the Cabinet of Damad Ferid Pasha and the immediate convening of the Chamber of Deputies. This demand was rejected but not ignored; the Congress was clearly a force to be reckoned with. An attempt was made, with the help of British agents, to rouse the Kurdish tribes against Kemal and his followers, but it was frustrated through efficient intelligence-work and a timely show of force. Repeated protests to the Sultan, against this 'treacherous and suicidal action against the fatherland and the nation', elicited no reply.

On 11 September, professing to regard this silence as due to the malevolence of the ministers rather than to the Sultan's own complicity, Mustafa Kemal telegraphed the following ultimatum to the Grand Vizier:

> Your reckless attempts to tread the nation's rights underfoot and to compromise the honour of H.M. the Sultan are known. The nation has no confidence in any of you apart from the Sultan; hence it is obliged to present its petitions to H.M. alone. Your Cabinet, fearing the perilous consequences of its unconstitutional actions, is coming between nation and Sultan. If your obstinacy in this matter continues for one hour longer, the nation will consider itself entitled to take any action it thinks fit, and will cut off all communication between the country and your unconstitutional Cabinet. This is our last warning.

On the expiry of the ultimatum, this threat was carried out; with very few exceptions all telegraph offices ceased to handle official messages to and from the capital.

On 2 October the Grand Vizier resigned, 'for reasons of health'. A new Cabinet was formed by Ali Rıza Pasha, who prepared for new elections and sent his Navy Minister, Salih Pasha, to confer with Kemal at Amasya. After three days of discussion they agreed on five principles which became known as the Amasya Protocol: the territorial integrity of Turkey was to be preserved; no special privileges were to be given to minorities; the government was to recognize the nationalist organization; the Turkish delegates at the Peace Conference were to be approved by the committee of the National Congress; and the new Chamber of Deputies was not to meet at Istanbul.

The Cabinet proceeded with arrangements for the election, but took no notice of the Amasya Protocol. The prudent Kemal moved his headquarters to Ankara, the capital of a province, with the advantages of railway communication with Istanbul, a central position in the country, and strong natural defences.

The elections gave the Nationalists a large majority, and the newly elected deputies joyfully prepared to hurry off to Istanbul, disregarding Mustafa Kemal's warnings. He himself had been elected deputy for Erzurum, but was too wily to enter the spider's parlour. Some thought him unduly pessimistic, others thought he was disgruntled at seeing his brief hour of glory fade. Outlaws no longer, but parliamentarians, at last they could go back to the flesh-pots of Istanbul and settle their country's future like gentlemen. Some of them promised to elect Mustafa Kemal President of the Chamber *in absentia*, but the promise was not kept.

So Kemal remained in Ankara and had the grim satisfaction of seeing his prophecies come true. The Chamber was opened on 12 January 1920. A week later, the Allied representatives procured the dismissal of the Minister of War and the Chief of the General Staff, whom they rightly suspected of complicity in the theft of arms from Allied depots, the Nationalists' main source of supply. This piece of interference, justifiable though it was except in Nationalist eyes, roused the deputies to vote on 28 January for the proclamation of the National Pact, which had been drafted by the Erzurum Congress and is still considered the basic document of Turkish foreign policy. Its provisions were these:

1. The destinies of those portions of the Ottoman Empire which are inhabited exclusively by Arabs and which were under enemy occupation on 30 October 1918 must be settled by free vote of the population. The remaining portions, inhabited by an Ottoman-Muslim majority, united by religion and race, linked to each other by feelings of mutual respect and self-sacrifice, form a whole which does not admit of division for any reason.

2. We accept that in the matter of the Three Sanjaks,[1] which attached themselves to the mother-country by a plebiscite, recourse should again be had if necessary to a plebiscite.

3. The determination of the legal status of western Thrace, which has been left to the Turkish peace treaty, must be in accordance with the vote which the local people shall freely give.

4. Provided that the city of Istanbul and the Sea of Marmara are kept immune from all harm, any decision that may be reached between us and all other interested Powers regarding the opening of the Dardanelles and Bosphorus to the commerce and traffic of the world is accepted.

5. The rights of minorities are to be guaranteed; this applies equally to Muslim minorities.

6. We accept no restriction that will hamper our political, judicial, and financial development. The settlement of our proved debts shall not be contrary to these principles.

Such bold words on the part of a defeated people did not please the Allied Powers. Still less did they like the continued thefts of arms from Allied dumps. On the night of 26 January, for example, a well-planned and well-executed raid on a French depot at Akbaş secured 8,000 rifles, 40 machine-guns, and 20,000 boxes of ammunition, which were dispatched to the Nationalist forces in the interior.

All the Allies had their own domestic post-war problems to contend with, and the demobilization of their armies was making it every day more difficult to cope with the Turks. On 3 March they forced the resignation of Ali Rıza Pasha and he was succeeded by Salih Pasha, who showed the same readiness to come to an understanding with Kemal as he had when Navy Minister. The Allies thereupon took the unwise step of formally placing the capital under military occupation and arresting and deporting to Malta such Nationalist deputies as were within their reach (16 March). Hearing the news, Mustafa Kemal said, 'Today, by the forcible occupation of Istanbul, an end has been made of the seven hundred years' life and sovereignty of the Ottoman empire'.

Salih Pasha, who resisted an Allied demand that he disavow the Nationalist movement, was obliged to resign on 2 April and the Sultan for the fourth time appointed his brother-in-law, Ferid Pasha.

Hüseyin Kâzım, the courageous Deputy Chairman of the Chamber, sought an audience with the Sultan and begged him to reconsider this decision, which could mean only disaster for the country. Enraged, the Sultan replied, 'If I wish I can appoint as Grand Vizier the Greek Patriarch or the Armenian Patriarch or the Chief Rabbi'. 'You can, Sire', replied Hüseyin Kâzım, 'but you will not be able to remain on your throne'.

On 11 April Ferid Pasha took a step which had previously been avoided: he declared the Nationalists to be rebels against the Sultan, having procured from the *Şeyhülislâm* a *fetva*[2] in support of this view. On the same day, the Sultan dissolved the Chamber of Deputies.

NOTES

[1] The three sub-provinces of Kars, Ardahan, and Batum, formerly part of the Russian empire. In accordance with Article 4 of the Treaty of Brest-Litovsk, a free vote of the inhabitants was taken in 1918 which decided on union with the Ottoman empire. Batum, however, was ceded to Georgia by the Treaty of Moscow of 16 March 1921.

[2] A *responsum* given by a mufti on a point of sacred law.

CHAPTER 7

The Grand National Assembly

THE OLD JEALOUSIES were for the moment set aside. Those deputies who had escaped arrest made their way to Ankara, and there, on 23 April, the Grand National Assembly of Turkey[1] began its first session. It was to have opened on 22 April, a Thursday, but the ceremony was deliberately postponed till the next day to give the lie to accusations that the Nationalists, who were defying the Sultan-Caliph, were enemies of Islam. The proceedings began with the Friday prayer at the mosque of Hacı Bayram. Mustafa Kemal was elected President of the Assembly, and the following statement of faith was proclaimed to the world:

> Sovereignty belongs unconditionally to the nation. The Grand National Assembly is the true and sole representative of the nation. Legislative authority and executive power are manifested and concentrated in the Grand National Assembly.

'Once the Sultan-Caliph has been delivered from the constraint he now suffers', said Mustafa Kemal, 'he will take his place within the constitution to be drawn up by the Assembly'. Probably a majority of Kemal's supporters, in and out of the Assembly, believed this. It is pretty certain that Kemal himself did not.

Soon the new government was fighting for its life. Copies of the *fetva* outlawing Kemal and his colleagues were dropped by Allied aircraft over inland towns, and anti-Nationalist riots broke out in a score of places, despite a counter-*fetva* given by the mufti of Ankara and other Ulema who were friendly to the Nationalist cause: 'Are the *fetvas* issued by a government under foreign duress binding, according to the sacred law, upon Muslims? – Answer: No'.

A court-martial held in Istanbul tried the rebel leaders *in absentia* and condemned them to death. Ferid Pasha raised a force of irregulars which he dignified by the title of 'The Army of the

Caliphate' and put under the command of Süleyman Şefik Pasha. For three months it fought the Nationalists in the Bolu-Düzce-Adapazarı region. The battle came close to Ankara itself, and more than once the vital telegraph-lines were cut. This particular force was put to flight on 4 June 1920, but others appeared in its place. Especially dangerous were the French-inspired rising of the Arab tribes along the southern frontier, and the two revolts at Konya in May and October 1920. Most of the local uprisings in north-western Anatolia were dealt with by the Nationalists' 'Mobile Forces' under Edhem the Circassian and his two brothers, who might have accomplished their task more easily had they not used methods of repression so savage as to cause new outbreaks to occur almost as fast as the old ones were put down. At the same time, the Nationalists were waging unrelenting war against the Greeks in the west, the Armenian Republic in the the north-east, and, in the south-east, against the French troops who had occupied Adana.

To say that Mustafa Kemal alone kept the Nationalists fighting would be unjust to the thousands of nameless Turks who fought, often with home-made weapons, to rid their country of foreign invaders and native dupes. But certainly it was his indomitable will and untiring energy which maintained the tenuous links of the Nationalist organization and saved it from piecemeal extermination.

The details of the military operations which confounded the pessimists are not essential to our story, though they constitute an epic of heroism and endurance. The town of Antep, besieged by 12,000 French troops, held out for over ten months. The inhabitants made rockets with crude gunpowder, they used unexploded enemy shells as grenades. They turned against the French an ancient muzzle-loading cannon which for many years had been used only to signal the end of the Fast of Ramadan. Hunger compelled them to surrender, in February 1921. The GNA conferred on the town the title of 'Warrior for the Faith' and it is known as Gaziantep to this day.

So hopeless did the Nationalist cause seem at first that even the London *Times* perpetrated what must ever remain a warning to all political prophets and Middle East experts. In its issue of 22 May 1920, a leading article stated authoritatively: 'Mustapha Kemal is no Hotspur, and his rabble lacks cohesion'. A month later its correspondent reported that the Nationalists controlled the greater part of Anatolia, with fully two-thirds of the literate and governing class behind them, including many thousands of officers who, with little to hope for from civilian life, had everything to gain from continuing the fight.

> But the attitude of the majority of the literate class, lawyers, politicians, journalists, above all officials, is less comprehensible. This class seems unconscious of the risk it is running.

'Heedless' would have been nearer the mark: the literate class supported the Kemalist movement because the alternative was national extinction; because there was no other way open to them if they wished to survive as Turks.

On 16 July 1920, a Greek communiqué announced that operations in Asia Minor had been concluded. East of the line occupied by the Greek troops (which ran southward from a point on the Sea of Marmara 9 miles east of Bursa, to the Menderes, 7 miles east of Nazilli), 'the Nationalists have lost all prestige and have been everywhere repudiated by the Moslem population'. The Turks were 'expressing absolute confidence and sincere gratitude towards the Greeks, whom they consider as their friends and protectors'.

In the summer of 1920, cushioned against the hardness of reality by their own cheerful communiqués, the Allied Powers decided to conclude a peace with the Sultan's government. The terms proposed were such that even Damad Ferid Pasha jibbed and it was only the personal insistence of Vahdettin that compelled the Ottoman delegates to sign (10 August 1920). The Treaty of Sèvres has been described as the death-warrant of the Ottoman empire. More; it would, if implemented, have meant the end of Turkey itself.

The Straits were to be demilitarized and administered by a permanent Allied commission sitting at Istanbul. The city itself was to be a hostage for the good behaviour of the Turks; it would be removed from their control if the rights of minorities were infringed. The eastern provinces were to be divided between an autonomous Kurdistan and an independent Armenia. Greece was to have İzmir and its hinterland, and Thrace. Italy's share would be the southern half of western and central Anatolia, while France would take the south-east. Rarely in history can so unrealistic a treaty have been signed. But its signing served only to inflame the Turks. From then on, although there were disagreements about who was to lead the Nationalist revolt, there was practically no argument about its necessity.

Still the Allies continued to misjudge the situation. On 27

September, *The Times* reported that the Sultan was seeking Allied financial help to pacify Anatolia:

> Nationalism is waning as a military force, but even so the Central Government must be enabled, after detaching the majority of the Angora Government's supporters by offers of amnesty, to deal with the minority of adventurers, criminals and fanatics whose crimes and follies exclude them from hope of pardon.

Fortunately for the morale of the Nationalists, *The Times* was not generally read round their camp-fires.

To turn for a moment to internal matters, a clear picture of Mustafa Kemal's ideas on government is afforded by a speech of his to the GNA on 4 November 1920. The original practice, codified in Law No. 3, of 2 May of that year, was for the GNA to elect ministers from among its own members by a simple majority vote. On 4 November, on Kemal's motion, the law was amended: 'Ministers are elected by absolute majority from among the candidates nominated by the President of the Assembly from its members'. The occasion for the change was that Nazım, the deputy for Tokat, had on 4 September been elected Minister of the Interior, by 98 votes to 89. Kemal mistrusted him as being 'in touch with foreign circles' (a euphemism for 'communist', which he was), and forced him to resign his ministry. Kemal's speech on the motion to amend the law included the following homily:

> Gentlemen, you know very well that in lands ruled by sultans and caliphs the greatest danger for the country and nation is that the sultans and caliphs may be bought by the enemy. This has usually proved very easy. In lands ruled by parliaments the most pernicious thing is that some deputies may be bought, to serve foreign interests. Historical examples compel us to judge that it would not be impossible to find unpatriotic individuals who have managed to find their way into national assemblies. Therefore the nation, when choosing its deputies, should be very careful and jealous. The only sound way of protecting the nation from error is for it to be given guidance by a political party which has won the nation's trust by its ideas and actions. Even if we suppose, for argument's sake, that the general run of citizens could have reliable information and an accurate opinion on which to base their judgement of every person who offers himself

as a candidate, abundant experience has shown incontrovertibly that this does not in fact happen.

The considerable Greek victories of 1919 and 1920 had been in part due to dissension among the Nationalist leaders. Kemal saw the futility of hoping to defeat a well-equipped modern army solely by guerrilla action. This conviction brought him into conflict with the principal guerrilla leader, Edhem, who when instructed to place himself under the orders of İsmet, Kemal's Chief of Staff, refused, thus precipitating open war between his 'Mobile Forces' and Kemal's regular forces. Defeated, Edhem went over to the Greeks, who took advantage of the apparent disunity among the Turks to advance eastward from Bursa, towards Eskişehir.

Their hopes were frustrated. The Turkish army on the western front, under İsmet, had been strengthened by reinforcements released by the cessation of hostilities in the east, where the Nationalist army commanded by Kâzım Karabekir had, with Russian help, taken Kars, Ardahan, and Artvin from the Armenians. On 10 January 1921, İsmet drove the Greeks back to Bursa, after a fierce engagement at İnönü.

For this success, İsmet was promoted to brigadier by the Grand National Assembly and was thereafter known as İsmet Pasha.

On 11 May 1920, a delegation had set out from Ankara for Moscow, which they reached late in July. Their discussions there led to the Russo-Turkish Treaty of 16 March 1921, in which the Russians accepted the provisions of the National Pact and in which some frontier revisions were agreed; notably, the port of Batum was ceded by Turkey to Soviet Georgia. What the Turks needed most of all was money. Lenin promised them 100 million gold roubles, which in the event were provided by the Asian Turkish government of the short-lived Republic of Bukhara. How this huge weight of gold found its way from Central Asia to Ankara is still something of a mystery, but when it did arrive the Nationalists' worries about how to finance the war were largely at an end.

Alarmed by the Greek reverse at İnönü, the Allies made an effort to finish the hostilities before the Turks could gain the initiative. A conference was called in London in February 1921, to which representatives of both Istanbul and Ankara were invited. Some modification of the terms of Sèvres was offered, but neither Turkish delegation would accept them. Britain, France, and Italy then announced their neutrality in the struggle on the western front, which thus became a straight fight between Greeks and Turks. To safeguard Allied comunications, a neutral zone was designated on either side of the Dardanelles, on which neither belligerent was to trespass.

Meanwhile the Grand National Assembly had passed the Provisional Law of Fundamental Organization (20 January 1921), whose terms may be summarized as follows:

1. Sovereignty belongs unconditionally to the nation.
2. Executive power and legislative authority are manifested and concentrated in the GNA, which is the sole rightful representative of the nation.
3. The Turkish State is administered by the GNA, and its government is entitled 'Government of the Grand National Assembly of Turkey'.
4. The GNA is composed of members elected by the people.
5. Elections are to be held once every two years. If it is impossible to hold new elections, the session may be prolonged for one year only. Each member of the GNA is a deputy not of the particular province electing him but of the whole nation.
6. To the GNA belong such fundamental rights as putting into execution the ordinances of the sacred law; the enactment, amending, and abrogation of all laws; concluding treaties and peace; proclaiming the defence of the fatherland (i.e. declaring a state of war). For executive matters, the GNA appoints and if necessary changes ministers.
7. The President elected by the GNA is authorized to sign in the name of the GNA. The Committee of Executive Ministers shall elect one of their number as President of the Committee.

The words 'putting into execution the ordinances of the sacred law' (*ahkâm-ı şeriyenin tenfizi*) call for some comment. They were included also in Article 26 of the 1924 Constitution and no one questioned their inclusion at the time. Although Kemal declared in 1927 that the words were redundant, meaning no more than 'giving effect to legal ordinances', and that he had argued against their insertion as liable to mislead, there is no possible ambiguity about them. Whoever drafted this clause was arrogating to the GNA the powers of the Caliphate. The reason why Kemal tried to explain this fact away was that he had no intention of letting the GNA be used to perpetuate the reign of the sacred law. The words were expunged from the constitution on 10 April 1928, on a motion signed by İsmet and 153 other members.

On 1 April 1921, İsmet inflicted another defeat on the Greeks in a second battle at İnönü. For the next three months the Greeks prepared and regrouped, and on 10 July began a general advance. The Turkish forces were inferior numerically and in equipment, particularly in transport. They gave ground before the Greek onslaught and the enemy swept eastward. With his army in danger of encirclement at Eskişehir, İsmet telegraphed for Kemal, who came at once from Ankara and gave his orders. The army was to fall back beyond the Sakarya river and thus lengthen the enemy's lines of communication. This abandonment of a hundred miles of Turkish territory to the invader would involve a terrific shock to public opinion; Mustafa Kemal would deal with that while İsmet was withdrawing his troops.

Back in Ankara, Kemal found that he had not overestimated the consternation that greeted the news of his decision. He faced an angry Assembly. The cry was raised that the man responsible for the imminent disaster ought to be at the head of the doomed army. With superb insolence, Mustafa Kemal agreed and formally accepted the 'invitation to become Commander-in-Chief', on condition that all the authority vested in the GNA be transferred to him personally. A storm of protest arose: supreme command belonged to the Assembly alone; at most he could be appointed Deputy Commander-in-Chief. He stood his ground; he would not accept this antiquated title so often conferred by the Sultans. If it was good enough for Enver it wasn't good enough for him; he would hold the supreme command in name as well as in fact. The following day, 5 August, the GNA voted him the powers he wished. Henceforth his orders had the force of law.

At once he decreed the confiscation (against payment 'at some future date') of 40 per cent of all food, clothing, bedding, petrol, oil, and motor-spares. A register was to be compiled of all mechanics, metal-workers, and men in other trades of military importance. 'Independence Tribunals' were set up to ensure that the Commander-in-Chief's orders were obeyed. These tribunals differed from similar bodies in revolutionary Russia only in holding their proceedings in public. There was no appeal against their verdicts. Kılıç Ali, a member of the first such tribunal to be created, tells in his memoirs, with a certain pride, how he sentenced his own foster-brother to fifteen years' imprisonment for carelessly allowing a prisoner to escape.

There were to be no more retreats. Mustafa Kemal enunciated this principle in an Order of the Day:

> There is no defence-line. There is a defence-area, which is the whole country. Not one inch of it is to be given up until it is wet with Turkish blood. Any unit, large or small, may be thrown out of its position. But it will face the enemy and continue to fight at the first point where a stand is possible. Units which see a neighbouring unit obliged to retreat will not follow it. They will stay where they are and resist to the end.

To regard these words as so much rhetoric is to mistake the nature of Mustafa Kemal and of those he was addressing. It is an old saying that if Satan were to order a Turkish soldier to bayonet his grandmother he would immediately do so, provided that Satan had taken the precaution of dressing in the uniform of a Turkish corporal. That Order of the Day was an order, and it was obeyed.

For three weeks the battle raged over a 60-mile front. On 13 September the Greeks fell back across the Sakarya and withdrew, burning and devastating, to their old positions round Eskişehir.

The news of the victory was greeted with wild rejoicing. The GNA promoted Mustafa Kemal to the rank of Marshal and gave him the title of Ghazi. Five weeks later, on 20 October, the Franklin–Bouillon Agreement was signed between Nationalist Turkey and France. Hostilities in the south-east were to end, thus releasing many thousands of Turkish troops for the western front. But more important than the actual terms of the agreement was the fact that, by signing it, France had recognized the GNA as the sovereign power in Turkey. Britain, who still recognized the Sultan's government, protested strongly, but to no avail.

For many long months the Greek army dug itself in north and west of Afyonkarahisar, not daring to risk an offensive, while Kemal drove his weary people to ever greater efforts. His position was by no means easy. Towards the end of 1921 the deputies who had been interned in Malta were released and made their way to Ankara, expecting a hero's welcome. But Mustafa Kemal made no secret of his feelings about them: they should have taken his advice not to go to Istanbul in the first place. Having gone, they should have had the sense to come back to Ankara as others had done, before the trap closed.

Some of them formed an opposition group, which tried to obstruct Kemal at every turn. His days were spent in talking down criticism of his conduct of affairs and where necessary he did not shrink from using force. When objections were raised to a motion renewing his tenure of the supreme command, he replied simply that no one but himself was fit for the job and that he did not intend to leave the nation without a leader.

For he was not given to false modesty. Here is his own appraisal of his services, from a speech he made in reply to a proposal that membership of the Assembly should be restricted to people born within the post-war frontiers of Turkey or who had lived in their constituencies for at least five years:

> Unfortunately my birthplace lies outside our present frontiers. That is not my fault . . . And if I have not lived for five years in any one constituency, that is because of the services I have been rendering to this country. Had I tried to comply with the conditions this clause lays down, I should have been unable to conduct our defence at Arıburnu and Anafartalar, which would have meant the loss of Istanbul. If I had been obliged to spend five years in any one spot, I should not have been able to go out to meet the enemy when he fanned out towards Diyarbakır after taking Bitlis and Muş; I could not have done my duty, which was to recover Bitlis and Muş. If I had wanted to fulfil the conditions these gentlemen impose, I should not have been able to form a front at Aleppo and defend it against the enemy, and establish the line which now we call our national frontier. I think my subsequent efforts are known to you all. I've been working too hard to stay five years in any one place. I think that I have won the affection and regard of my nation – perhaps of the whole Muslim world – for these services of mine. So it never occurred to me that anyone might try to deprive me of my rights as a citizen.

In March 1922 representatives of the Allied Powers, meeting in Paris, made proposals for an armistice between Turkey and Greece. These were rejected out of hand; Mustafa Kemal would not accept any armistice unless the Greeks began immediately to evacuate Turkish territory. As they would not do this of their own accord, they must be made to go.

At dawn on 26 August the Greek positions were pulverized under an intense artillery bombardment. Then the Turkish infantry, with fixed bayonets, poured forth from their trenches. The Greek army broke and fled. A portion of it made a stand at Dumlupınar, but by the evening of the 30th there was no Greek army left. Its battered remnants were rushing headlong for İzmir and the waiting ships.

On 9 September, Mustafa Kemal rode into İzmir. As more and more Turkish troops entered the city, terror spread among the

Greek population. For days the streets were hideous with murder and pillage. Then fire broke out, a fire which destroyed half the city and whose marks are still visible today.

A Greek army still remained in Thrace. The Turks marched northward to deal with them. Entering the neutral zone at Çanakkale, they found the Allied Army of Occupation, under General Sir Charles Harington, barring their way. The situation was grave, containing the seeds of a new war, a war in which Turkey could probably count on Soviet help. On 19 September, Harington's French and Italian contingents discreetly withdrew. Slowly the Turks moved closer to the British positions, each side wondering when the other would open fire. Then dramatically, in the nick of time, word came that an armistice had been arranged.

The armistice that was signed at Mudanya on 11 October 1922 represented a complete Allied surrender to the demands of the Nationalists. The agreement made no mention at all of the Sultan. Istanbul, the Straits, and eastern Thrace as far as the Maritsa were to be handed over to the government of the Grand National Assembly, though Allied forces would remain in Istanbul until the signing of a definitive peace treaty.

Lloyd George's policy of encouraging Greece's imperialist adventure in Asia Minor had borne strange fruit. A week after the Mudanya Armistice, he handed in his resignation.

NOTE

[1] *Türkiye Büyük Millet Meclisi*. Its English name may conveniently be abbreviated to 'GNA'.

CHAPTER 8

From Sultanate to Republic

THE MUDANYA ARMISTICE had been the work of professional soldiers. Now the professional politicians took over. On 27 October 1922, invitations to a peace conference at Lausanne were sent both to the Grand National Assembly and to 'the Government of His Imperial Majesty the Sultan'. This ill-considered action precipitated the end of the Sultanate. On 1 November 1922, a long and heated debate took place in the Assembly. Few if any members had a good word to say for Vahdettin, and the obvious move was to depose him and appoint his successor as Sultan-Caliph. But Mustafa Kemal had a more radical proposal. Sovereignty belonged to the nation; the Sultanate should be abolished and the Caliphate alone should be conferred on Vahdettin's successor.

It was decided to refer the question whether the Sultanate could legally be separated from the Caliphate to a joint meeting of the Assembly's Judicial and Constitutional Committees and the Committee for the Sacred Law.

For hours the *hocas* – the learned doctors – wrangled, while Mustafa Kemal sat in a corner, listening to them. Finally his patience gave way. He asked the chairman's leave to speak, jumped on a bench, and shouted:

> Sovereignty and Sultanate are not given to anyone by anyone because scholarship says so; because of debate or discussion. They are taken by strength, by power, by force. By force the Ottoman dynasty seized the sovereignty and sultanate of the Turkish nation; they have maintained this usurpation for six hundred years. The Turkish nation has called a halt; it has rebelled and taken the sovereignty into its own hands. This is an accomplished fact. The question is not whether or not we are going to leave the sovereignty to the nation; the question is merely how to give expression to the accomplished reality. This is going to be, come

> what may. If those who are present and the Assembly and everybody see the problem in its natural light, I believe they will agree. If not, the truth will still be given proper expression. Only maybe some heads will be cut off. As for the academic side of the matter, the learned gentlemen need be in no doubt or anxiety. Let me give you a scientific exposition of the facts.

The words about cutting off heads were a piece of grim humour, not a literal threat. Kemal was perfectly ready to hang his opponents if necessary, but decapitation was no longer in vogue. Nevertheless, these words may well have had more effect on his audience than the scientific exposition which followed. At all events, when he had finished, one of the *hocas* rose to his feet and said, 'Your pardon, Sir. We had been examining the question from a different viewpoint. We have found your explanation enlightening'.

A resolution was hurriedly prepared and read at a second sitting of the Assembly that same day. There were dissenting voices, but they were shouted down. The resolution declared that the Turkish people regarded 'the form of government in Istanbul, which is based on the sovereignty of an individual, as having for ever passed into history as from 16 March 1920'. That was the date of the Allies' official occupation of Istanbul.

On 16 November 1922, Sultan Mehmed VI Vahdettin wrote to General Harington, Commander-in-Chief of the occupation armies:

> Considering my life in danger in Istanbul, I take refuge with the illustrious English State and request my transfer as soon as possible from Istanbul to somewhere else.

He signed the letter as 'Caliph of the Muslims'.

The next morning he stole out of his palace and boarded a British warship, which took him to Malta. That he saved his life by so doing is suggested by a passage in Mustafa Kemal's great apologia, the six-day speech which he delivered to the GNA in October 1927.

> A weak and mean creature, devoid of sensibility and perception, may enter the protection of any foreigner who will take him, but surely such a creature cannot be said to possess the qualities necessary for the Caliph of all the Muslims . . . We Turks are a people who, throughout our history, have been a byword for freedom and independence. We have shown ourselves capable of removing from the stage the puppet-show of Caliphs who

regard as permissible any humiliation which enables their worthless lives to drag on in dishonour for two and a half days longer.

On 18 November, Vahdettin's cousin Abdülmecid became Caliph, by a vote of the Grand National Assembly.

For a little while, Vahdettin toyed with the idea of going to the Hijaz and establishing himself there as Caliph. But the Arab world was too busy dividing itself up into nationalist states to bother with the living symbol of the unity of Islam. The thirty-sixth and last Sultan of the House of Osman died at San Remo, on 16 May 1926.

At the Peace Conference which opened at Lausanne on 21 November 1922, Turkey's chief delegate was İsmet Pasha, who had been appointed Foreign Minister three weeks before. If anyone still thought that the Allies would be dictating terms to a conquered people, half an hour at the conference table must have sufficed to dispel the idea, İsmet fought at Lausanne as hard and as obstinately as he had fought on the field of battle. He was fortified by the knowledge that the Allies were far from united in their aims, despite the appearance of unity presented by the opening words of the draft treaty: 'The British Empire, France, Italy, Japan, Greece, Roumania and the Serb-Croat-Slovene State of the one part and Turkey of the other part . . .'.

İsmet argued every point, until everyone's patience but his own was at an end. Lord Curzon, the head of the British delegation, broke off the Conference on 4 February 1923, as İsmet refused to accept certain economic clauses which he regarded as limiting Turkish sovereignty. To the journalists who asked him what had happened, İsmet replied, 'Nothing. We have refused to accept servitude'.

For some weeks the Allies waited hopefully for İsmet to change his mind, and then, seeing they might wait for ever, they invited him to reopen discussions. The Conference resumed at Lausanne on 23 April. On 24 July, eloquence having beaten in vain against İsmet's imperturbability, the Treaty was signed, embodying virtually all of Turkey's demands. The major provisions of the Treaty and its accompanying Conventions were:

1. The frontier with Greece was to be the river Maritsa, but Turkey would be given an enclave west of the river opposite Edirne, containing a section of the Edirne–Istanbul railway, by way of reparations from Greece.
2. The frontier with Iraq would be settled by subsequent

discussions with Britain. If this proved impossible within a period of nine months, the matter would be decided by the Council of the League of Nations.

3. The Greek and Turkish populations of Turkey and Greece respectively were to be exchanged, except for the Greeks of Istanbul and the Turks of western Thrace.

4. Gallipoli was to be restored to Turkish sovereignty, but the Straits were to be demilitarized. Conditions for the passage of foreign warships in peace and war to be settled later.

5. The Capitulations were to be totally abolished.

The exchange of populations, which was arranged in a Convention signed on 30 January 1923, was well meant but caused a great deal of unhappiness, because the criterion of 'Greek' and 'Turkish' was religion. As a result, many Greek-speaking Muslims and Turkish-speaking Christians found themselves living in virtual exile among their co-religionists of alien speech. As for the Capitulations, the Ottoman government, with German approval, had declared them abolished from 1 October 1914, but this act was not recognized by the Allied Powers.

Thus Turkey won the last campaign in the War of Independence. İsmet Pasha preferred a different metaphor: this time, when the journalists asked him for a statement, he said, 'We've finished the exams and now we're graduating'. Now Kemal could concentrate his attention on building a new nation.

The framework of the Nationalist movement had been the League for the Defence of Rights, founded by the Sivas Congress. The victories of the War of Independence and the final triumph of Lausanne had left the League with no rival for the mastery of Turkey. Opposition to the growing personal power of Kemal appeared as a splinter-group within the League, known as the 'Second Group' in contradistinction to the original 'Group', 260 strong, of his closest adherents. The Second Group, who numbered about forty, half of them belonging to the Ulema, set themselves firmly against him, objecting to each renewal of his supreme command and insisting that the absolutism of the Sultan must not be replaced by the absolutism of the Commander-in-Chief.

What particularly exercised them was their fear that if Kemal remained in control Islam was in for a rough time. There was a severe shortage of residential accommodation in Ankara at that period, and a number of deputies, including some of the Second Group, occupied a dormitory in a school opposite the Assembly building. Two notices were hung on the dormitory wall. One read: 'The playing of backgammon etc. is prohibited'; the other: 'Prayers are compulsory'. Those who did not choose to pray resented having their sleep regularly broken by the call to prayer, which was recited right inside the dormitory; they complained to Kemal and the practice was discontinued. None of the Second Group stood at the 1923 elections.

At a congress held in April 1923 the League transformed itself into a political party, to be known as the People's Party (*Halk Fırkası*). Although it was the only party in the new GNA, there were groups and individual members of the Assembly who did not belong to it. Even inside the Party there was opposition to Kemal's plans, and if he succeeded almost invariably in carrying the Assembly with him, it was because the deputies knew that he had the backing of the professional and officer classes. As for the ordinary people, 'obedience to those in authority among you' was an established principle of Islam. They had always been accustomed to getting on with their work while the Sultan-Caliph 'maintained the order of the world by his prayers', and the overwhelming majority of them were prepared to do the same under the man who had brought them out of the valley of the shadow.

On 13 October 1923, the Assembly voted that Ankara should be the permanent seat of the government. This action had not been taken until the Treaty of Lausanne was safely signed. Although the Nationalists would never have allowed the old capital to be wrested from them, there was clearly no sense in running into trouble if it could be avoided. To have shifted the centre of government from Istanbul would have weakened the Turkish position at the Conference, if the Allies chose to revive the old claim that Istanbul was a predominantly Greek city. As a matter of fact, İsmet Pasha had thought it necessary to mention at Lausanne that the Turks were in a majority at Istanbul and had no more fear of a plebiscite there than in any other part of their country. This contention was not disputed; and it is notable that Lord Curzon mentioned, as a factor in the Allied decision on the future of the Straits, 'the existence of the capital of Turkey and the seat of the Caliphate on the shores of this waterway'. But the move had been under consideration for some time, as appears from an understandably tendentious manifesto published by the deposed Vahdettin in the Cairo newspaper *al-Ahram* as early as 26 April. In it he referred to the Kemalists' desire to make Ankara the capital, and ascribed it to their desire for closer proximity to the Bolsheviks 'with a view to putting Istanbul spiritually into Russian hands'. It is probably safe to set aside the ex-Sultan's explanation and take it that the decision to move the capital into central Anatolia was in recognition of the fact that Anatolia now was Turkey, unencumbered by European, Arab, or African provinces. The shift to Ankara symbolized a clean break with the Ottoman past.

On 2 October the occupation forces had left Istanbul. Four days later, Turkish troops entered the city, and with them went a delegation to represent the Grand National Assembly at the ensuing celebrations. The delegation had a hostile reception from the crowds; it was not that this fact persuaded the GNA to remove the seat of government but that the ineluctable nature of the rumoured move had become generally realized a week before, with a newspaper report of an interview given to a foreign journalist by Kemal, in which he stated flatly that Ankara was the capital.

The decision to make Turkey into a republic, though hotly contested, did not come as a surprise. The existing system clearly could not last. The ministers, being at that time appointed by and responsible to the GNA, were subjected to constant criticism, not only from members who genuinely disapproved of their decisions or actions, but also from members who thought it was time they had a turn at running a ministry themselves.

The announcement by an Ankara newspaper on 9 October 1923, that a republic would soon be proclaimed, aroused violent controversy in and out of the Assembly. In accordance with Mustafa Kemal's carefully laid plan, the Cabinet presided over by Fethi resigned on 27 October, and the deputies tried to agree on a new Cabinet which might have a chance of general acceptance. Jealousies made this impossible; the opposition were hopelessly divided. Mustafa Kemal and his immediate circle were the only people who knew exactly what they wanted. Kemal drafted the alterations he desired to make in the Law of Fundamental Organization, and waited his moment.

Though several members tried to pin Fethi down, he would not state the reason for his resignation. He could hardly have told the truth, which was that the Ghazi Pasha had instructed him to resign in order to precipitate a constitutional crisis. On 29 October, when the deputies had talked themselves to a standstill, it was decided to seek guidance from Mustafa Kemal, who was in his house at Çankaya, where over dinner the previous evening he had told his guests, who included Fethi and İsmet, 'Tomorrow we're going to proclaim the Republic'. He came down to the Assembly and said, his tongue well in his cheek, 'Gentlemen, I understand there is some divergence of opinion about the election of a Cabinet. If you will excuse me for one hour, I shall find a solution and submit it to you'.

He used that hour to present his proposals to certain key men and, sure of their support, returned to the Assembly. Mounting the rostrum, he explained his conviction that the trouble lay in the constitution, which he proposed to amend. Then he handed his draft proposal to a clerk, to read aloud, and left the rostrum.

> The form of government of the Turkish State is a Republic. The President of the Turkish Republic is elected by the whole Assembly from among its members . . . The President is the Head of the State. As such, he may, if he thinks fit, preside over the Assembly and the Council of Ministers. The Prime Minister is chosen by the President from among the members of the Assembly . . . The other Ministers are chosen by the Prime Minister from among the members of the Assembly and the whole Council of Ministers is then submitted to the Assembly by the President for approval.

Everybody tried to speak at once. After a great deal of quibbling, one member put the realist point of view:

> Once you've said, Sovereignty belongs unconditionally to the nation, you can ask anyone you like; it's a Republic. That is the name of the new-born baby. We're told some people don't like the name. Then they can lump it'.

The motion was put to the vote. There were many abstentions, but it was carried. The Assembly was then asked to approve the nomination of Mustafa Kemal as President of the Republic. One hundred and fifty-eight members voted for him, out of a total of 287. The rest abstained, and he was declared elected. İsmet Pasha became Prime Minister and Fethi President of the GNA. At last Mustafa Kemal had the power he wanted to set his seal on the new Turkey. Only one obstacle remained.

CHAPTER 9

The End of the Caliphate

MUSTAFA KEMAL'S PURPOSE was to make Turkey into a modern state fit to take its place among the civilized countries of the Western world. In his view, the native virtues of the Turks had been strangled for centuries in the toils of the religion of the Arabs. He took no account of the fact that Islam had been the unifying force which enabled the Ottomans to build their great empire; other Turks had built empires before them, without the help of Islam. It is probable that he did not hope to eliminate Islamic worship; if he did, that was something for the remote future. The primary task was to sever the bonds between Islam and the state, and then to replace Islamic by Western civilization. The first step was to get rid of the Caliph.

It is not without significance that the decision to abolish the Caliphate was taken while Kemal was attending manoeuvres at İzmir in January and February of 1924; he acted only when he was sure that the army was solidly behind him.

Abdülmecid, who had been appointed Caliph after the deposition of Vahdettin, took his duties seriously. The conditions under which he was to hold office had been clearly laid down. He was to use the title 'Caliph of the Muslims' and no other. He should issue a declaration to the Muslim world, expressing his pleasure at being elected Caliph by the Grand National Assembly of Turkey and his disapproval of the conduct of Vahdettin. He was to quote the substance of the Law of Fundamental Organization and speak appreciatively of the achievements of the new government of Turkey.

Never dreaming that the Caliphate itself was in danger, and confident in the knowledge that he had lent his support to the Nationalists during the War of Independence, Abdülmecid did not hesitate to defy Kemal. He signed himself 'Caliph of the Messenger of God' and 'Servitor of the Two Holy Places'. In his declaration to the Muslim world he did not mention Vahdettin, considering that to denigrate his predecessor 'would manifestly accord ill with my office and my disposition'. He proposed to attend the Friday prayer wearing a robe and turban of the type worn by Mehmed the Conqueror. Large crowds gathered to cheer his public appearances; he held court, receiving foreign diplomats and official visitors. Until the proclamation of the Republic took the wind out of their sails, many deputies had favoured making him titular Head of State, thus preserving for Turkey the distinction of being the personal domain of the Caliph.

Kemal's biting rhetoric did not spare the unfortunate authors of this last suggestion.

> For centuries our people have been compelled to act in accordance with this absurd point of view. And what happened? Millions of them died, in every land they went to. Do you know how many Anatolian boys perished in the sweltering heat of the deserts of Yemen? How many men died to keep Syria and Iraq, to stay in Egypt, to cling on to Africa; do you know that? And do you see what good it all did?

Yet a large body of opinion in the country was against him, and Kemal knew it. Many ordinary people who cared not a scrap whether they were ruled by a Sultan or a President, so long as he was a Turk, cared very much about the Caliph of Islam.

Unwittingly two distinguished Indian Muslims came to the Ghazi's aid. On 24 November 1923, the Agha Khan and Mr Ameer Ali, a Privy Councillor, wrote to İsmet Pasha, respectfully urging

> the imminent necessity for maintaining the religious and moral solidarity of Islam by placing the Caliph-Imamate on a basis which would command the confidence and esteem of the Muslim nations, and thus impart to the Turkish State unique strength and dignity.

The letter was published in three Istanbul newspapers on 5 December. The journalists responsible were arraigned before an Independence Tribunal for high treason, but were acquitted on 2 January 1924.

The fact that the Agha Khan had consistently supported the Nationalist cause was not generally known in Turkey. Since he was not an orthodox Muslim, but head of a heretical branch of the Ismailis, who are a heretical offshoot of the Shi'ites, whom orthodoxy regarded as heretical, he had about as much right to a say concerning the future of the Caliphate, in the eyes of such Turks as had heard of him, as Catholics might have conceded to Brigham Young in a debate on the future of the Papacy. By his intervention, therefore, he frustrated his own purpose. The Kemalists spread the story that his prestige in India had been largely manufactured by the British in order to set him up as a native leader of Islam in opposition to Abdülhamid, during the time when the latter was trying to assert his authority over Muslims everywhere.

On 3 March 1924, the GNA voted for the deposition of Abdülmecid, the abolition of the Caliphate, and the banishment from Turkey of all members of the Imperial family (this last provision was rescinded in June 1952). Abdülmecid left that night for Switzerland. He died on 23 August 1944 in Paris and was buried at Medina.

In the course of the debate, a deputy who had been travelling in India and Egypt on behalf of the Red Crescent (the counterpart of the Red Cross in Muslim countries except Persia, where its counterpart is the Red Lion and Sun), declared that a number of representative Muslim bodies in both those countries had authorized him to offer the Caliphate to Mustafa Kemal. The Ghazi's head was not turned. Thanking those concerned for their goodwill towards him, he said:

> You know that the Caliph is a political leader. How can I accept? Those who made this offer are subjects of a King, an Emperor. If I accept, will their rulers consent? . . . Have those who wish to make me Caliph the power to execute my orders? Would it not therefore be ridiculous to assume an empty title with no reality behind it?

At the same sitting two more blows were struck at the supremacy of Islam. The Law of Unification of Instruction gave into the charge of the Ministry of Public Instruction all educational institutions within the boundaries of the Republic. Now the *medreses* were under the direct control of the government, which shortly afterwards closed them, thus putting a drastic end to the old grievance of the Westernizers, that schools and *medreses* produced two different nations, one European, one Asian.

The other business before the Assembly on that eventful day was a law which replaced the Ministry of the Sacred Law and Pious Endowments (*Evkaf*) by a new department of the Prime Minister's office, the Directorate of Religious Affairs.

The religious courts were abolished on 8 April. The next day saw the repeal of a law prohibiting the use of intoxicants, which the GNA had passed on 14 September 1920.

The changes so far made were embodied in a new constitution, accepted by the GNA on 20 April 1924. Its fundamental provisions were these:

1. The Turkish State is a Republic.

2. The religion of the Turkish state is Islam. Its official language is Turkish. Its capital is the city of Ankara.

3. Sovereignty belongs unconditionally to the nation.

4. The Grand National Assembly of Turkey is the sole rightful representative of the nation and exercises, in the name of the nation, its right of sovereignty.

5. Legislative authority and executive power are manifested and concentrated in the Grand National Assembly.

6. The Assembly exercises its legislative authority directly.

7. The Assembly exercises its executive power through the President of the Republic, whom it elects, and a Cabinet to be chosen by him. The Assembly has at all times the right to keep a check on the actions of the Government or to overthrow it.

8. The judicial function is exercised in the name of the nation by independent courts in accordance with the law.

CHAPTER 10

The First Opposition Party and the Kurdish Revolt

MUCH AS THE constitutional lawyers might amuse themselves by analysing the structure of the new Turkish state, the plain truth is that it was a dictatorship. And, although one's liberal sentiments may revolt at the thought, this dictatorship was the best possible thing that could have happened to the Turks. Fully 80 per cent of them were peasants : patient, hard-working, disciplined, honest; the salt of the earth, but illiterate and living brutally primitive lives, as incapable of participating in the business of government as they were of regulating the rhythm of the spheres. Defeated in the First World War, their land overrun by foreign troops, their morale would inevitably have collapsed had there been no Mustafa Kemal to make a nation of them.

Kemal was the master, and few dared criticize him to his face – to his great regret, for he loved nothing so much as a good argument. There is an agreeable tale of how he visited a girls' school and one of the girls asked him whether the foreign Press were right in describing him as a dictator. 'If they were', replied Kemal, 'you wouldn't dare ask me'. But obviously it was easier to criticize İsmet, so he became the general target. Nor was this wholly unfair, because he had made himself responsible for financial matters, of which he knew nothing. Trade was at a virtual standstill, partly through world conditions, partly through the departure of many Greek businessmen by the transfer of populations agreed on at Lausanne, but partly also because of the irritating bureaucratic restrictions which discouraged foreign shipping from visiting the port of Istanbul. Lausanne had barred foreign ships from the coastal trade, and port services had been nationalized.

The membership of the People's Party in the Assembly was ill-assorted. Besides those who unswervingly followed Kemal there were many sincere republicans who disapproved of autocracy. Then there were the *hocas*, who were bitterly antagonistic to the government's laicist policy and had been ready even to have Mustafa Kemal as Caliph, rather than to see the total disappearance of the Caliphate. These men began to beat the democratic drum and to wave the banner of liberalism as soon as the establishment of the Republic showed them that any other form of opposition was foredoomed. Lastly there were those former Ottoman officials and deputies who saw no hope of personal advancement under the new order.

Early in October 1924 a wave of resignations began from the People's Party, headed by Hüseyin Rauf, İsmail Canbulat, and Dr Abdülhak Adnan. In November, however, İsmet won a vote of confidence from a party meeting by a comfortable majority. It was subsequently decided to add the word 'Republican' to the name of the party (*Cumhuriyet Halk Fırkası*, 10 November 1924). Two distinguished soldiers, Kâzım Karabekir Pasha (who had always been jealous of Kemal) and Ali Fuad Pasha, resigned their military inspectorates to return to their seats in the Assembly and to take over the leadership of the rebels, who on 17 November formed themselves into the Progressive Republican Party (*Terakkiperver Cumhuriyet Fırkası*).

Four days later, İsmet's Cabinet resigned and in an attempt at reconciliation the premiership was given back to Fethi, an intelligent, cultured, gentle, and transparently honest liberal. The Istanbul newspapers began a concerted attack on the People's Party, regarding Fethi's reappointment as a confession of weakness.

In February 1925 a great insurrection broke out among the Kurds in the east of Turkey. The Kurds are a pastoral, semi-nomadic Muslim people whose homelands are divided among Turkey and her southern and eastern neighbours. Those in Turkey number something under 3 million. Their ethnic origin used to be glossed over; thus a history textbook published by the Turkish Ministry of Education in 1950 spoke of those involved in the 1925 insurrection as 'a gang of ignorant villagers in the eastern provinces'. A Turkish encyclopaedic dictionary published as late as 1971, while correctly defining 'Kurdish' as 'an Indo-European language spoken by the Kurds, who live in Turkey, Persia, Iraq, Syria, and the USSR', cheerfully explains 'Kurds' as 'a people of Turkish origin, living in Hither Asia'. The term 'Mountain Turks' used to be applied to them, but if it is now used at all, it is only as a wry joke. Yet the term appeared in a somewhat Delphic passage in a report in *The Times* on 21 October 1966, about a Press conference held by Amnesty International in London. To make sense of it would require more research than its peripheral interest warrants; it is therefore reproduced here with no attempt at emendation or expansion.

> A protest was made about 'the attempt to attack Dr. Salahadin Rastgeldi as a non-European'. He is a Kurd who left Turkey at the age of 16, and has become a distinguished medical specialist in Sweden. Because he was worried that the Arabs might find this out and refuse to talk to him (Kurds are not popular in Cairo) he asked Amnesty to say that he was 'a mountain Turk'.

The tribal organization of the Kurds is strong but they have no articulate national voice and seem unlikely ever to have a land of their own. The stillborn Treaty of Sèvres had envisaged an autonomous Kurdistan, but although Lord Curzon expressed his support for this plan at Lausanne, nothing came of it.

The revolt of 1925 was due in part to resentment at Turkish rule and to a positive desire for Kurdish independence, and in part to outraged religious feeling at the abolition of the Caliphate. In a desire to play down the element of Kurdish nationalism, the government stressed the religious-reactionary nature of the insurrection and used it as grounds for muzzling the opposition Press and Party. And apparently with some reason, for although positive information is scanty, it seems clear that however loudly the Progressive Party leaders proclaimed their loyalty to the Republic, some of them were in communication with the insurgents. It is significant that the Party's first branch office was opened in the east, at Urfa.

The leader of the insurrection was Sheikh Said of Palu, the hereditary chief of the Nakşibendî order of dervishes, who on 11 February 1925 announced that the time had come to put an end to the Republic and restore the Sultanate and Caliphate. His candidate was Mehmed Selim Efendi, the eldest son of Abdülhamid, at that time fifty-three years old and living in Beirut. The Kurdish tribesmen flocked to his banner and for some weeks the situation was critical indeed, with the insurgents in control of large areas of the provinces of Muş, Bitlis, Bingöl, Elâzığ, and Diyarbakır. Martial law was proclaimed in thirteen eastern provinces, but things went so badly that the People's Party passed a vote of censure on Fethi's Cabinet, and İsmet's strong hand resumed control on 3 March. Before the end of the month the back of the revolt was broken. The last flickers of organized rebellion were stamped out by the end of April. Information that came to light during the trial of the ringleaders was declared to be clear evidence of a link between the insurgents and the Progressive Party, which was accordingly suppressed on 5 June, under the provisions of a hastily passed Establishment of Order Act. On 29 June the Independence Tribunal at Diyarbakır condemned Sheikh Said and forty-six others to death and ordered the *tekkes*, the dervish lodges, of the eastern provinces to be closed.

There was some talk in Turkey and abroad of British machinations, on the basis of a *cui bono?* argument, because the ruthless measures taken by the Turkish authorities did not endear them to the Kurds of Mosul, whose views were canvassed by the League of Nations commission which ultimately recommended that Mosul become part not of Turkey but of Iraq (see below, p. 131). But even Pandit Nehru, who was not conspicuously pro-British at that time, had to concede that there was no evidence of British involvement in the insurrection.

Sporadic unrest continued in the east for many years. In June 1930 a number of Kurdish chieftains who had fled into Persia after the 1925 rising returned with several hundred horsemen and established themselves on Mount Ararat, whence they succeeded in defying the authorities for some months.

In 1936 the province of Tunceli was placed under martial law and 3,000 Kurdish families were deported to western Turkey. Ten years were to pass before the government felt satisfied that there was no more danger of a Kurdish insurrection. On 30 December 1946, civil administration was restored in Tunceli and the deported families were permitted to return home.

Almost all the Kurds of eastern Turkey have now settled down; large numbers of them will be found, for example, living round the city-walls of Diyarbakır.

CHAPTER II

The Progress of the Reforms

ALTHOUGH THE KURDISH revolt had a partly religious motive and a wholly religious colour, it had won no support from the Turks of the eastern provinces, among whom Islamic feeling was, and is, traditionally strong. They seem to have felt no sympathy with the racially and linguistically alien Kurds, brother-Muslims though they were. But this fact did not lull Mustafa Kemal into complacency. The power of religion over the minds of the Turks had to be broken, or at least weakened, if his plans were to succeed. The body of Muslims, those who believe that there is no god but Allah and that Muhammad is His messenger, is divided into two great sections, Sunnite and Shi'ite. The schism began soon after the death of Muhammad (A.D. 632), over the succession to the leadership of the new Islamic community. The Sunnites believe that the office of Caliph belongs to the man most capable of fulfilling its duties. Theoretically it is conferred by the Ulema as representatives of the community. Although most Caliphs designated a son or brother as successor, the formal approval of the Ulema had to be obtained at the beginning of each reign.

The Shi'ites are the partisans of Ali, the Prophet's son-in-law, and have always held that the Imamate (their term for Caliphate) belonged exclusively to his line. They consequently regard as usurpers all the Caliphs acknowledged by the Sunnis, except of course Ali himself, who held the office from 656 to 661. Whereas one of the theoretical bases of Sunnite Islam is the consensus of the community, Shi'ism is authoritarian, being based on blind obedience to the Imams, who are sinless and infallible.

Although Turkish official statistics pay no heed to this division, lumping all Muslims together, there is in Turkey a large Shi'ite (or *Alevî*, to use the Turkish term) minority. It is commonly said that the religion of many *Alevîs* is Islamic only in name, while in reality they follow the shamanistic practices of their forefathers. In the absence of an up-to-date study of popular religion in Turkey, it is impossible to estimate the truth in this assertion, which is mainly made about certain of the nomadic and semi-nomadic tribes collectively known as *Yürüks*.

But the position is further complicated. Even among the nominally Sunnite majority, Islam in Turkey has always existed on two different planes. There was the Islam of the state, with its salaried hierarchy speaking with the voice of orthodoxy, and there was the heterodox Islam of the people (and not only of the common people), embodied in the great dervish orders (*tarikat*, literally 'Way'). The most flourishing of these were the popular Bektaşi and the more aristocratic Mevlevî orders. The former was firmly entrenched in the Corps of Janissaries, who were sometimes called 'Sons of Hacı Bektaş', after the semi-legendary founder of the order. Before the abolition of the *tarikats*, of which we shall presently speak, a network of Bektaşi lodges (*tekke*) covered the Ottoman empire, each, it is said, no more than 15 miles from the next. The doctrines of the order were mystical and tinged with Shiʿism. One remarkable feature which attracted much hostile attention from the orthodox was that women attended Bektaşi ceremonies unveiled, on equal terms with men. Bektaşi apologists plausibly claim this to be a survival of Turkish pre-Islamic custom.

The comparative indifference and calm with which the abolition of the Caliphate had been greeted among the Turkish population contrasts strangely with the widespread disorders which followed Mustafa Kemal's next move. Although many Turks had revered the Caliphate and deplored its passing, it was too remote and exalted an institution to mean much to the average Anatolian peasant. But the clothes he wore, especially his headdress, meant a great deal to him, distinguishing him as they did from the Christian. The Ulema wore turbans, members of the *tarikats* wore distinctive conical caps, officials and townsmen generally wore the fez. Worn in conjunction with a black frock-coat, which constituted formal dress for civilian officials from the reign of Abdülmecid onward, the fez has been well described as giving the wearer the appearance of a wine-bottle with red sealing-wax on the cork. Villagers usually wore a fez with a cloth wrapped round it, turban-wise. The essential was that the headdress should not prevent the wearer's forehead from touching the ground during prayer. During the War of Independence the Nationalists had worn the tall lambskin *kalpak* (decree of the GNA, 12 April 1921), and after the abolition of the Caliphate the army exchanged their *kalpaks* for peaked caps.

During the month of August 1925, Mustafa Kemal paid an

official visit to the Black Sea coastal region. He and the civilians who acompanied him wore Panama hats. Addressing an open-air meeting at Kastamonu, a town which still has a name for conservatism, he gently broached the subject of dress. He pointed out that the traditional Anatolian male attitre of full gown and baggy trousers took far more material than a suit of European cut, while the fez, with its skull-cap beneath and its cloth wrapped around, was far more expensive than a European hat.

A few days later, at İnebolu, he developed the theme in more forceful terms: 'We are going to adopt the civilized international mode of dress... including a headdress with a brim; this I wish to say openly. The name of this headdress is "hat" '. These words may strike the reader as slightly ridiculous. The courage it demanded to say them in a hidebound Anatolian town may be judged from the fact that in the Turkish idiom of that time *şapka giymek*, 'to put on a hat', meant 'to apostasize from Islam' or 'to enter the service of a foreign power'.

Mustafa Kemal then dealt with those who maintained that the hat, an alien form of headdress, was unnatural for Turks.

> To these people let me say that they are very unobservant and very ignorant. I should like to ask them why it is permissible to wear the fez, which is a Greek headdress, and not the hat. Further, when, why, and how did they come to wear the gown, which is the garment peculiar to Byzantine priests and Jewish rabbis?

Still treading on dangerous ground, he went on:

> In the course of my trip, I have seen that our women comrades – not in the villages but particularly in towns and cities – are careful to muffle up their faces and their eyes. I should think this habit must cause them great discomfort, especially now, in the hot weather. Men, this is to some extent the result of our selfishness... Let them show their faces to the world and let them have the chance to see the world for themselves. There's nothing to be afraid of in that.

On 30 September he returned to Kastamonu and in an address to Party members there was even more outspoken:

> The aim of the revolutionary measures we have been taking is to bring the people of the Turkish Republic into a state of society

which is entirely modern and civilized, in every sense and in every way... It is essential that we bring about the utter rout of mentalities incapable of accepting this fact.

In the same memorable speech he lashed out at most of the old Muslim modes of conduct, which the vast majority of Turks would have considered immutable and unassailable. He touched on the exaggerated veneration paid to the tombs (*türbe*) of holy men: 'It is disgraceful for a civilized society to seek help from the dead'. Then he passed on to give the first warning of what was in store for the *tarikats*.

I take it that the aim of the orders can only be the wellbeing of their followers, in worldly and spiritual life. I cannot accept the existence, in the civilized Turkish community, of people so primitive as to seek their material and spiritual wellbeing through the guidance of any old sheikh, today, when they stand in the radiant presence of learning and science, of civilization and all that it means. Gentlemen, I want you and the whole nation to understand well that the Republic of Turkey can never be the land of sheikhs, dervishes, disciples, and lay-brothers. The straightest, truest Way [*tarikat*] is the Way of civilization. To be a man, it is enough to do what civilization dictates and demands. The heads of the orders will grasp this truth I have stated and will at once close their *tekkes*, of their own accord. They will acknowledge that their disciples have at last attained right guidance.

He modified this hectoring tone when going on to speak of the position of women, well knowing the damage that might be done by over-precipitate action.

A society or nation consists of two kinds of people, called men and women. Can we shut our eyes to one portion of a group, while advancing the other, and still bring progress to the whole group? Can half a community ascend to the skies, while the other half remains chained in the dust? The road of progress must be trodden by both sexes together, marching arm in arm as comrades...

In some places I see women who throw a cloth or a towel or something of the sort over their heads, covering their faces and their eyes. When a man passes by, they turn away, or sit huddled on the ground. What is the sense of this behaviour? Gentlemen, do the mothers and daughters of a civilized nation assume this curious attitude, this barbarian posture? It makes the nation look ridiculous: it must be rectified immediately.

If the Ghazi had hoped for a positive response to his eloquence, he was disappointed. The majority of educated women had discarded the veil years before, particular impetus being given to this trend by the First World War, during which many women had entered the Civil Service. Mustafa Kemal's speech was a factor in the disappearance of the veil from the big country-towns, and the process was accelerated by increased knowledge of, and interest in, Western fashions. But, outside the big towns, the generality of women remained shut off from the equality which the Ghazi had invited them to enjoy. Many people, even in Turkey, believe that he outlawed the wearing of the veil, but he never did; he had the good sense to see that it was not legislation but time that would overthrow this last citadel of Islamic conservatism. So even today the visitor to Anatolia may see women put their shawls over their faces as he passes, or cringe with their faces to the wall, just as Mustafa Kemal saw them fifty years ago, though they grow fewer as the years go by.

Shortly after this Black Sea tour, all officials were ordered to replace their fezzes by hats, a special allowance being given to them for this purpose. On 25 October 1925, a law was passed compelling all male citizens to wear hats; the wearing of the fez became and remains a punishable offence.

It is a strange irony that whereas few Turks were prepared to do anything to preserve the Caliphate, an institution venerated by Muslims for 1,300 years, many of them fought like tigers to save the fez, which had been introduced less than a century before. So grave were the disorders in the north-east that a cruiser was ordered to Rize, on the Black Sea, and the Independence Tribunals went into action. Not a few *hocas* were hanged for preaching against the new law. The government, presumably feeling that it would be best to get all the rioting over at once, pushed through a law dissolving all the dervish orders and closing their lodges and the tombs of holy men. The same law, which was passed on 30 November, forbade fortune-telling, sorcery, and the preparation of amulets for purposes of divination or of obtaining the fulfilment of wishes. The Tribunals did their work with ruthless efficiency. The reforms continued.

Three separate systems of dating had been in use in the Ottoman empire. For general purposes there was the Islamic *Hicrî* calendar, which begins with the Prophet's departure from Mecca in A.D. 622. It is lunar, with no intercalary months, so that when we hear of Muslim centenarians we must remember that they have lived for only ninety-seven of our years. The beginnings and ends of the months were fixed in each separate locality by observation of the new moon. The obvious disadvantages of this system for fiscal purposes led to the adoption by the Treasury, in 1740, of the *Malî* or financial calendar, which was the Old Style or Julian year but with an era reckoned from the Islamic year of its inception. The *Malî* year was used by other government departments and for civil purposes from 1840 on, side by side with the *Hicrî*. Thus the 'Thirty-first of March Incident' of 1325 took place on 13 April 1909, corresponding to 22 Rabi' al-Awwal 1327 of the Islamic era. In 1917 it was enacted that '16 February 1332 should be counted as 1 March 1333', i.e., that the *Malî* year be brought into step with the Gregorian by dropping thirteen days, for it must be borne in mind that the Julian year began in March.

All this tangle was swept away with effect from the beginning of January 1926 by the adoption of the Gregorian calendar for all purposes. On tombstones and in obituary notices, however, the Turks still have the disconcerting habit of giving the birth-year of the deceased in the old reckoning if it occurred before 1926; thus one may read of a man born in 1305 and dying in 1970. The inscription on the statue of Mustafa Kemal at Seraglio Point includes the words 'Proclamation of the Republic 1339. This statue erected 1926'. A law of 14 January 1926 set the beginning of the state's financial year at 1 June. In 1944 this was changed to 1 January, but it was found that this did not allow sufficient time for the budget proposals to be debated and a further change was made in 1949: starting in 1950, the budgetary year now begins on 1 March.

From 1 December 1925 the international method of reckoning time, which had been allowed for official purposes just before the First World War, replaced the Islamic reckoning whereby clocks and watches are set at 12 every evening at sunset.

It was obvious that Mustafa Kemal, having done away with so many of the outward signs of Islam in Turkey, would not long tolerate the existence of Islamic law as the law of the land. Between 1870 and 1877, the doctrines presented in the canonical works of the great Muslim legists had begun to be promulgated in a well-classified Turkish translation known as 'The Code', *Mecelle*. Before the committee which was preparing it could deal with family law and the law of inheritance it was dissolved by Abdülhamid, in 1888, so that in these matters Jews and Christians were still governed by their own religious laws. The continuance of this state of affairs was guaranteed by Article 41 of the Treaty of Lausanne:

> The Turkish Government undertakes to take, as regards non-Muslim minorities in so far as concerns their family law or personal status, measures permitting the settlement of these questions in accordance with the customs of these minorities.

In October 1925 the leaders of the Jewish and Armenian communities formally renounced this privilege, 'in view of the forthcoming introduction of a Western civil code'.

On 5 November, Mustafa Kemal opened the new School of Law at Ankara. In his inaugural speech he spoke of the government's intention of bringing into existence 'completely new laws' and eradicating the old ones.

In January 1926 the Greek community, reluctantly making a virtue of necessity, followed the example of the Jews and Armenians. The radical nature of the reform, when it came, surprised most foreign observers: the Turkish legal experts did not waste time trying to tinker with the existing laws; instead the Swiss Civil Code was adopted *en bloc* on 17 February, an adaptation of the Italian Penal Code on 1 March, and a Commercial Code based chiefly on those of Germany and Italy on 29 May. The new Penal Code came into effect on 1 July, the other two Codes on 4 October. Henceforth all Turkish citizens were subject to the same laws.

The opposition made one last effort. In June 1926, Mustafa Kemal was to visit İzmir. A few days before, a conspiracy came to light, one of its members having turned informer. A bomb was to have been thrown into Kemal's car as it passed along a narrow street, and gunmen would be standing by to finish the work if necessary. The ringleader was Ziya Hürşid, a former deputy who had aroused Kemal's anger in the Assembly by voting against the abolition of the Sultanate.

Kemal made this conspiracy the excuse for hanging or exiling virtually every prominent man known to be irredeemably opposed to his policies. Evidence is lacking to show how many of them had really been implicated.

Now that the opposition leaders were gone, Mustafa Kemal had no fear of what the rank-and-file might do. In 1927 he paid his first visit to Istanbul since 1919, taking up his residence in Dolmabahçe, the summer palace of the Sultans.

On 10 April 1928, the clause 'The religion of the Turkish State is Islam' was dropped from Article 2 of the constitution.

CHAPTER 12

The Language Reform

THE STRONG DIDACTIC streak in Kemal's temperament was never more clearly revealed than in the next part of his campaign to change the face of Turkey.

The Arabic alphabet is ill-suited to the writing of Turkish, particularly because Turkish has eight short vowels, while the Arabic alphabet at best distinguishes only three; 'at best', because the Arabic letters are all consonants; the three short vowels can be indicated by the use of accents above or below the letters, but these are regularly employed only in the Koran and school-books and sometimes in poetry. Hence the gloomy but realistic dictum with which Western teachers of Arabic are fond of scaring their would-be pupils: that it is impossible to read an Arabic sentence unless one knows what it says. The position is no better when the Arabic letters are used for Turkish, since the consonant-systems of the two languages are not alike: the Arabic letter *kaf*, for example, was used by the Turks to represent *k*, *g*, *ng*, *y*, and *v*. Thus if one sees the Arabic letters *kl* in an Ottoman text it is not always immediately obvious which of the eight possible words is intended: the Turkish *kel* 'scabby', *kül* 'ashes', *gel* 'come', or *gül* 'smile'; the Arabic *kall* 'weariness' or *kull* 'whole'; the Persian *gil* 'clay' or *gul* 'rose'. At no time was there a universally recognized rule about the spelling of Turkish words. Words borrowed from Arabic and Persian, on the other hand, retained their original spelling, although their pronunciation changed, sometimes beyond recognition, on Turkish lips.

Its unsuitability for Turkish apart, the Arabic alphabet is intrinsically difficult. Most of its twenty-eight letters change their shape according to whether they are initial, medial, final, or isolated, for they are joined together in printing as well as in writing.

In 1857 Feth-Ali Ahundzâde, a well-known literary figure of Azerbayjan, wrote an essay on how the Arabic alphabet might be improved. He came to Istanbul in 1863 and explained his ideas to the Grand Vizier, Fuad Pasha, who asked the Ottoman Scientific

Society to assess them. The Society approved them but thought the printing industry would find excessive difficulty in implementing them. Feth-Ali then proposed that the Arabic alphabet be abandoned and Latin letters introduced, but got nowhere with this suggestion. Still, the desirability of a change continued to exercise people's minds. Enver Pasha played with a scheme for modifying the Arabic alphabet by eliminating the initial, medial, and final forms and writing each letters separately. He also devised a way of indicating the vowels within the body of a word. But his ideas did not catch on.

The possibility of scrapping the Arabic alphabet and introducing the Latin was a topic of conversation among Ottoman officers during the Gallipoli campaign.[1]

In February 1924, Şükrü Saracoğlu, a prominent member of the GNA, said during a debate on education:

> I am convinced that the heaviest responsibility for this lamentable situation rests with the alphabet... The Arabic letters are not suited to the writing of Turkish. In spite of so many years, indeed centuries, of self-sacrificing labour on the part of our learned men and officials, only two or three per cent of our people are literate.[2]

He went on to ask the Minister of Education what his views were, but was howled down and his question remained unanswered.

For the next few years there was sporadic discussion of the problem with no tangible result, until Mustafa Kemal had time to devote himself to it. In 1927 the Soviets set up an 'All-Union Committee for a New Turkish Alphabet', and the 'Unified Turkic Latin Alphabet' which it devised came into use among the Turkish peoples of the USSR in 1929–30 (though it was replaced by an adaptation of the Russian alphabet at the beginning of the Second World War). Kemal beat them to it. The replacement of the Arab numerals by the Western numerals for official purposes was decreed by the GNA on 24 May 1928, with effect from 28 May. But already on 20 May had come an official intimation that the Arabic letters were going to be not modified but superseded, in the course of a statement by the Minister of Education in the Assembly:

> If we have been slow in this matter, it is because we are waiting for the findings of the special Commission we are appointing. The question of the alphabet will naturally be resolved in accordance with the principles accepted by the civilized world.

The obvious objection to this course, that it would cut off the younger generation from all the vast heritage of Ottoman literature, had no weight at all with Kemal; it was precisely his purpose to do this, and so to divert their attention from East to West. In fairness to him it must be remembered how very few of the Turks could read enough to share in that heritage.

The Commission did its work well. The new Turkish alphabet, though not perfectly phonetic, is a good deal more so than that of most European languages, and is immeasurably superior to any other form of writing that has been applied to Turkish.

The gardens round the old palace of Topkapı had been turned into a public park, containing a *gazino* – not a place for gambling, but something more like a *café-chantant*, a restaurant and bar with variety-turns. It was there, late in the evening of Thursday 9 August 1928, that Mustafa Kemal chose to inaugurate the new era. He told the crowd that he would like someone to read out something he had written down. A young man rushed forward but retired baffled at the sight of the Latin letters. 'Our friend is confused', said Kemal, 'because he doesn't know real Turkish writing'. Then he explained the purpose of the change. Shortly afterwards he went on tour, setting up his blackboard and easel in village streets and giving spelling lessons. To his confidant and biographer Falih Rıfkı Atay, who suggested that the change might be spread over five or even fifteen years, he replied 'It'll either happen in three months or it won't happen at all'.

Between 8 and 25 October all civil servants had to pass a test in the use of the new letters. On 1 November the GNA approved a law introducing the new alphabet and forbidding the use of the Arabic letters in works published after the end of the year. Communications from private citizens to government departments would have to be in the new script after 1 June 1929. The deputies to the Grand National Assembly suddenly found that Article 12 of the constitution had taken on a sinister importance for them; among those it excluded from membership of the Assembly were 'those who are unable to read and write Turkish'. They hastened to raise themselves out of the state of illiteracy into which they had so abruptly thrown themselves.

But the language reform did not rest there. Ottoman Turkish, the official and literary language of the Ottoman empire, was manifestly unsuited to be the language of an avowedly populist republic, because it was too difficult. Readers of Robert Burton's *Anatomy of Melancholy* will know how he adds to the difficulty of his already heavily Latinized English by dropping without warning into Latin. In the same way, Ottoman writers considered themselves free to draw on all the vast resources of the Arabic and Persian vocabularies. The 'Turkish' dictionary of Sami Bey Fraschéry, *Kamus-u Türkî* (1901), included some 30,000 words, of which 11,300 were Arabic and 4,400 Persian. Frequently one finds Ottoman sentences in which only the final auxiliary verb is Turkish, the remainder being Arabic and Persian words strung together in accordance with the laws of Arabic and Persian syntax. The Ottoman Chamber of Deputies was known as *Meclis-i Meb'usan*: *meclis* and *meb'us* represent the Turkish pronunciations of the Arabic words *majlis and mab'ūth*, meaning 'assembly' and 'deputy' respectively. The *–i* is the Persian for 'of', the *–an* is the Persian plural termination. For many years Turks had protested against this fantastic hotch-potch but without achieving any radical change. The Ottoman language, affected and obscurantist though it may seem to modern taste, developed naturally out of Ottoman culture, which was equally hybrid, and it maintained its sway until the emergence of the Turkish nation, which preferred to speak and write Turkish.

The measures taken by the pioneers of this change, always with the active interest and encouragement of Mustafa Kemal, have come in for a good deal of criticism, not all of it justified. Their first enthusiastic attempts to eradicate all Arabic and Persian words from the language confronted them with the need for 'genuine Turkish' words to put in their place. Where none could be found ready to hand, recourse was had to ancient Turkish vocabularies and to those of related languages. Thousands of words were deliberately coined from existing roots (just as in English the entirely artificial 'foreword' was manufactured in the nineteenth century to replace the Latin 'preface').

The Turkish Linguistic Society,[3] founded by Kemal in July 1932, turned out glossary after glossary of 'genuine Turkish' terms. It has been accused, unfairly, of trying to force people to alter their speech-habits. The method in fact used was not legal sanctions but education. The Ottoman schoolchild was taught to call an isosceles triangle *müselles-i mütesâviy-üs-sakeyn* ('triangle equal as to the two legs'), which is pure Arabic except for the Persian *–i* at the end of the first word. It may be doubted whether there is now a single Turkish child to whom this would convey anything at all, because on 1 September 1929 Arabic and Persian were deleted from the lycée curriculum. As every Turkish schoolboy knows, a triangle with two sides equal is an *ikizkenar üçgen*; the *gen* is a neologism, but the rest of the term was made up of words familiar to every Turk. But there were many words of foreign origin that were too much a part of everyday speech to be superseded, such as those for 'fire', 'stairs', 'blue', 'religion', and 'government'. To heal the damage done to their national pride by their failure to expel all these, the reformers cooked up a new philosophy of language. The 'Sun-Language Theory' was propounded at the Third Turkish Linguistic Congress,[4] held in 1936. It taught that all the languages of mankind derived from Turkish, so that in using any foreign word they needed the Turks were only reclaiming their own.

This remarkable notion was of a piece with the thesis regularly advanced at that time by Turkish historians, that most of the great peoples of antiquity were either Turks themselves or had been elevated out of their natural anarchy and brutishness by the spread of Turkish civilization. Mustafa Kemal, who was a keen amateur of history, regrettably lent his support to some of the wilder manifestations of this belief.

The history taught in pre-Republican Turkey had been mainly that of the Islamic dynasties, including the Ottomans, so that Turkish history began in 1299, the legendary date of the Ottomans' attaining their independence from the Seljuks. Now the study of Islamic history was dropped from school curricula, and the history of the Turks, from the time of the 'Hun-Turks', was taught instead. This innovation was beneficial to the Turkish ego at a critical time and did no great damage. Survivals of it are to be seen in the names of two big Turkish banks, *Eti* (Hittite) and *Sümer* (Sumerian), as also in the lasting fashion of calling children by such names as Attilâ and Tomris in preference to Islamic names like İsmail and Fatma.

To revert to the language reform: one must remember that, although it was marred by many absurdities (as all Turks now agree), it did an inestimable service in making the written language accessible to any Turkish-speaker who takes the trouble to learn the alphabet. While we may smile at the zealot who says 'Tongue-Moot' for 'Linguistic Congress', we should at the same time appreciate the change for the better that has come over the written language generally. The Republican civil servant will now write, 'I have been thinking about your suggestion'. His Imperial predecessor would have written, 'Your slave has been engaged in the exercise of cogitation in respect of the proposals vouchsafed by your exalted person'.

For many years now the Turkish Ministry of Education and private publishers have been producing popular editions, in the new letters, of Ottoman classics, and scholarly transliterated texts with modern Turkish glossaries. Consequently the treasures of the old poetry, history, and *belles-lettres* are open to a higher proportion of Turks than ever before. If the younger generation, in Turkey as elsewhere, prefers to read tough detective stories and coloured comics, that is not the fault of the Turkish language-reformers.

The most depressing feature of the modern Turkish linguistic landscape is the vast mass of unnecessary borrowings from French and, to a lesser extent, English. Where no 'genuine Turkish' word was available, it was understandable (though not necessarily right) that the Westernizers should exchange Arabic for European words. Thus in 1935 the Republican People's Party changed its name from *Cumhuriyet Halk Fırkası* to *Cumhuriyet Halk Partisi*, preferring the French *parti* to the Arabic *firka*, though the other two words in the title are still of Arabic origin. But it is impossible to justify the sort of snobbery that can put up a notice reading *İzmir Enternasyonal Fuarı Enformasyon Bürosu* or can engage on a campaign for the *eradikasyon* of malaria. Although there are perfectly good Turkish words for 'horse-race' and 'winner', the Turkish punter will go to the *konkuripik* in the hope of becoming a ganyan. 'Pill' in Turkish is *hap*; 'contraceptive pill' is *antibeybi hap*. Before building a bridge or a railway it is now *normal prosedür* to commission a *fizibilite raporu*. The appendix 'On foreign nonsense' to George Borrow's *The Romany Rye* is still worth reading in this connection.

NOTES

[1] Verbal communication from Mr Taufiq Wahby to the author in June 1972.

[2] The speaker was overstating his case. The true figure at that time was a little under 9 per cent.

[3] *Türk Dili Tetkik Cemiyeti*. In 1936 the name was de-Arabized into *Türk Dil Kurumu*.

[4] *Türk Dil Kurultayı*. A more literal rendering of its official title would be 'Turkish Tongue-Moot'.

CHAPTER 13

The Liberal Republican Party

THE END OF 1928 found Turkey full of resentment against the Republican government. The Republican People's Party could hardly be held responsible for the run of bad harvests which had brought great hardship to many parts of Anatolia, but hungry men are not disposed to be reasonable. And the Party was certainly to blame for some of the decline in trade, which was worsened by İsmet's illiberal financial policy.

There was much to be said for the state's undertaking the creation and exploitation of industry, at a time when domestic capital was scarce and foreign capital shy, but the government, with the memory of the Capitulations fresh in its mind, positively discouraged foreign investors. Moreover, it had erred from the first in devoting so much time and money to building up Turkish industry at the expense of agriculture.

There were two strong motives at work to make the Republicans aim at industrial self-sufficiency; one economic, one emotional. Turkey simply could not afford to buy all the manufactured goods she needed; but more than that, the new Turks, whose constant cry was (and indeed still is), 'What will Europe think of us?' did not wish to be considered a nation of peasants. 'Turkey is a Western country. Western countries are industrial . . .' And out of the completion of this dubious syllogism there arose the great blast-furnaces of Karabük.

The programme of industrialization, economically unsound though it may have been, was justifiable on patriotic grounds. Not so the deliberate attack on the wealth and trade of Istanbul. From the beginning, the Republic had treated the former capital as a milch-cow. Discriminatory taxation and the creation of state monopolies in sugar, salt, petrol, alcohol, tobacco, matches, and shipping had bankrupted many old-established Istanbul firms and raised the cost of living to fantastic heights. The prices of some basic foodstuffs were said to have risen to 14,000 per cent above their pre-war level.

The widespread discontent at the secularist reforms was accentuated by a rumour spread by elements hostile to the government, to the effect that Kemal intended to 'abolish Islam altogether'. In December 1928 numerous arrests were made in Bursa of members of an organization calling itself 'The Revolutionary Committee for the Protection of the Muslim Religion', five of the accused being condemned to death for plotting against the state.

In the first four months of the following year some forty communists were arrested in Istanbul and İzmir, but the government, soberly judging that they had no mass support, announced on 4 March that the validity of the Establishment of Order Act would not be prolonged.

But although communism represented no immediate danger, trouble was coming to the boil. In addition to the disaffected elements referred to above, there was the small but influential class of well-intentioned liberals for whom Paris was the heart of the world. The rigorous state control of commerce and industry went against their principles, as did the single-party system and the adulation of Mustafa Kemal.[1] They had taken it for granted a republic would be democratic, and were bitterly disappointed.

Early in 1930 a new journal called *Yarın* ('Tomorrow') began to appear in Istanbul. It rapidly gained a large circulation by its attacks on the Prime Minister, particularly for his economic policy. To everyone's surprise, the authorities did not immediately clamp down on it. On 6 April it was suspended, but for one issue only, and although its editor, Arif Oruç, was arrested for having published articles 'calculated to trouble public opinion', he received quite a mild sentence. The rumour ran that the Ghazi himself was not displeased at the attacks on İsmet, who was prodded by the episode into announcing that the government was preparing a new economic programme.

In a letter to Mustafa Kemal, dated 9 August 1930, the former Prime Minister Fethi, who since 1925 had been ambassador in Paris, complained that the government's financial policy was imposing an excessive burden of taxation on the people. The failure to protect home industries and agriculture was leading to a drop in exports, while there was less and less real debate in the Assembly, owing to the reluctance of Party members to criticize the Cabinet, which had therefore become quite irresponsible. The remedy as he saw it was to create a new party. In his reply, two days later, Kemal assured Fethi that he would not stand in his way:

> I have always been wholeheartedly in favour of the system of free discussion of national affairs and the seeking of the nation's best interests by the efforts of all men and parties of goodwill... I am happy to see that you are with me on the essential principle of a secular republic.

Thereupon Fethi announced the formation of his Liberal Republican Party (*Serbest Cumhuriyet Fırkası*). He made known his programme in a letter to the newspaper *Yarın*. Among the ends he promised to work for were: freedom of thought and the Press, reduction of taxes, a lessening of state control, speed in dealing with business in government departments, and a merciless war against corruption.

During August, Fethi conferred with Kemal, repeatedly and at great length. The Ghazi's sister, Makbule, was the first woman to join the new party, a fact which was seized on as confirming the gossip of a rift between him and İsmet. But this conclusion was not justified by the evidence, partly because the Ghazi's relations with his sister were not always of the best, partly because he wanted Fethi's creation to prosper *qua* opposition party; whether or not it succeeded in wresting power from the Republican People's Party was of minor importance. The schoolmasterly spirit in which he approached the experiment is shown by his words to Fethi at dinner on 10 August:

> I am sure you'll argue a great deal with the leaders of the People's Party. But these arguments will ensure the strengthening of the foundations of the Republic and I shall be happy to watch them. I can tell you now that when you're quarrelling most I shall bring you together round my table and then I'll ask each one of you individually, 'What did you say? Why did you say it? What was your answer? What was it based on?' I confess that this is going to give me enormous pleasure.

It is uncertain whether İsmet was at heart in agreement with this scheme to convert Turkey into a parliamentary democracy, but he saw the advantage of having his opponents out of the Party and clearly identifiable; moreover, he was too good a soldier to do otherwise than conform to Kemal's wishes; so he and Fethi ostentatiously remained on the best of terms, to the mystification of the general public, unacquainted with the niceties of parliamentary behaviour.

But the Ghazi soon realized that his experiment was premature. In September, Fethi went to İzmir to begin his election campaign. He was given a tumultuous welcome. Cabbies and waggon-drivers provided free transport into town for those wishing to attend his meetings. Pictures of İsmet were ceremonially torn up by the crowds, the İzmir headquarters of the Republican People's Party was attacked, and the office windows of the Party's local newspaper were stoned.

Here at last was a situation the local authorities could understand. The talk of an Official Opposition seemed irrational to them; the sight of the Prime Minister walking arm in arm with Fethi, who spent all his time finding fault with him, passed their comprehension. But a mob breaking windows was within their competence. The police fired over the heads of the crowd, but a stray bullet killed a fourteen-year-old boy. Only the presence of a large force of soldiers prevented further bloodshed.

The gentle Fethi himself was appalled by the violent passions of the crowds who turned out to cheer him. At Akhisar he was hailed as the man who was going to save Islam from the godless Republic; the crowd bore banners inscribed in Arabic with the Profession of Faith.

Municipal elections were held in October; they were to have been Fethi's first test, but he failed utterly. The local authorities everywhere may have been uncertain whether the government had gone raving mad or was merely playing a deep game, but they did their duty as they saw it: to save the government from itself. In a vigorous speech to the GNA, Fethi protested against the conduct of the elections; there had been intimidation of voters and barefaced trickery. He attacked the government party for branding all his followers as 'reactionaries and communists'.

> If reactionary movements are so widespread in our principal towns and cities, how is it that the local officials did not detect any such movement before the municipal elections and warn the government? If a one-party government uses state officials and the forces of law and order to strengthen its own position . . . the ethical foundations on which the government is based are shaken and, by preventing demonstrations of national sovereignty, the political foundation is uprooted.

It is true that the elections had been rigged from start to finish, but Fethi was wrong to play down the strength of the reactionary elements which had eagerly joined his party. This he soon realized for himself and, when he saw that he was in danger of becoming a figurehead for the opponents of the Ghazi, he wrote to the Minister of the Interior on 17 November 1930, announcing that he had decided to dissolve the Liberal Republican Party. Turkey was not yet ready for democracy.

Two more new parties had been formed in September, the first at Adana by a lawyer and former deputy, Abdülkadir Kemalî, who in 1924 had published an article urging that Istanbul not Ankara should be the capital. His 'Popular Republican Party' (*Ahali Cumhuriyet Fırkası*) announced that its chief aim was to bring prosperity to the people. This it proposed to do by restricting government expenditure and permitting the property of the state to be sequestered 'to pay its debt to the people'. The organizer had no time to develop this interesting theme before the Party was dissolved by order of the Council of Ministers. The second new party never got off the ground. It was the 'Workers' and Farmers' Party (*Amele ve Çiftçi Fırkası*), which was refused leave to function on the grounds that is displayed communist tendencies, although it declared itself opposed to 'any religious fanaticism and to organizations harmful to the country's structure, such as Bolshevism and communism'.

Any lingering regrets on the part of the liberals at the speedy finish to the experiment in parliamentary democracy were dispelled on 23 December 1930, when a hideous manifestation of religious reaction occurred at Menemen, north of İzmir. A large crowd was demonstrating against the 'impious Republic' when a twenty-four-year-old second lieutenant, Mustafa Fehmi Kubilây, courageously ordered them to disperse. The ringleader was Mehmed the Dervish, a Nakşibendî who claimed to be the Mahdi, the Redeemer who is going to appear at the end of time. He brought Kubilây down with a bullet and unhurriedly decapitated him. Two municipal watchmen who tried to intervene were also murdered while the crowd looked on, some approving, some indifferent. A mob then ran wild through the streets with Kubilây's severed head. Troops were called in by the local authority, and Mehmed the Dervish and two others were killed on the spot. Of the 144 who were arrested, 67 were acquitted, 49 were imprisoned, and the remaining 28 were hanged.

Mustafa Kemal decided to give the common people a token representation in the Assembly by nominating some handpicked labouring men and small shopkeepers as candidates of the Republican People's Party at the forthcoming general election. That was the maximum measure of democracy for which Turkey was ready; for the next fifteen years there was no organized opposition to the rule of the Party.

NOTE

[1] A writer in the newspaper *Cumhuriyet* of 9 September 1930 referred to *him as ezelî ve ebedî Şefimiz*, 'our Chief, from all eternity to all eternity'; the context suggests that the appellation was already familiar.

CHAPTER 14

The Last of the Reforms

WITH THE PROMULGATION of the new Civil Code in 1926 the disabilities imposed on women by Islamic law were swept away. Polygamy, admittedly infrequent even before the Revolution, was now illegal. A wife now had the same rights as her husband in the matter of divorce; he could no longer repudiate her by pronouncing a brief formula. Henceforth only civil divorce and civil marriage were recognized. The right of women to serve as judges had been acknowledged by the Ministry of Justice in 1924 and the first woman judge was appointed in 1932. As early as 1924, too, a number of deputies had made a spirited attempt to give women full political rights. The occasion was the debate on Article 10 of the constitution, of which the first draft ran : 'Every Turk over eighteen years of age is entitled to participate in the election of deputies.' After this had been carried unanimously, it was pointed out that 'every Turk' included women. Although the secretary of the drafting committee was applauded when he said that such had been the committee's intention, opposition was then expressed. Recep (who later took the surname of Peker and was Prime Minister 1946–47) spoke out strongly : if Turkey was a republic, a people's state, it was wrong to exclude half the people. A motion to insert the word 'male' before 'Turk' was declared carried, on a dubious show of hands. A similar but shorter argument took place over the next Article : 'Every Turk over thirty years of age is eligible to be a deputy'. When a motion to amend this to 'Every Turk, male or female' was defeated there was applause, whereupon Recep said 'You haven't given women their due; at least have the grace not to applaud!' This gallant failure seems all the more commendable when we think of the weight of the centuries of tradition that pressed on the legislators' minds, and of the fact that women did not get the vote in France till 1945, in Italy till 1946, in Belgium till 1948, and in Switzerland till 1971.

The Municipalities Act of 16 April 1930 gave women the right to vote at municipal elections. Their political emancipation was completed on 5 December 1934, by a law entitling them to vote in the election of deputies and to stand for election themselves. In a notable speech, İsmet Pasha urged the Grand National Assembly not to regard this measure as a favour generously conferred, but as rectification of an ancient injustice. 'In a country whose women strove side by side with the men, under the invaders' fire, labouring to bring food from the earth to sustain and defend that portion of the land which remained free – surely these people have a right to their say'.

The right was first exercised in the general election of February 1935, as a result of which seventeen women were elected to the GNA out of a total membership of 399.

A minor innovation of some interest was the request made in 1930 by the Turkish government to the world at large, that only the Turkish names of cities should be used in addressing letters to Turkey: thus Ankara, İstanbul, İzmir, Edirne; not Angora, Constantinople, Smyrna, Adrianople. Two years later it was announced that letters addressed to the old names would not in future be delivered. It is noteworthy that in this matter the Turks' nationalistic pride outweighed their strong desire to be Western in all things.[1]

At the 1931 Congress of the Republican People's Party, the principles which had been implicit in the Turkish Revolution from its beginning were formulated for the first time. They are these: Republicanism, Nationalism, Populism, Étatism, Laicism, and Reformism. The last, *İnkılâpçılık*, may also be translated 'Revolutionism'. These six principles, which were written into the Turkish constitution in 1937, are symbolized in the badge of the Party, a fan composed of six arrows.

A feature of the 1931 Congress was the determination shown to make the Revolution reach the people, to inculcate patriotism and to eradicate the sort of ignorance which had given rise to the Menemen incident. It was decided to set up a 'People's House' (*Halkevi*) in every city and town of any size. The activities of these *Halkevis* were to be organized in nine different sections: (*a*) Language, Literature, and History, (*b*) Fine Arts, (*c*) Dramatics, (*d*) Sports, (*e*) Social Assistance, (*f*) People's Classrooms and Foreign Language Courses, (*g*) Library and Publications, (*h*) Rural Activities, (*i*) Museum and Exhibitions. Any Turk, whether a Party member or not, would be entitled to use facilities provided by the *Halkevis*, though the chairman of each *Halkevi* would be chosen from the local committee of the Party.

It was emphasized that internationally-minded people and reactionaries would be equally out of place in the *Halkevis*, which were to function 'in a sincere spirit of brotherhood, embracing all citizens of a nationalist outlook and loyal to the Revolution'.

The first fourteen People's Houses were opened in February and twenty more in June of the same year. In 1949, the last full year of their existence, there were 478. The quality of their contribution to Turkish cultural life naturally varied from place to place; so much depended on the local organizers. But, broadly speaking, they proved a blessing to Turkey, serving as true Community Centres. They arranged lectures, excursions, athletics-meetings, film-shows, and concerts. Many of them published books and reviews descriptive of local dialects, customs, and folklore.

From 1940 onward their work was supplemented by 'People's Rooms' (*Halkodaları*) in small towns and villages, performing the same kind of function but with a smaller range of activities. By 1950 there were 4,322 of them.

The Village Institutes (*Köy Enstitüleri*) may be conveniently mentioned here, although the first of them was not opened till 1940 and they were all closed in 1954. What prompted their creation was an awareness of the impossibility of providing enough qualified teachers for all of Turkey's 40,000 villages. It was not just a question of numbers; it had been found that town-bred teachers, when posted to village schools, tended to panic at the sight of their future homes.

At the Institutes, children of either sex who had completed their course at a village primary school were trained as teachers. The period of instruction was five years. The boys were taught such crafts as building and carpentry, the girls were taught midwifery and the care of children, in addition to general subjects. All had to join in the work of the Institute farm. Those who failed to show promise as teachers were allowed to specialize in a craft or trade that would enable them to serve their community. The work of these Institutes was of inestimable value; in many cases the buildings were put up by the students themselves, whose enthusiasm and faith were unbounded. The best of them went back to their villages qualified not only as schoolteachers, but also as pioneers of scientific farming. They were pledged to serve as teachers for at least twenty years after graduation.

On 18 July 1932 it was decreed that the *ezan*, the call to prayer, must be recited in Turkish instead of Arabic. To show how beautifully this could be done, a gramophone-record made by Hafız Sadettin, chief muezzin of the Sultan Ahmed Mosque, was circulated. The following February, when Kemal was visiting İzmir, word was brought to him that a mob at Bursa had rioted in protest and that a muezzin at the Great Mosque there had recited the *ezan* in Arabic. He cancelled his engagements and rode through the night to Bursa to investigate the matter for himself. Finding that the local authorities had been slow to take action, he delivered himself of some impromptu remarks to the effect that the defence of the reforms was the business of the young; if they saw them threatened they would not wait for the authorities to act but would defend the reforms themselves with whatever weapons came to hand. These words, later to be known as the Bursa Speech, were to prove a thorn in the flesh of authority a generation later.

The use of the metric system, which had been legalized as early as September 1881, was made compulsory from the end of 1932. The coinage remained anomalous, with 40 *para* to the *kuruş* and 100 *kuruş* to the *lira*, until the early 1950s, when the increase in world prices drove the *para* out of circulation.

Another radical change which affected all citizens was brought about by the Surnames Law, which came into effect on 2 July 1934. Previously the Arab system of nomenclature had been in general use and it was given official force in 1881, from which year identity documents had to show one's father's name: Ahmed son of Mehmed. To distinguish among all the Ahmeds whose fathers were called Mehmed, a word might be added denoting the birthplace or a physical peculiarity: Ahmed of Sivas, son of Bald Mehmed. Men of ancient lineage might have a family-name, but most people did not. Now every family was given two years in which to choose a surname; otherwise one would be chosen for them. Surnames could be compounded with *-oğlu* ('-son') and had to be taken 'from the Turkish language'. The latter provision was often ignored and half-Arabic names such as Müezzinoğlu and Hocaoğlu abound. Sometimes brothers who could not agree on a choice, or had lost touch with each other, chose different surnames. Kemal gave İsmet Pasha the surname of İnönü, after the scene of his two great victories in the War of Independence, and he himself became Atatürk ('Father-Turk') by a law published on 24 October. Another law was published on 17 December, about which all one needs to know is the title: 'Law ordaining that neither the name "Atatürk" given to the President of the Republic, whose given name is Kemal, nor any name made by prefixing or suffixing any word to the name

"Atatürk", shall be adopted by anyone else'. His sister Makbule was married to a man surnamed Boysan. When their marriage ended, she took the surname Atadan ('From the Father').

On 29 October 1934, the titles Pasha, Efendi, Bey, and Hanım were declared obsolete, being replaced by the ill-conceived terms Bay and Bayan, for men and women respectively. Bay is a very ancient word for 'rich'; Bayan is a less ancient word for 'clever', also alleged to be the name of a pre-Islamic male deity. But old customs are not so easily altered by decree. Although Hasan the baker receives letters addressed to Bay (or, more frequently nowadays, Sayın, 'Honoured') Hasan Ekmekçi, his customers still call him Hasan Bey; while his wife, officially Bayan Ekmekçi, is still Fatma Hanım for social purposes. Indeed, the Istanbul telephone-directory was classified by alphabetical order of first names until 1950. When the new directory appeared, arranged by surnames, some extreme Republicans joined the extreme conservatives in deploring the change, for they argued that it contravened Article 2 of the Surnames Law: 'In speech, in writing, and in signatures, the given name shall be used first, the surname last'.

On 3 December a new law forbade the wearing of distinctive dress by clerics of any religion outside their places of worship. By a special dispensation, however, the President of the Directorate of Religious Affairs, the Greek and Armenian Patriarchs, and the Chief Rabbi appeared in their canonicals at the official opening of the Bosphorus Bridge in October 1973.

In June 1935 it was decreed that all official establishments should have a weekly holiday from 1 p.m. on Saturday till Monday morning. Since 1924, Friday had been the official weekly holiday: Friday is the Muslim day of obligatory congregational prayer but is not a day of rest. Muslims find shocking the implication of the Judaeo-Christian Sabbath, that God needed to rest after His labours. The feelings of the pietists at having the infidel Sabbath thrust on them may be imagined, but the innovation was well received by the working population. Nowadays all official departments and many private establishments hang out the Turkish flag at week-ends, a pleasing custom which adds to the brightness of city streets.

Ever since the inauguration of the Grand National Assembly in 1920, the opening speech of each new session had been delivered by Mustafa Kemal. When the Assembly met on 1 November 1938, the speech he had written for the occasion was read by the Prime

Minister, Celâl Bayar. The President himself was confined to his bed by an illness from which he did not recover.

He had suffered from kidney-trouble on and off for at least twenty years, but he never let it affect his mode of life. He presented to the world an appearance of great physical toughness. But in 1937 a decline in his health became apparent. He suffered from frequent nose-bleeds, he looked pale and drawn, and his old vigour departed. His remarkable memory began to fail him, and whereas before he had always been tolerant of honest disagreement, he now grew touchy and cantankerous. The diagnosis was cirrhosis of the liver, a disease whose connection with over-indulgence in alcohol is well known. He died on November 1938, in his fifty-seventh year. His body was laid to rest in a temporary tomb at the Ethnographical Museum in Ankara. In 1953 it was moved to an imposing new mausoleum on the outskirts of the city.

The nature and magnitude of his achievement have been outlined in the preceding pages and need not be recapitulated at length. He had forced the Turks to emerge from the crumbling ruins of the Ottoman empire and become a nation, at a time when many European and Asian peoples were lapsing into demoralization and despair amidst the wreckage of ancient empires. With an unconquerable faith in the potentialities of his people, he drove them along the road to Western civilization, which, as we read his speeches, we see that he came close to deifying.

> Resistance to the flood-tide of civilization is in vain; she is pitiless towards those who ignore or disobey her. Civilization pierces the hills, soars in the skies, sees and illuminates and studies all things, from the invisible atoms to the stars. Nations which try to function with medieval minds, with primitive superstitions, in the presence of her might and her sublime majesty, are doomed to annihilation or, at best, to servitude or ignominy.

And again:

> We have got to be men, from every point of view. We have suffered; and the reason has been that we did not understand the way the world was going. Our thoughts, our mentality, are going to be civilized. We're not going to pay any attention to what this one or that one says; we're going to be civilized and proud of it. Look at the state of the rest of the Turks and Muslims! What catastrophes and disasters have come upon them, because their

> minds could not adjust themselves to the all-encompassing and sublime dictates of civilization! This is why we too remained backward for so long, and why we finally plunged into the last morass. If we have been able to save ourselves in the last few years, it has been because of the change in our mentality. We can never stop again. We're going on, whatever happens; we can't go back. We must go on; we have no choice. The nation must understand this clearly. Civilization is a blazing fire that burns and obliterates those who will not acknowledge her.

His personal equipment for his task consisted of a fanatical belief in the Turks' high destiny, an overriding strength of will, a quick wit, great powers of leadership and oratory, enormous personal charm, and the patience to bide his time.

It would be idle to pretend that he was a plaster saint, when it is common knowledge that he loved drink and gambling and women. His vices were a part of him, a manifestation of his tremendous vitality. But self-deception was not among his failings. He was no brash young revolutionary but an Ottoman officer and gentleman who happened to have a revolutionary fire in his soul. He well knew that few of those he had to work with shared his fervour. All too often they paid only lip-service to his dreams and ideals, even to his concrete plans. He occupied the centre of the stage while the rest of the cast stood around and applauded him instead of playing their own parts. It was his awareness of this that in his later years made him drink to excess, made him storm out of a room filled with polite yes-men to seek low company who, when he roared at them, had no inhibitions against roaring back. It was this awareness too that made him say what he said in the heat of the moment at Bursa in 1933, as well as what he said coolly and deliberately at the end of his six-day speech in 1927:

> Turkish youth! Your first duty is to protect and defend Turkish independence and the Turkish Republic to all eternity... By force and guile all the fortresses of the dear motherland may one day be seized, all its arsenals penetrated, all its armies scattered, and every corner of the country occupied. Even more painful and more perilous, those in power within the country may be negligent and in error, even traitorous; they may even identify their personal interests with the political ambitions of the invaders. The nation may be ruined and helpless, in destitution and want. Children of the Turkish future! Your duty, even under

these conditions, is to save Turkish independence and the Republic. The strength you need is in the noble blood within your veins.

At the moment of Atatürk's death, Abdülhâlik Renda, Chairman of the Assembly, automatically became acting President. On 11 November 1938, the Assembly unanimously elected İsmet to be President of the Republic.

İsmet İnönü was born in İzmir on 24 September 1884. His father, Hacı Reşid Bey, was a judge; his mother came of a Turkish family that had long been settled in Bulgaria. His education was almost exclusively military. Graduating from the Staff College in 1906, he was posted to the Second Army at Edirne, where he soon became a leading figure in the local branch of the CUP, but withdrew from active association with it after the proclamation of the constitution, sharing Mustafa Kemal's belief that the army should thenceforth not meddle in politics.

In 1910 he was sent to Yemen, and in 1912 was appointed Chief of Staff of the forces in that province, at the same time receiving his majority, a rank then rarely conferred on one so young. He served on the commission which drafted the peace terms with Bulgaria in 1913; a small rehearsal of the part he was to play ten years later at Lausanne. For some time during the First World War he was Mustafa Kemal's Chief of Staff. By the end of the war, İsmet was a colonel. He worked at the Ministry of War until the Allies occupied the capital, when he escaped to Ankara, where the Grand National Assembly made him Chief of Staff of the Nationalist forces. Of his great services during the War of Independence some account has already been given. True to his principles, he resigned from the army once the Republic was on its feet.

His qualities tend to be underrated. Opponents of the regime used to blackguard him on principle, while ardent Kemalists played down his abilities in order to enhance the glory of Atatürk. He has often been criticized, in particular, for his blinkered vision; 'a good staff officer and nothing more' is one common verdict. But few staff officers, of whatever nationality, could have conducted the brilliant campaign which İsmet won at Lausanne, against the great European masters of diplomacy. The slogan 'Sèvres, death; Lausanne, life' is not yet forgotten in Turkey. Nor have any of his political opponents, in a land where politicians do not go about their business wearing kid gloves, ever questioned his devotion to his Chief or to the Republic.

NOTE

[1] *Istanbul*, the name by which the former capital has always been referred to in spoken Turkish, is generally explained as deriving from the Greek εἰς τὴν πόλι ('in the City'). The objection to this is the *a* where one would have expected an *i*. An alternative explanation is that *İstanbul* is simply a corruption of *Constantinopolis*; this will not seem so far-fetched if it is remembered that *Nicomedia* has been corrupted to *İzmit*. It may be that the first etymology is the right one but that the influence of *Constantinopolis* has changed a hypothetical *İstinbul* to its present form. On Ottoman coins the city is variously called *İstanbul, İslâmbol* ('Muslims abounding', a punning variant), or the Arabic name *Qostantiniyya*.

1 Sultan Abdülhamid (with parasol) walking in the grounds of the old Topkapı Palace, in his day a residence for harem ladies who had lost his or his predecessors' favour

ربیع الآخر ٢٧ — تشرین اول ٣٠

سنه ١٢٧٧ — نومرو ٤

درسعادت ایچون
فیئات
بریللغی — التی ایلغی
١٥٠ — ٨٠
٣ برنسخه‌سی
٣ اعلانات سطری
اعلاناتک تکرارنده فیئاتی دخی تنزل ایدر

طشره ایچون
فیئات

بریللغی	التی ایلغی	(درسعادتدن)
١٧٤	٩٢	قرق ساعت یره قدر
١٩٨	١٠٤	یوز ساعت یره قدر
٢٢٢	١١٦	یوز ساعتی متجاوز یره قدر

طشره فیئاتنده پوسته اجرتی ضم اولنمشدر

(١٢٧٧)

اشبو غزته احوال داخلیه و خارجیه‌دن منتخب بعض حوادث و معارف و صنایع متنوعه ایله تجارت و سائر مواد [illegible] متعلق مباحثی شامل اولدیغی حالده شنبه‌دن [illegible] هفته‌ده برکره بازار گونلری چیقار — بوکا [illegible] معینه ایله مشتری اولمق مراد ایدنلر درسعادتده ایسه بالذات ویاخود بالواسطه [illegible] اسم و رتبه و مأمور بلرینه محل اقامتلرینی (استانبولده باغچه قپوسنده [illegible] ترجمان احوال مطبعه‌خانه‌سنه) بیان ایتملری لازم‌در [illegible] کنارده جدول مخصوصنده کوستریلمشدر — نشر اولنمق ایچون [illegible] حوادث کوندرن اولورسه قبول اولنور — کتاب و سائره طبع ایتدرمک استه‌ینلر [illegible]

حوادث داخلیه

(استانبول خبرلری)

* توجیهات *

صنف اول ایله تجارت مستشارلغی خارجیه مکتوبجیسی سابق سرور افندی حضرتلرینه

مکتوبجیلق رتبه اولی صنف ثانیسیله سعادتلو [illegible] بک افندی‌یه

[illegible] اولکی حرم همایون تبردارلرندن سلیمان اغایه

[illegible] ثانیلکی قصر همایون بکجی باشیسی حسین اغایه

[illegible] قپو کتخدالغی ترجمه اوطه‌سی خلفاسندن عزتلو صبری افندی‌یه

[illegible] قپودانه همایون سعادتلو محمد پاشا حضرتلرینه اوستریا [illegible] رتبه‌سنک بر قطعه معتبر نشانی ایله [illegible] همایون سواریسی علی بک ایله [illegible] رتبه‌سی دیگر علی بکه دخی شوالیه‌لک رتبه‌سندن بر قطعه نشانلر اعطا قلنمشدر

درسعادتده مقیم ناپولیسان مصلحتگذاری موسیو (حونوت) ایتالیه‌یه عودت [illegible] دولت خارجیه ناظری طرفندن بالتلغراف امر و اشعار اولنمش اولدیغندن قونسلوس وکیلی موسیو (استللا) ایله برابر موسی الیهک [illegible] گون انقرم درسعادتدن حرکت ایتمش اولدیغی و سفارت مزبوره ایشلری بالش ترجمانه حواله اولنمش ایدوکی خبر آلنمشدر

مجمع حوادث نام ارمنی غزته‌سندن عیناً النان بر بنددر

بکن هفته پاریسدن کلان تلغراف خبرینه نظراً استقراض بندی دیو [illegible] پنجشنبه کونی برملت غزته‌سی دخی بوخبر صحیحه چیقمدی [illegible] نهرم بازار ایرتسی تکمیل طوغری بدرنه آلک لکن آنک بکلشی یازدن [illegible] یلرزه‌حیزوقت لمه استقراض واقعا اولمش ایدی دفعه بارسده شو شرط [illegible] ایله یاره [illegible] برقوبنیاسیا حاضر ایدی لکن شرطلر [illegible] باب عالی‌یه معلوم اولمدیغندن احتمالدر باب عالی بو شرطلری قبول ایتمزدی و اووقت استقراض [illegible] شمدی ایشیدیورز که بکن بازار کلن واپور ایله بو شرطلرک صورتی پاریسدن کلمشدر که بو راده [illegible] تکرار پاریسه کوندریله‌جکدر [illegible] نشرینی [illegible] اون بشندن اعتبارا اعلان اولنه‌جقدر شمدی‌یه دکین بو شرطلر قبول اولنمامش دیه‌جک بر سبب یوقدر و کندی اعتقادیمزه قالورسه استقراض بو راجه دخی بیتشدر مأمول ایدرز و امارزکه وقوعات بزی تصدیق ایده‌جکدر لکن بعضیلری ظن ایدرسه که استقراضک بندیکی کون [illegible] آلتون [illegible] اوبه مأمول نکلدر استقراض حصه حصه اولوب صاتیلور و تقسیط تقسیط ویریلور و انجق برسنه‌ده آرقه‌سی آلنور بو وجه ایله استقراضک بندیکی کون هرقاچ ملیون لیرا ایسه اوقدرشی حاضر اقچه صاتیلور

ملاحظه

٢ نومرولو غزته‌مزده دولت علیه‌نک اوروپاده [illegible] بعض [illegible] دردست تسویه بولندیغنی و بونک ایکی شیدن عبارت اولدیغی حالده اوا یکیسی اولان خارجدن نقود [illegible] حقنده جانب سلطنت سنیه‌دن تدابیر لازمه‌یه تشبث بیورلمش اولدیغی بیانیله بکن صره‌ده ایلروده بونلرک تفصیلاتی دخی اعلان ایده‌جکمز دیو وعد ایتمشدک بو دفعه دولت علیه‌نک ایتمش اولدیغی استقراضه متعلق برخبر رسمی هیچ بر غزته‌یه هنوز ویرلمش اولدیغی جهتله بونک معاملات اجرائیه‌سی تکمیل اولوب انجه‌سی آلنه باشلانجه‌یه قدر و تفاصیلی سکوت ایتمک لازمه‌دن ایدی مادامکه ارتق ارمنی و روم غزته‌لری بونه دائر مباحثات ایلمه‌یی [illegible] آفاق و دیکر طرفندن دخی خلق بوخصوصک معناسی [illegible] آشوری مرتبه مراق ایتمکده بولنمش ایکن بزدخی حفظ سکوتده دوام ایتمش اولمق اولسان استقراضک اصلی تصدیق ایتمش اولورز شو ملاحظه‌یه مبنی تفصیلات و شرائطی ینه ایلرویه براقه رق شمدیلک استقراض مذکورک بالکز دیمت اجرا بولندیغی بیان ایله اکتفا ایدرز

اون درت کون اول پیرودن حرکت ایتمش اولان قطعه [illegible] قپاق یوز بیش نفر یوچی عساکر شاهانه ایله پنجشنبه کونی آستانه‌یه مواصلت ایتمشدر

شامدن رودوسه نقل اولنمش و اینکی صنف مجرملردن بولنمش اولان [illegible] کورک قونلسه‌یچون درعلیه‌یه کوندرلمسی خارجیه ناظری دولتلو فؤاد پاشا حضرتلری طرفندن اشعار [illegible]

تفرقه

[illegible] ایجاد طبعی اولان قومدیانک بکنجی فصلی

(هفته کی ٣ نومرونک تفرقه‌سنه مربوطدر)

١ (اخطار)

[illegible] سوز جانبنه علامت اولنور

(التنجی فقره)

مشتاق بک — زیباطوطی — جبه قادین

ابو القلقه — باناق امه — محلل

ابو القلقه (باشنده برداداده ایله تبدیل قیافت [illegible] عیلری یانلانه رق [illegible] یانلانه رق) — صانکه برتلاش ایله [illegible] اوبقودن قالدیرونده کبیر [illegible] وار [illegible] اوبو [illegible] جیقار کی باقلق شوقیافتمه عیب کورلتو کز تولویور ز

زیباطوطی (آتاریسنک اوت [illegible] اولدیغی حالده ابو القلقه‌نک الی اوپر) —

امانک افندم کویکی اوله‌جق شو حریف [illegible] حاجی‌باشی بولدی او شوله طورسون [illegible]

سزه نقل ایتمکسه اوتانیورم

ابو القلقه (مشتاق بکه) — وای تومسز وای

مشتاق بک — افندم کیم ایدیکز بنده‌کز نه‌یلدیکم قدر حقیقتی سزه آکلاته‌یم

ابو القلقه — سن صوص سفیه قادین نمله کی بیچاره خاتون بلاغی سویلیه‌جک

زیباطوطی — افندم بوقزی مطلقا آلمه ایدر

ابو القلقه — [illegible] آلمازسه عرضنه لکه سورمش دیمک اولور (محلله) [illegible] اویله دکلمی قومشولر

محلل — های های

مشتاق بک — آه نم افندم بونده بر یاکلشلق وار زیرا نکاح ایتدیکمز قز بو دکلدر بونه [illegible] بنا وفی استدم

ابو القلقه — [illegible] نکاح ایتدیکم [illegible]

مشتاق بک — [illegible] دکلدر

ابو القلقه — وای سن [illegible] جیقار یورسونه بونه یوزسزلکدر

باناق امه — افندی بیلیو [illegible] بونک [illegible] [illegible] طورک [illegible] [illegible] اولدیغندن ایچون [illegible] طولاشورکن [illegible] [illegible] کلیور [illegible] [illegible] اولدم [illegible] [illegible] دمسونی [illegible] یاقلق شوا حقنه

مشتاق بک — وای فرانسزلی آدم وای

باناق امه — [illegible] آدم [illegible] اوغلان [illegible] سویلیوب طورمه [illegible]

2 Front page of Turkish newspaper, *Tercüman-ı Ahval*, 1860

Harîçten gazel

Mithat PERİN

DÜNYA

ŞUBAT 10 PAZAR 1974

HAVA DURUMU

100 Kr.

Program eleştiriliyor

«Bütün ekonomi devlet tekeline alınmaktadır»

★ ANKARA TİCARET ODASI BAŞKANI AYDOĞAN «ANAYASAMIZIN ÖNGÖRDÜĞÜ KARMA EKONOMİ İLKESİNİN, EN İYİMSER YORUMLA, UNUTULDUĞU İNTIBAI VERİLMEKTEDİR» DEDİ.

Menteşe ve Bilgehan cevap verdi

★ «CHP TEBLİĞİ VE GÜVEN'İN DEMECİ HADİSELERİ SAKLAMA GAYRETİNDEN İBARETTİR»

AP yöneticileri Ecevit ve Erbakan'ı ziyaret ederek 'başarı dileklerinde bulundular

Demirel: İktidar ile diyalog lüzumludur

«Medenî münasebetleri başından beri biz savunduk»

MSP'nin Ortak Pazarla ilgili görüşü değişmemiş

Keskin sirke..

Türkeş MHP'nin 26. yılı için demeç verdi

Tural istifa etti

Teknik personel için tedbirler alınacak

Millî Piyango dün çekildi

Sultanahmet Camiinde «ses-ışık» gösterisi

ANKARA NOTLARI

Pazar günü için fıkralar

Tütün üreticileri sigara fabrikası kurmak istiyor

Başbakan ve Adalet Bakanı açıkladı

«Af, en yakın zamanda çıkarılacaktır»

★ ADALET BAKANI ŞEVKET KAZAN, BOLU CEZAEVİNDE TUTUKLU VE MAHKUMLARLA KONUŞTU

İngiltere'de kömür işçileri greve başladı

Vodvil gibi..

Bedii FAİK

Tehlikeli başlangıç..

M. Emin AYTEKİN

Turizm Bakanı bazı kurumları ziyaret etti

3 Front page of Turkish newspaper *Dünya*, 1974

4 Enver Pasha, the Minister of War, at attention before Kaiser Wilhelm on board the *Yavuz*, previously *Goeben*, in the Bosphorus, during the Kaiser's tour of the eastern front in 1917

5 Women workers in an improvised munitions factory during the War of Independence, checking cartridges for size

6 Turkish soldiers in the War of Independence
7 Mustafa Kemal addressing the first Grand National Assembly in 1920. The several *hocas* among the deputies are distinguishable by their turbans. Most of the others, including Kemal, wear the *kalpak*

8 The Lower House of the new Grand National Assembly building, completed in 1960

9 Atatürk driving through Istanbul with King Edward VIII in September 1936. In several respects they were two of a kind, and the visit was a great success

10 Atatürk hammering home a point in discussion with İnönü at the Third Linguistic Conference, held at Dolmabahçe Palace in Istanbul in 1936. He was greatly interested in language reform

11 Turkish refugees arriving from Bulgaria in December 1950. It is remarkable how few of them look like most people's idea of a typical Turk

12 Premier Adnan Menderes (*right*) and his Foreign Minister, Fatin Rüştü Zorlu, at the opening of the Baghdad Pact Conference in London on 28 July 1958. Both were hanged three years later

13 General Cemal Gürsel

14 Süleyman Demirel, Prime Minister 1965-71 (waving hat), on tour at Isparta. The grey horse on the flags above him is the symbol of his Justice Party

15 İsmet İnönü congratulating the new President, Fahrî Korutürk, in April 1973. The President and his entourage are wearing tails and black waistcoat, the ceremonial dress favoured by Atatürk

16 At the ballot-box in a small country town

17 Voting in a provincial town, under the eyes of the returning officer and party representatives. The badge worn by the lady in black marks her as representing the RPP

Y. T. P.

YENİ TÜRKİYE PARTİSİ

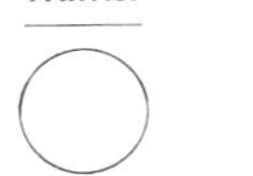

İSTANBUL İLİ ADAYLARI

1 — Sadi Bekter
2 — Ömer Canca
3 — Ali İhsan Çelikkan
4 — Füruzan Eksat
5 — Reşit Erkmen
6 — Sırrı Öktem
7 — Mehmet Ali Gökberk
8 — Cahit Çaka
9 — Tevfik Hamdi Ander
10 — Suha Ali Bolton
11 — Selâhattin Konuralp
12 — Asiye Kitapçıoğlu
13 — Vecihi Divitçi
14 — Şevket Yalovalı
15 — Mihriban Avşaroğlu
16 — Haçik Eram
17 — Mehmet Şerafettin Özdil
18 — Mediha Gezgin
19 — Niran Kursan
20 — Oya Süzen
21 — Hazer Baler
22 — Erdoğan Öztüregen
23 — Elie Hayun
24 — Boğoz Sariçyan
25 — Abdullah Kalkavan
26 — Sadık Öner
27 — Samim Paker
28 — Hüseyin Sami Yağcıoğlu
29 — Ali Yalçın
30 — Mehmet Ertaş
31 — Cemil Güngör

C. K. M. P.

CUMHURİYETÇİ KÖYLÜ MİLLET PARTİSİ

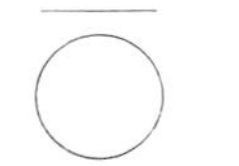

İSTANBUL İLİ ADAYLARI

1 — Ahmet Tahtakılıç
2 — Mustafa Kaplan
3 — Fuat Uluç
4 — Selâhattin Şar
5 — Bedia Seven
6 — Ş. Muammer Günel
7 — Mümtaz Seçkin
8 — Memduh Tarhan
9 — Necati Alper
10 — Erdoğan Zorlu
11 — Oğuz Küçükkutlu
12 — M. Turan Koçal
13 — İlhan Tandoğan
14 — Edip Sezgin
15 — Suphi Cebe
16 — Ahmet Özel Türkay
17 — İsmail Hakkı Pulat
18 — K. Bekir Kuntak
19 — Süleyman Ateş
20 — Mehmet Kırpat
21 — Enver Malcan
22 — Hüsnü Zaim
23 — Merih Gökmen
24 — F. Celile Olgaç
25 — Hüseyin Şentürk
26 — Edip Asya
27 — Hüseyin Yusuf Atayman
28 — Mahmut Özçay
29 — S. Niyazi Resnelioğlu
30 — Yaşar Öke
31 — Necmettin Durdabak

A. P.

ADALET PARTİSİ

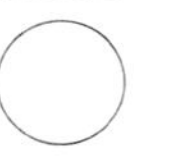

İSTANBUL İLİ ADAYLARI

1 — Sadettin Bilgiç
2 — Aydın Yalçın
3 — Ali Fuat Başgil
4 — Ferruh Bozbeyli
5 — Tekin Erer
6 — İsmail Hakkı Tekinel
7 — Muhittin Güven
8 — Osman Özer
9 — Nuri Eroğan
10 — Ali Esat Birol
11 — Orhan Seyfettin Orhon
12 — Kaya Özdemir
13 — Mehmet Yardımcı
14 — Osman Nuri Ulusay
15 — Nurettin Bulak
16 — Mustafa Ertuğrul
17 — Mustafa Kara
18 — Mustafa Gürpınar
19 — Mehmet Ali Yalçın
20 — Faruk Ilgaz
21 — Orhan Cemal Fersoy
22 — İbrahim Abak
23 — Ali Ulvi Yenal
24 — Turan Gürsoy
25 — Orhan Koraltan
26 — Fethi Başak
27 — Naci Öktem
28 — Enver Üstün
29 — Mustafa Sabahattin Tanman
30 — Abdurrahman Yazgan
31 — Niyazi Yıldırım

M. P.

MİLLET PARTİSİ

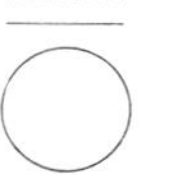

İSTANBUL İLİ ADAYLARI

1 — Hüseyin Ataman
2 — Abdurrahman Şeref Laç
3 — Fehmi Cumalıoğlu
4 — Mustafa Kemal Ekşi
5 — Tahsin Kitapçı
6 — Suat Uluğ
7 — Eser Deliorman
8 — Suphi Altan
9 — Varujan Tutuoğlu
10 — Zafer Poroy
11 — Mehmet Fırat
12 — Süleyman Güner
13 — Refik Işın
14 — Nadir Aksoy
15 — Bekir Sıtkı Keçeli
16 — Zeynel Özdil
17 — İbrahim İsti
18 — Hadi Börü
19 — Hayrettin Çiçekdağ
20 — Harun Karakaş
21 — Fikret Düzgünses
22 — Zehra Hepanıl
23 — Hasan Basri Maviengin
24 — Galip Murat
25 — Musa Kâzım Öner
26 — Selâhattin Saygı
27 — Dimitri Karavasopulo
28 — Namık Dinçcan
29 — Ahmet Niyazi Başyurt
30 — Hurrem Işık
31 — Saibe Mürenler

T. İ. P.

TÜRKİYE İŞÇİ PARTİSİ

İSTANBUL İLİ ADAYLARI

1 — Mehmet Ali Aybar
2 — Çetin Altan (Bağımsız)
3 — Sadun Aren
4 — Yaşar Kemal Gökçeli
5 — Kemal Nebioğlu
6 — Yılmaz Halkacı
7 — Nazife Cemgil
8 — Mehmet Aziz Erkmen
9 — İbrahim Güzelce
10 — Ahmet Şen
11 — Mahmut Makal (Bağımsız)
12 — Zaven Biberyan
13 — Moris Gabbay
14 — Burhan Cahit Ünal
15 — Müşerref Hekimoğlu (Başarır)
16 — Rasih Nuri İleri
17 — Hilmi Özgen (Bağımsız)
18 — Metin Erksan (Bağımsız)
19 — Süreyya Gülgün
20 — Cavit Zengin
21 — Orhan Namık Güner
22 — Hüseyin Biber
23 — Celâl Beyaz
24 — Selâhattin Hilâv
25 — Avni Erakalın
26 — İsmail Kenan Aydeniz
27 — İhsan İşcan
28 — Müzehher Vâ-Nû
29 — Ahmet Cansızoğlu
30 — Nâzım Sarıyavuz
31 — Emin Tüver

C. H. P.

CUMHURİYET HALK PARTİSİ

İSTANBUL İLİ ADAYLARI

1 — Fuat Sirmen
2 — İlhami Sancar
3 — Orhan Erkanlı
4 — Suphi Baykam
5 — Orhan Eyüpoğlu
6 — Reşit Ülker
7 — Selim Sarper
8 — Coşkun Kırca
9 — Orhan Birgit
10 — Vedat Dicleli
11 — Oğuz Oran
12 — Cihat Baban
13 — Nermin Neftçi
14 — Fehmi Atanç
15 — Erol Ünal
16 — M. Kâzım Özeke
17 — Sedat Börekoğlu
18 — Abdullah Vehbi Uğur
19 — Günseli Özkaya
20 — Şahin Gürol
21 — Sabri Vardarlı
22 — Şeyda Güley
23 — Mümtaz Özarar
24 — Kenan Bayraktar
25 — Vahyi Özarar
26 — Kemal Mert
27 — Enver Sökmen
28 — Suat Ulagay
29 — Kemal Çilingiroğlu
30 — Hayri Hayırlıoğlu
31 — Uğur Kalafatoğlu

18 A Turkish ballot paper of October 1965. The Justice Party symbol was placed askew by arrangement with the printer, to enable illiterate voters to identify it, failing recognition of the horse

19 Nomads on the road in eastern Anatolia

20 Atatürk's mausoleum at Ankara. The architect of this starkly beautiful building, completed in 1953, was Emin Onat

21 In a village mosque. The position of the hands shows that the worshippers have finished the ritual prayers and are engaged in private thanksgiving

22 Ararat, an extinct volcano, perpetually snow-capped, rises above the plateau, a little to the west of the Russian and Persian borders

23 The Bosphorus Bridge which joins Europe and Asia, opened on 30 October 1973. The Ortaköy Mosque on the European shore was built in 1714, in the reign of Ahmed III

CHAPTER 15

Foreign Policy and the Second World War

IN THE SUMMER of 1940 a Turkish friend of the author's was staying in a small town in western Anatolia. One morning, as he was sitting outside a café, reading the paper, an elderly man stopped and asked him if there was any news. 'Indeed there is!' he answered. 'The Soviet Union has annexed Estonia, Latvia, and Lithuania'. 'What are they?' asked the old man. 'Countries in northern Europe'. 'How strange!' was the reply. 'When I was a boy, there were only two countries. There was the Ottoman empire and there was Moscow'.

Russian dreams of capturing Constantinople began over a thousand years ago, and a glance at the map will show why. It has always been vitally important for Russia to have her outlet to the Mediterranean unimpeded, independently of her neighbours' good-will. During the Armenian riots of 1896, when the Russian ambassador in Constantinople was told that British warships might be coming there to protect British interests, he is reported to have said, in great agitation, 'We shall never give up the key of our front door!' Catherine the Great, who had cast covetous eyes on the Sultan's Bulgarian and Serbian provinces and desired to be acknowledged as 'Protector' of his Orthodox Christian subjects, named a gate in Moscow 'The Way to Constantinople' in token of her ambitions. In the eighteenth and nineteenth centuries, Russia and Turkey were at war at least a dozen times.

The continuity of Russo-Turkish hostilities was broken by the revolutions that came in the train of the First World War. It was natural for the new republics to be thrown together; the Soviet Union, with every man's hand against it, and Turkey, the defeated power which refused to admit defeat. In the Russo-Turkish Treaty of Friendship and Brotherhood, signed in Moscow on 16 March 1921, the GNA was recognized as the only legitimate ruler of Turkey.

Russia had been giving financial and military aid to the nationalists.

An Islamic Bolshevist Committee had been formed at Eskişehir, of which *The Times* wrote on 6 July 1920: 'Nationalist leaders cynically avow the artificiality of the movement, created with the object of intimidating the Allies'. The truth of this view is confirmed by the curious episode of the two Communist Parties of Turkey.

The first of these was founded on 18 October 1920, by a number of generals and members of the GNA, acting on orders from Kemal. It was unsuccessful in its application for membership of the Third International and engaged in no political activity; its sole purpose was to show the Russians how friendly the new Turkey was to the ideas of the new Russia. The second Communist Party of Turkey was founded two months later. It was affiliated to the Third International and aimed at establishing an orthodox dictatorship of the proletariat. Its leader, Mustafa Suphi, and fifteen other influential members were all 'accidentally' drowned at Trabzon on 28 January 1921. In July 1922, when the Nationalists were certain of victory over the Greeks, all communist activity was proscribed. For Mustafa Kemal never swerved from his aim: Turkey was to become a Western state, a European state; France and Britain were his models, not Russia. But there was no change in Turkey's external policy, of which Kemal spoke in the following terms on 1 November 1924, in a speech to the GNA:

> Our amicable relations with our old friend the Soviet Russian Republic are developing and progressing every day. As in the past, our Republican government regards genuine and extensive good relations with Soviet Russia as the keynote of our foreign policy.

These words were loudly applauded.

The two countries were brought even closer together by the question of Mosul. At the Lausanne Conference, İsmet had fought hard and long for possession of this former Ottoman province, ostensibly because its population was largely Kurdish, and the Ankara government felt that the integration of the Anatolian Kurds within the Turkish Republic would be rendered more difficult by the proximity of close on half a million unintegrated Kurds outside. Curzon had insisted that Mosul belonged to Iraq, on historical, economic, racial, and military grounds (giving Mosul to Turkey would have meant bringing the Turkish frontier to within 60 miles of the Iraqi capital, Baghdad), but the Mosul oilfields were uppermost in the minds of both parties; this is obvious from the vehemence with which both denied it.

It will be recalled that the Treaty of Lausanne had left the destinies of Mosul to be settled by Turco-British discussions, within nine months of the Treaty's coming into effect. As no agreement had been reached within the time stipulated, the question was referred to the Council of the League of Nations, which on 16 December 1925 decided to attach the disputed territory to Iraq. A factor in the decision was the strong anti-Turkish feeling engendered in the Kurds of the Mosul area by the Draconian methods the Turks had used to suppress Sheikh Said's revolt earlier in the year.

The Turks refused to accept the Council's ruling, and on the very next day signed a Pact of Non-Aggression and Security with the USSR. A triumph of diplomacy, however, persuaded Turkey to conclude a treaty with Great Britain and Iraq on 5 June 1926, accepting the League's decision. By 1929 the breach was sufficiently healed for units of the British Mediterranean Fleet to pay a highly successful visit to Istanbul.

Even more remarkable was the *rapprochement* with Greece. On 30 December 1930, a Treaty of Friendship, Neutrality, Conciliation, and Arbitration, and a Convention for Establishment, Commerce, and Navigation, were signed. By the latter, Greek nationals were given special privileges to enable them to live and work in Turkey. On 14 September 1933 came a Pact of Cordial Friendship, and on 27 April 1938 a Treaty of Friendship, both additional to the 1930 Treaty.

On 18 July 1932, Turkey was admitted to membership of the League of Nations, while maintaining friendly relations with Russia, who during that year gave her a credit of 8 million gold dollars for industrial development. Kemal's watchword was 'Peace at home and peace abroad'; he was determined not to let Turkey be drawn into any risk of conflict with anybody. On the tenth anniversary of the foundation of the Republic, 29 October 1933, the government newspaper *Hâkimiyet-i Milliye* wrote thus: 'The Turkish friendship for the Russian Soviet Republic is rooted in Kemalism. This friendship was begun by Lenin and Mustafa Kemal and is now confirmed'.

The greatest worry of Turkish statesmen in the 1930s arose from the aggressive policies of Bulgaria, and of Italy, whose wartime designs on southern Anatolia had not been forgotten. Turkey therefore entered into a defensive alliance, the Balkan Entente, with

Yugoslavia, Greece, and Romania, on 9 February 1934. The signatories undertook to preserve the Balkan frontiers and to consult together in the event of any threat to peace in their area.

The fear of Italian aggression is referred to in the Note which Turkey sent to Great Britain in 1936, asking for revision of the Dardanelles Convention of 1923, which forbade the fortification of the Straits: 'The situation in the Black Sea is reassuring in every respect, but uncertainty has gradually arisen in the Mediterranean'.

In response to this Note, the Lausanne Powers held a conference at Montreux, which, by the Convention of 20 July 1936, restored full Turkish sovereignty over the Straits, subject to the following conditions:

> In peacetime, merchant shipping of all nations may pass freely, as may warships of Black Sea Powers. The total tonnage of warships which other nations may send through the Straits is restricted, as is the length of time for which they may stay in the Black Sea.
>
> If Turkey is at war, she may forbid the passage, not only of enemy ships, but also of neutral merchantmen carrying troops or material in support of the enemy.
>
> In time of war, Turkey being neutral, no belligerent warships may pass the Straits, except under orders from the League of Nations or in fulfilment of a treaty of mutual assistance to which Turkey is a signatory. Neutral ships may pass, provided that they respect the laws of neutrality.
>
> If Turkey considers that there is a threat of war, she may close the Straits to foreign warships and compel foreign merchantmen to pass during the hours of daylight.

Italy did not accede to the Convention until 1938, a year after Turkey recognized her conquest of Ethiopia. In 1935, after Italy had invaded Ethiopia and fortified the Dodecanese, Turco-Italian relations had been broken off, but were now resumed.

On 8 July 1937, the Saadabad Pact was signed at Teheran, by representatives of Turkey, Persia, Iraq, and Afghanistan. The signatories undertook to preserve their common frontiers, to consult together in all matters of common interest, to commit no aggression against one another's territory, and to prevent the formation within their own territories of political associations aiming at the disturbance of the peace of any of the other signatories. Some commentators interpreted Turkey's adherence to this Pact as a return to

Pan-Islamism. They were wrong. Mustafa Kemal, who had set out to make Turkey a Western nation, had succeeded to a large extent in overcoming the facts of history. The facts of geography are less submissive. Turkey may not be oriental, but she cannot help being Eastern. It was because Kemal wished to cut her off from her oriental and Islamic past that the several Islamic Congresses held between 1926 and 1931 had received no support from Turkey. But this purely defensive Pact, which helped guard her eastern frontiers, and promised to discourage further Kurdish insurrections, did not constitute a threat to the principle of laicism.

Turkey's frontiers did not assume their present shape until 22 July 1939, when Turkish troops took possession of Hatay, the former sanjak (sub-province) of Alexandretta. This had been annexed to Syria after the collapse of the Ottoman empire, and the Turks had accepted this situation in the Ankara Agreement with France in 1921. In 1937, Turkey took advantage of France's desire for friendship with her to press for the cession of the region, at least 40 per cent of the population being Turks. Atatürk, still obsessed with the theories of the Nationalist historians, declared: 'The land which has been Turkish for 4,000 years cannot remain captive in foreign hands'. France expressed her willingness to grant autonomy to the region, but the Turks were not satisfied and fighting broke out in the summer of 1938. On 3 July, a Franco-Turkish condominium was agreed upon. Elections for a local Assembly were held in August, the Turks securing twenty-two out of forty seats. On the strength of this majority, they proclaimed an independent Republic of Hatay. France, being eager to win Turkey's support in the coming struggle, raised no objection when the inevitable next step was taken: on 29 June 1939, the Hatay Assembly voted for union with Turkey.

France saw the reward of her forbearance on 19 October 1939, when the Anglo-Franco-Turkish Treaty was signed at Ankara. It provided that Turkey would give Britain and France every aid and support in her power, in the event of an act of aggression by a European power which led to a war in the Mediterranean area in which Britain and France were involved, or if they had to go to war in fulfilment of their guarantees given to Greece and Romania in April 1939. Britain and France, for their part, would aid Turkey to the limit of their power if she were the victim of aggression by a European state, or if she were involved in a war in the Mediterranean area occasioned by any such aggression.

Within a year, an act of aggression by a European power had

indeed brought war to the Mediterranean. One of Turkey's allies had laid down her arms, and the other was fighting alone against a monstrous enemy, while Turkey looked on.

Mustafa Kemal was dead and lesser men were in control. They had signed the Treaty because they overestimated the strength of France; they broke it because they overestimated the strength of Germany. The Nazi propaganda machine had been active and many Turks, including the General Staff, found its message plausible: Britain was doomed and soon it would be Russia's turn; there was no further need to maintain the unnatural friendship with her which it had previously been expedient to profess. So in June 1941 Turkey negotiated a Non-Aggression Pact with Germany and continued to sit adroitly on the fence.

On 27 August 1942, the German ambassador, Franz von Papen, asked Prime Minister Şükrü Saracoğlu for his views on 'the Russian problem'. Saracoğlu replied that as a Turk he longed for the annihilation of Russia, which would be an epoch-making act on the part of the Führer and had been the Turkish people's dream for centuries.[1] As Prime Minister, however, it was his business to see that nothing occurred which might furnish the Russians with an excuse to slaughter their Turkish minorities; hence the need for a strictly neutral attitude. He also considered it necessary not to compromise Turkey's position because the approaching collapse of Russia was bound to prompt a desire for peace on the part of the British. This opportunity to restore peace to Europe must not be missed.

The influence of Nazi ideas was certainly in some measure responsible for the shameful episode of the 'Property Tax', *Varlık Vergisi.* At the time of the French collapse in the summer of 1940 the Turkish army was mobilized, imposing a heavy burden on the economy. At the same time the worldwide rise in prices was being felt in Turkey. The farmers benefited enormously, but they paid no tax whatsoever on the income from their produce; some 40 per cent of the revenues of the Ottoman empire had come from tithes, but these had been abolished in February 1925.

The government decided that the times called for extraordinary measures. By a law passed on 11 November 1942 the GNA ordained a capital levy on all property-owners, 'big farmers', and business-men. In the preamble to the law, the levy was declared to be

> aimed at those who have amassed inflated profits by exploiting the difficult economic situation but do not pay commensurate taxes. Its purpose is to compel them to participate in the sacrifice

demanded by the extraordinary circumstances in which we find ourselves, to an extent commensurate with their profits and capacity.

These stern but righteous sentiments were unfortunately vitiated by the manifest intention of the promoters of the law that it should weigh very much more heavily on non-Muslims than on Muslims. The amounts to be paid were fixed by local committees of government officials, according to their own estimates of the individual's ability to pay. There was no appeal against their assessment; the property of those who could not pay was sold at public auction and, if the price obtained was insufficient, they were sent away to forced labour under the direction of the Ministry of Public Works. The names of those liable to pay in each locality were placed in one of two lists, the *M* list or the *G* list; *M* standing for *Müslüman*, 'Muslim', and *G* for *Gayrimüslim*, 'non-Muslim'. It being a principle of international law that a state may not tax foreign subjects more heavily than its own nationals, orders were given that foreign residents in Turkey were to be treated like the *M*s, except for Jewish subjects of the Axis Powers. In practice, not only these but many other foreigners were assessed as *G*s; citizens of Greece, in particular, tended to be lumped together with the indigenous Greeks of Turkey, because of the defective system of identification records then in operation. In general, the non-Muslim paid up to ten times the amount levied from a Muslim of the same estimated wealth. Later a *D* list was instituted, for *Dönmes*,[2] who paid twice as much as Muslims.

This disgraceful chapter in Turkish history was ended by a law of 15 March 1944, releasing the defaulters from their forced labour and writing off amounts still unpaid. The Treasury had benefited by some 221 million *liras* (at that time roughly equivalent to £20 million), but against this must be set the dislocation brought about in the commercial life of the country through the ruin of many old-established businesses. Worse still was the blackening of the good name which the Republic had been winning for itself abroad by its scrupulousness in the payment of its share of the Ottoman Public Debt and the yearly instalments of the purchase price due to former owners of state-owned enterprises, as also by its humane reception of so many refugees from Nazi Germany.

The end of the *Varlık Vergisi* coincided with the general realization that Germany had lost the war. In April 1944 an Allied *démarche* brought about a suspension of supplies of chrome to

Germany; after the USSR, Turkey was at that time the world's largest producer of this essential war material.

The following month the government at last took action to suppress a Nazi-inspired racialist Pan-Turanian movement which had been winning converts amongst university students in Ankara.

On 14 June 1944, it was announced that Turkey had consented to ban the passage through the Straits of the thinly-disguised German naval auxiliaries which had long been going through to the Black Sea, in defiance of the Montreux Convention and the 1939 Treaty with Britain and France.

The black-out regulations in Istanbul and the Black Sea towns were intensified when Bulgaria capitulated to the Red Army in September 1944. A joke that went the rounds in Istanbul at the time is worth recording as illustrative of the Turkish state of mind. The story was that the Russian ambassador had called on the Turkish Foreign Minister, to say: 'I am instructed by my government to assure you that there is no need for you to inconvenience your people by this black-out. When we attack, it will be in the daytime'.

The 1925 Treaty with the USSR had been renewed for a further ten years in 1935, but in March 1945 the Soviet government gave notice that they would not renew it again in the following November, when it was due to expire. In June the USSR declared her willingness to negotiate a new Treaty of Friendship if Turkey would agree to hand over Kars and Ardahan to Armenia and Georgia respectively and to accept Russian participation in the defence of the Straits. This suggestion was immediately turned down.

On 22 February 1945, Turkey declared war on Germany and Japan with effect from 1 March, as the Yalta Conference had decided that only those nations which had declared war on the Axis by the latter date would be invited to take part in the inaugural Conference of the United Nations at San Francisco.

NOTES

[1] 'Als Türke ersehne er die Vernichtung Russlands, die eine säkulare Tat des Führers darstellte, und die seit Jahrhunderten der Traum des türkischen Volkes sei'. *German Foreign Office Documents: German Policy in Turkey 1941–1943* (Moscow, 1948), 87–91.

[2] Descendants of the Jewish followers of the false Messiah, Sabbatai Zevi (1632–75), who ostensibly became converts to Islam with him in 1666 when

he was forced by the Sultan to renounce his pretensions. They long maintained their identity as a sect, not intermarrying with Jews or Muslims and secretly following certain Jewish practices as well as some peculiar to themselves, notably a liturgical recitation in praise of Sabbatai Zevi. In recent years they have done their utmost to be assimilated into the Muslim community, abandoning their non-Muslim practices.

CHAPTER 16

The Rise and Fall of the Democrat Party

THE LACK OF success of the various attempts to break the Republican Party's monopoly of power had not discouraged those who, for one reason or another, were opposed to the existing order.

The repressive measures that had been taken during the war, in an effort to keep the Press in conformity with the government's delicately ambidextrous policy, had intensified the liberals' desire for a loosening of the reins. The commercial class, enlarged and enriched by Turkey's wartime neutrality, wanted more outlets for their capital than state socialism allowed. The wealthy landowners had been alarmed by the creation of the Village Institutes in 1940 and were still more alarmed in 1945 by a law distributing land to landless peasants. In the event, this did not affect the big private holdings. Nor did it greatly help the landless, because it increased the number of uneconomically tiny farms. The peasants, for their part, were resentful at İnönü's use of forced labour to build village schools. Labouring men, suffering from inflated prices and forbidden by law to strike, were ready to support any party strong enough to challenge the government. The minorities, still reeling under the savage and unexpected blow of the *Varlık Vergisi*, felt that any change could only be for the better. The fanatically religious were, as ever, watchful of a chance to undo the Kemalist reforms.

The first attempt at organizing the opposition came from the National Recovery Party (*Millî Kalkınma Partisi*), founded in September 1945 by Nuri Demirağ, an outspoken advocate of free enterprise on the American model. It attacked the étatism of the Republican People's Party and accused it, quite unjustly, of being pro-Russian. Whereas Turkey's face had been set resolutely westward by Mustafa Kemal and the Republican Party, the new party proposed to establish close ties with the Muslim states of the East. The absence of popular response to this programme may be attributed to two reasons. In the first place, national pride, born during the years of revolution, had swamped, in the majority of Turks, any feeling of kinship they may have had for the Muslim world. Secondly, many of those who might have been sympathetic hesitated to link themselves to the new party because of memories of the fate of previous attempts at opposition.

These same fears persisted until 1 November 1945, when İsmet İnönü, addressing the GNA at the beginning of the new session, declared himself in favour of having an opposition party: the Republican government, he said, had never yet been in a position to permit argument about what needed to be done, but now that the war was over there was more room for democracy in Turkey.

This speech had been prompted by a serious split within the Republican ranks, which began in the summer of 1945 and culminated in the expulsion from the Party of three prominent members – Adnan Menderes, Mehmed Fuad Köprülü, and Refik Koraltan – and the resignation of a fourth—Celâl Bayar. On 7 January 1946, these four men founded the Democrat Party (*Demokrat Parti*).

Mahmud Celâl Bayar was born in 1884, the son of a mufti of enlightened views who gave the boy a European education, partly at the school of the Alliance Israélite at Bursa. He was deputy for İzmir in the last Ottoman Parliament and made his way to Ankara when that body closed. He held several cabinet posts and in 1937 became Deputy Prime Minister and then Prime Minister, a post he held till January 1939.

Adnan Menderes, born in 1899, was educated at the American College in İzmir and the Faculty of Law at Ankara, but devoted much of his time to farming his large estates, on which he introduced a number of modern improvements. The premiership which he held from 1950 to 1960 was his first and last public office.

Refik Koraltan, born in 1891, was also trained as a lawyer. He presided over one of the Independence Tribunals and held several provincial governorships, returning to parliamentary life in 1942. He was known to be rather slow and unimaginative. A reasonably well authenticated piece of malicious gossip ran as follows. On 18 December 1946, while Menderes was speaking during the Assembly debate on the 1947 budget, Âkil Muhtar, a Republican deputy who was also a medical man, having watched him intently for some time, turned to his neighbour, the Prime Minister, Recep Peker, and whispered, 'The man's a psychopath!' – *psikopat*. The Prime Minister rose and tactlessly informed the House of this diagnosis, whereupon Refik Koraltan jumped to his feet and shouted indignantly, 'Arkadaşımız piskopos değil!' – 'Our colleague is not a bishop! He's a good Muslim!'

Mehmed Fuad Köprülü, born in 1890, was a descendant of the great Köprülü dynasty of Grand Viziers, whose stern efficiency staved off the collapse that threatened the empire in the seventeenth century. Before entering public life, Mehmed Fuad was Turkey's most outstanding scholar. His work on the history and literature of the Turks had won him an international reputation; the Universities of Heidelberg, Athens, and Paris had conferred honorary doctorates on him. The decision he made, in 1943, to devote himself exclusively to politics was a great loss to scholarship.

These, then, were the men who, in 1946, broke away from the Republican People's Party. They considered that the need for étatism was passing and that Turkey's economy could best be served in future by the encouragement of private enterprise. They claimed also that the traditional concentration of power in the hands of the executive, with all the restriction of personal freedom that it involved, was inconsistent with Turkey's claim to be a modern Western state and with her support of the Charter of the United Nations.

The correctness of the latter belief was immediately demonstrated by the repressive measures taken against the new party, especially in the eastern provinces, where Governors regarded opposition as synonymous with insurrection. It must be recorded to the everlasting credit of İsmet İnönü that he published an unequivocal statement of his desire that the opposition party be allowed to work without hindrance from over-zealous officials. He then made a tour of the eastern provinces to press home the point, accompanied by a representative of the Democrat Party.

İnönü's sincerity in this matter can scarcely be questioned, but he failed to persuade the local authorities to follow his statesmanlike lead. Nor is this really surprising. The officials had, for twenty years and more, been enforcing the dictates of the government, which was but a manifestation of the party to which they all belonged. They could not be expected to facilitate a new party's efforts to unseat that government.

Elections were held in July 1946, in which Democrats stood for 273 of the 465 seats. Even in a fair election they would probably not have gained a majority; as it was, they won 62 seats.

The new Republican Cabinet, headed by Recep Peker, did not long enjoy the ill-gotten fruits of office. It was assailed by the Democrat opposition in the Assembly and by the popular ex-Chief of the General Staff, Marshal Fevzi Çakmak, who had been elected as an Independent. But it had also to face the attacks of a group of young Republicans, who accused it of impeding President İnönü's efforts to liberalize Party policy and so to steal the Democrats' thunder. The government did yield on one important matter of principle: from 2 July 1947, Muslim religious schools were allowed to reopen, but attendance at public elementary schools remained obligatory.

In September of the same year Recep Peker resigned, although he had recently won a vote of confidence, because he felt that İnönü was on the side of the rebels, several of whom were given portfolios in the ensuing Cabinet headed by Hasan Saka.

The Democrat Party underwent an even more serious split than its rival, resulting in the emergence of the National Party (*Millet Partisi*) in July 1948. Its founders regarded the Democrat leaders as wanting in vigour, and certainly their refusal to come out openly against the Kemalist reforms was disappointing to many who had seen in the rise of the new party a chance to undo the work of the 'godless Republic'. Some Republicans also joined the National Party, of which Marshal Çakmak accepted the honorary presidency. The government made another concession to public opinion by introducing lessons in the principles of Islam as an optional subject in the fourth and fifth classes of primary schools – i.e., for children aged ten to twelve.

At the 1949 Congress of the Democrat Party, many speakers rose to advocate revolt in the event of a repetition, at the next election, of the malpractices of 1946. Celâl Bayar was far too prudent to listen to such hot-headed talk, but it may have helped persuade the Republicans of the vanity of hoping to cling to power by perpetually rigging elections; and certainly the Republican officials who had falsified the returns in 1946 knew better than anybody the strength of the opposition in the country.

In February 1950, the GNA passed a new electoral law, which had been drafted with the approval of both major parties. It provided for secret ballot and public counting of votes (a reversal of the procedure previously in force), equality of parties in the allocation of political broadcasts, and supervision of the elections by the judiciary. The National Party deputies voted against the new law, because it did not meet their demand for proportional representation.

Both Republicans and Democrats adopted the innovation of permitting the constituency parties to nominate the great majority of candidates. On 14 May 1950, Turkey went to the polls.

The results were variously described in the next day's newspapers as a landslide and a bloodless revolution. The Democrats had won 408 seats, the Republicans 69, the National Party one, and Independents 9. Details will be found in the table on page 146. The striking disproportion between the number of votes and the number of seats won by each party was due to the list-system, whereby every voter had to choose among the lists of candidates nominated by the various parties for all the seats allocated (on the basis of one deputy for every 40,000 people) to the province in which he lived.

The reasons for the Democrats' success were not hard to find. Once İsmet İnönü had assured the electorate that there wasn't a catch in it, all the elements desirous of change hastened to strike their blow against the Party which had ruled them for a quarter of a century. The Democrats, however, had not passively waited for this to happen; for many months before the elections their organization was hard at work, particularly in country districts, promising everyone everything. Farmers were assured that a Democrat victory would mean higher prices for their produce, the religiously-minded were promised a relaxation of the anti-Islamic ordinances, the minorities were told they could expect compensation for their losses under the *Varlık* law, the industrial workers were promised the right to strike.

So the Republican People's Party went down, and with it went its leader. The Democrats had suggested before the election that İnönü should resign from the Party and retain the Presidency. But that stubbornness in him that had served his country so well would not let him take out this easy insurance. By a majority vote of the GNA, on 22 May 1950, Celâl Bayar was elected President of the Republic, and Adnan Menderes became Prime Minister.

Cynics may say that in permitting free elections İnönü was only making a virtue of necessity. Yet it must be remembered that had he wished to cling to office he could have used the perennial fear of Russian intentions as an excuse to delay the election. His refusal to adopt this course must stand to his credit; the dignified way in which he abdicated the power he had wielded for so long compels our admiration.

The reader will have gathered that the author does not share the dislike of İnönü displayed by many Turks, which is as intense and, to the foreigner, as startling as the dislike some Americans still express for Franklin D. Roosevelt. İnönü deserves to go down in history as one of the world's great statesmen. His sagacity or, if you will, craftiness is almost proverbial in Turkey; a favourite saying about him is 'İsmet Pasha has nine foxes running about inside his head, and their tails don't even touch'. What makes him virtually unique among politicians is that he changed his mind and was not afraid to admit it. For most of his Presidency he was as tough as the country's situation demanded, and tougher. Some time between 1946 and 1949 he decided to allow free expression to the popular will. His defeat in the 1950 elections ranks with his achievement at Lausanne as one of his greatest victories.

The most remarkable immediate consequence of the change of government was an outbreak of fez- and turban-wearing in the eastern provinces. This may sound trivial, but its significance must not be overlooked: it carries the clear implication that the Democrats were expected to be more tolerant than their predecessors of reversions to the old way of life, and it is not unreasonable to conclude that this expectation was based on the pre-election promises of Democrat canvassers. From 17 June 1950, which was the first day of Ramadan, the month of fasting, the call to prayer was permitted to be recited in Arabic instead of Turkish, and the Turkish version has seldom if ever been heard since. In March 1952, religious instruction was added to the curriculum of the Village Institutes.

Another pre-election promise was implemented in August 1951, when the State Maritime Administration was handed over to a new Maritime Bank (*Denizcilik Bankası*), 51 per cent of its capital being subscribed by the government and the remainder by private investors. Private firms were also allowed to participate in the manufacture of wine, and in May 1952 the state monopoly of the match industry was ended.

August 1951 also saw the passage through the GNA of a Bill to encourage foreign investment. By the end of 1955 some 150 applications from foreign firms had been received, but the country's worsening economic position discouraged all but thirty from actually putting their money into it.

For this situation a combination of chance and human error was to blame. Where chance came in (though Democrats saw it as a mark of divine approval) was that for the first few years of Democrat rule weather conditions were exceptionally favourable. From 1951 to 1953, harvests were the best in living memory and Turkey became a major exporter of wheat. But in 1954 harvests reverted to normal, or worse; not until 1958 was there another wheat surplus.

The error was on the part of Menderes. He was a man of great personal magnetism and high intelligence, with a deep understanding of the mind of the peasant. But his understanding of the mind of the intellectual – a category which in Turkey includes the officer – was not so profound. He had two other defects, which brought his country to insolvency and himself to the gallows: his addiction to free enterprise blinded him to Turkey's need for a planned economy if she was ever to develop her potentiality to the full, while his pathological vanity made him deaf to argument and intolerant of criticism.

His domestic policy was to maintain himself in power by giving the peasants what they wanted: loans for farm equipment, public works in country districts, a relaxation of the official antipathy towards the more obscurantist manifestations of Islamic religious feeling. His economic policy was simple, ingenious, and, to the economist, horrifying. It was to build up Turkey's agriculture and industry to the limit by importing all the necessary capital equipment without worrying about how to pay for it, in the sure knowledge that Turkey's allies would foot the bill. The end of the run of bumper harvests should have been the signal to cut back on spending, but Menderes paid no heed. By the end of 1952 Turkey's debt to the European Payments Union amounted to $147.5 million. Inflation grew; with the official rate of exchange standing at 7.84 *liras* to the pound sterling, the black market rate was 12 in 1953, 15 in 1954, and 30 in 1956.

Opposition criticism was loud against him, and this he would not endure. As early as 1951 the *Halkevis* had been closed and their assets confiscated to the Treasury. This meant a heavy loss to the Republican People's Party, both financially and in terms of its ability to influence the electorate. The cessation of the educational, cultural, and social work of the *Halkevis* constituted an even heavier loss to the people at large.

In July 1953 action was taken against the National Party, which was working for a restoration of the Caliphate and a reversion to the use of the Arabic alphabet and to the veiling of women. In this it was going a bit too far and might make inroads on the Democrat vote, so it was suspended from activity and its offices were closed. The Republican People's Party protested against this action, regarding it as the thin end of the wedge; rightly so, because on 14 December came a Bill confiscating all its property, except as much as the Minister of Finance might deem essential to the Party's activities. The Democrat Party claimed that its rival had embezzled huge sums during its long monopoly of power. The Republicans argued, not unreasonably, that all the leading Democrats had been members of the Republican Party in their time and bore their share of any guilt there might be. That party funds and government funds had been mixed up is hardly surprising; the Republicans had not regarded themselves as temporarily exercising the powers of government. The Party *was* the government and, until 1946, had not seriously considered the possibility that things might some day be different.

On 16 December 1953, the premises and plant of the leading Republican newspaper, *Ulus* ('The Nation'), which Mustafa Kemal had founded in 1920 under the title of *Hâkimiyet-i Milliye* ('National Sovereignty'), were taken over by government representatives. The Party's 200-odd branch headquarters throughout the country were also closed down. İsmet İnönü protested that this action was unconstitutional, and demanded the creation of a supreme court, with power to decide on the legality of measures passed by the Grand National Assembly. The government's answer was a threat to treat this speech as treason against the sovereign Assembly.

The Village Institutes, which had given the peasant his first glimpse beyond his own horizon and were the one development in Turkish education to attract admiring visitors from all over the world, had long been anathema to the conservatives, who saw them as hotbeds of vice where innocent village children were corrupted by lectures on Lenin, Freud, homosexuality, and atheism, or alternatively as places where a lot of smelly ragged peasants came to watch Shakespeare and grand opera and get ideas above their station. On 28 January 1954, the GNA abolished the Village Institute programme. It may be added here that in 1963, after the Democrats' downfall, a Minister of Education, Şevket Raşit Hatipoğlu, produced yet another stick with which to beat the Institutes. Teachers trained in them, he said, were supposed to be carpenters, farmers, blacksmiths, charcoal-burners, and village factotums. 'In the twentieth century everything has become specialized. Is such an education possible?' Like his predecessors and successors, he refused to countenance a restoration of the Institutes.

The leaders of the National Party had been brought to trial and on 27 January 1954 judgement was delivered: the Party was dissolved and the leaders sentenced to one day's imprisonment and a nominal fine. They were understandably not deterred and on 10 February they founded a new party, the Republican National Party (*Cumhuriyetçi Millet Partisi*), which ostensibly accepted the principle of the division between religion and state, as it had done in its previous avatar, but demanded the recognition of 'full religious liberty'. It also seconded İnönü's demand for a supreme court.

On 9 March, a new Press Law was passed, increasing from one to three years' imprisonment the maximum penalty for libel or for spreading inaccurate information 'calculated to endanger the political and economic stability of the country'. It was in a strained and unhappy atmosphere that Turkey went to the polls on 2 May 1954.

Besides the parties already discussed, there were two new contestants, neither of which won a single seat. The Democratic Workers' Party (*Demokrat İşçi Partisi*) was founded in 1950 by a lawyer, two fitters, and a mechanic. Membership was numbered in the hundreds. It sought to 'give the working class political power'. The Peasants' Party of Turkey (*Türkiye Köylü Partisi*) was founded in Ankara in 1952 by a number of intellectuals, including several ex-Democrat deputies. Its aim was 'to bring all citizens who work, and peasants above all, into a new life; new in culture, technique, and prosperity'.

But the real fight was between the two big parties. The results, which are tabulated below, showed the success of Menderes's policy of improving the lot of the Turkish villager at the expense of the British, French, West German, Italian, and American taxpayer.

Name of party	*Percentage of votes*		*Seats won*		*Gain or loss in seats*
	1950	*1954*	*1950*	*1954*	
DP	53.3	56.6	408	503	+95
RPP	39.9	34.8	69	31	−38
NP/RNP	3.1	4.8	1	5	+ 4
PP	—	0.6	—	0	—
Independents	4.8	1.5	9	2	− 7

Once again a clear majority of the country had decided against the Republican People's Party. Because of the list-system, the small drop in its percentage vote had cost it over half its representation in the Assembly.

With his mandate renewed, Menderes continued his efforts to silence the opposition. It was not enough for him that he had a majority of the electorate behind him; he seemed to regard each vote cast against him as a personal blow. Shortly after the election a Bill was introduced to change the constituency boundaries in such a way as to eliminate the province of Kırşehir, which had returned the five National Party deputies. (The province was restored to existence in June 1957 and again returned the National Party's candidates.)

The opposition certainly had a great deal to criticize. The trade-gap, 382.1 million *liras* in 1953, rose to 401.6 million in 1954. By the end of the latter year, British exporters alone were owed £15 million, not because Turkish businessmen wanted to cheat them but because the Central Bank simply had no sterling. According to the Istanbul Chamber of Commerce, the city's cost-of-living index, on the basis of 100 in 1950, was 129 in 1954. By August 1955 it was 143. Newspapers were forbidden to publish photographs of queues outside shops. Tradesmen were forbidden to use the word *zam*, 'price-increase'; instead they had to use *ayar*, 'adjustment'. Nor, when asked for goods which had vanished from the market, could they say *yok*, 'there isn't any'; the officially imposed substitute was *gelecek*, 'it'll be coming'. The current name for Turkey was *Yokistan*, 'the Land of Not', but journalists who used it in print felt the weight of the Press Law, as they did if they ventured to give details of corruption in ruling circles. In October 1955, thirteen Democrat deputies proposed to amend the Press Law so as to give anyone accused under it 'the right of proof'; i.e., the right to justify his allegations. They subsequently announced that their purpose was to enable the Press to publicize 'the misdeeds and crimes of people in the public service'. They were soon joined by six of their colleagues. A Party congress, on 15 October, expelled nine of them, and the other ten resigned.

Among the misdeeds and crimes they wanted to publicize was a fresh one. On 29 August, tripartite talks on Cyprus had opened in London. As far as the story can be reconstructed, the Turkish Foreign Minister, Fatin Rüştü Zorlu, was stung by the Greek delegation's remarking that there did not seem to be much popular feeling in Turkey about the Cyprus situation. He cabled home a request for a popular demonstration. (The author may here mention his personal belief that there has never been a spontaneous riot in the whole of Turkish history.) On 5 September an explosion damaged the Turkish Consulate in Salonika and the adjoining house, in which Mustafa Kemal was born. The next night, riots occurred simultaneously in the three chief cities of Turkey. The rioters travelled in lorries and had lists of addresses to visit. But soon the amateurs took over, and what had begun as anti-Greek became anti-minority, then anti-foreign, ending as anti-rich. Churches, houses, and shops were sacked; there was much looting but more wanton destruction. İstiklâl Caddesi, formerly the Grande Rue de Péra, the main shopping-street of Istanbul, was littered with the wreckage of furniture, refrigerators, and radios. The police were slow to realize that the planned demonstration had changed its nature; by the time they and the military intervened the damage was done. Three thousand people were arrested but subsequently released. The government paid compensation, but the minorities' faith in the Democrats was shaken and there were many resignations from local Party branches. There was a reminder of this terrible night ten years later, in November 1965, when Prime Minister Ürgüplü said, 'If a single Turk is killed in Cyprus I cannot give any guarantee about what may happen in Istanbul. I fear another incident like that of 6–7 September'. He was immediately slapped down by President Gürsel : 'Turkey isn't a tribe, it's a state. I cannot imagine what possessed the Prime Minister to talk like this. It is distressing even to be reminded of the events of 6–7 September'.

On 13 November 1955, local elections were held. The RPP and National Party put up no official candidates, in protest against alleged malpractices in the 1954 general election, but independent opposition candidates won eight of the sixty-six provinces, while two went to the liberal-led Peasants' Party. The awareness of the government's unpopularity was such that several Democrats resigned to fight the election as independents, then rejoined the Party when they had been elected. The nineteen rebels, led by a former Minister of the Interior, Fevzi Lûtfi Karaosmanoğlu, formed a new Freedom Party (*Hürriyet Partisi*). Most of the Cabinet resigned, and ten days passed before Menderes could form another, which won a vote of confidence on 16 December with at least fifty Democrats abstaining. Apparently chastened, Menderes promised that the Press Law would be amended to permit 'the right of proof', but instead, in June 1956, when he felt that the fuss had blown over, it was strengthened : a new amendment made it an offence to summarize or comment on any speech made in the Assembly except according to the official record. On 28 June a new law virtually prohibited political meetings except for the forty-five days before an election.

The previous month, sixteen judges had been placed on the retired list before reaching the retiring age of sixty, the opposition alleging that some of them had incurred the government's displeasure by acquitting journalists accused under the Press Law.

In August, leaders of the three opposition parties decided to unite their efforts at the next general election, due in May 1958. It came, however, on 27 October 1957, and a month before that date the hopes of the opposition had been frustrated by an ingenious piece of *ad hoc* legislation. It ordained that every party must present a list of candidates in every province in which it had a party organization. No one could be a candidate for two parties. Nor could anyone be included in any party's list who had resigned from another party less than six months before a normal election, or two months before an early election. As might have been expected, the election campaign was heated. In Ankara and Istanbul the police used tear-gas to break up demonstrations. Strict security measures were taken on polling day.

There is little doubt that honest elections would have given Menderes the victory; his hold on the peasants was still strong. But he took no chances and the elections were rigged. In Istanbul, for example, the results were announced before counting was complete. Here they are, for what they are worth:

Name of party	*Percentage of votes*	*Seats won*	*Percentage of seats*
DP	47·3	424	69.50
RPP	40.6	178	29.18
RNP	7.0	4	0.66
FP	3.8	4	0.66
Independents	0.1	2	0.33

After the election, the RNP amalgamated with the Peasants' Party, to become the Republican Peasants' National Party (RPNP).

To say that Menderes was heading for destruction is not mere hindsight. Confident in the backing of the peasants, he underestimated the hatred he had roused in the intellectuals.

All intellectuals in theory, and some in practice, are idealistically eager to educate their underprivileged brothers into equality with themselves. But Menderes courted the peasants for the sake of their votes; he let them believe that they were all right as they were and needed no improvement. Above all, although he never dared say openly that he thought Atatürk had gone too far and too fast in his reforms, he let it be known that reversions to the old ways would be winked at. He did not try to repeal the Hat Law, but anyone who wanted to could wear a turban and get away with it. Polygamy was condoned. Restaurateurs who did not voluntarily close their premises during the daylight hours of Ramadan were intimidated into doing so, and the police took no action. In Kemalist eyes, Menderes had betrayed Atatürk's revolution and his own class.

The roots of the movement which led to the *coup d'état* of 27

May 1960 go back to late 1946, when ten Staff colonels and majors decided that it was their duty to overthrow the government which had so shamelessly rigged the elections that year. They approached a general commanding a corps at Gallipoli and asked him to join them, but he advised against the violent remedy they had in mind; they should wait and see what happened at the next elections. The honest elections of 1950 caused them to relax and they prepared, like so many of their countrymen, to enjoy the new era of liberal democracy.

But as time passed, more and more officers became discontented with the Menderes regime. Like their forebears under Abdülhamid, they knew Western languages and were in touch with Western colleagues. Many had served abroad, in Korea and with NATO. They knew there was more to democracy than the name. They had a tradition, deriving from the day when the army was Prussian-trained, that it was their business to keep an eye on the government. This did not conflict in their minds with Atatürk's injunction against interfering in politics; this injunction they interpreted as applicable only so long as the civilians were following the lines laid down by Atatürk. The cocktail-party joke one heard after 27 May really wasn't fair: that the Menderes government fell because, with all its faults, it was the only civilian government the Turks had ever had and the army couldn't tolerate this anomaly any longer. Like other people on fixed incomes the officers were suffering from inflation and rising prices.[1] Their duties took them to every corner of the land and they saw how far short the poor peasants were of the civilized Western standard of living which was the Kemalist goal. At the same time they were of a social position to see how well the rich were doing under Menderes. The Democrat Party neglected to woo the officers who, under the electoral laws of 1946 and 1950, did not have the vote. A minority of officers, notably Alpaslan Türkeş, believed sincerely that military discipline was the best instrument for governing a country. Lastly, there was a strong undirected desire to do something, no matter what, so that the splendid weapon of which they were part should not rust from lack of use; Korea had whetted their appetite for action and for glory.

In November 1954, Orhan Kabibay and Dündar Seyhan, two captains at the Anti-aircraft School in Ankara, agreed to work to form an organization among their brother-officers. Seyhan was posted in October 1955 to the Istanbul War College as a Staff candidate, and there he continued what he had begun in Ankara. He created an organization called *Atatürkçüler Cemiyeti*, the

Society of Atatürkists, of which he became Secretary. At that stage the purpose did not go beyond a reform in the army so that the power in it should not lie with senior officers prepared to kowtow to Menderes. Doubtless there were other such secret organizations all over the country; it is known that one was founded in Ankara at the beginning of 1956. One of its members was an artillery officer called Talât Aydemir. Posted to the War College in Istanbul, he put Seyhan and his group in touch with his friends in Ankara. By this time Seyhan had decided that a reform in the army would not mend the nation's ills and that a revolt was necessary. In the autumn the courses finished and the conspirators were posted to units all over the country. Aydemir was all for a revolution before the 1957 elections. An approach was made to İsmet İnönü, but he refused to see the officers, knowing how vigilant the secret police were.

On 20 December 1957, nine officers were denounced by an informer but were acquitted for lack of evidence. The result, however, was to introduce an element of caution into the movement's activities, and for a while recruiting was slow.

In February 1959, General Cemal Gürsel, recently appointed Commander of Land Forces, consented to head the movement, but insisted that revolution must be a last resort. All agreed that there would be no alternative to revolution if the next elections were not conducted honestly. Some of the officers must have felt they were experiencing a *déjà vu.* And after the revolution, what then? A minority led by Alpaslan Türkeş, a racialist Pan-Turanian of whom we shall hear more later, wanted a military government. Some were for handing power over to the RPP, but this course was rejected by the majority, who saw their duty as the protection of the constitution and not the furtherance of one party's interests. The eventual decision was that a provisional government should be set up to hold free elections as soon as possible.

On 27 February Menderes flew to England for the London conference on Cyprus. The aircraft crashed at Gatwick, killing fifteen of the twenty-five people on board. Menderes escaped with bruises. When radio interviewers came with their recording apparatus to see him and the other survivors in hospital, he told them 'No voice but mine is to go out to Turkey'. His escape was presented as a miracle by the Turkish State Radio and the Democrat Press; the other nine survivors were pushed into the remote background.

Since the 1957 elections there had been a change in the nature of the Democrat membership of the Assembly. The Party's constitution laid down that candidates should be chosen in local primaries, but that the Leader of the Party could set aside these choices and nominate whom he wished. Menderes had exercised this power to such effect that the government benches were occupied almost exclusively by yes-men. One of these exclaimed, on Menderes's return to Ankara, 'We are grateful to England. We sent her a prime minister; she has sent us back a prophet!' A few people muttered the old proverb, more apposite than they knew, 'The man born to hang will not drown', but their voices were not heard among all the cheering.

Puffed up by the adulation, Menderes became quite unable to endure the sight of any support given to the opposition. İnönü visited Konya in February 1960 and the police used tear-gas and truncheons to disperse the Republicans who turned out to meet him. The next month he was to visit Kayseri and the government took it into their heads to prevent this. The Governor of Kayseri had his train stopped and ordered him to abandon his intention. İnönü took no notice and eventually the train took him on to his destination. The next day the Governor called on the troops to prevent him from going on to Yeşilhisar, half-way to Niğde. A colonel and two majors resigned their commissions in protest against being ordered to deprive a citizen of his constitutional right to travel where he pleased. They were at once arrested. General Gürsel tried to secure their release but failed; he thereupon asked to be relieved of his duties pending his retirement under the age-limit (sixty-five) in September.

It is probable that the government were planning to hold elections about this time, but abandoned the idea when ministers who had been touring the provinces made their reports about the state of feeling in the country. Menderes could still command his solid block of 4 million votes, but the opposition was becoming militant. Most of the Press was against him and so were the universities, incensed by the legislation, some of it *ad hominem*, designed to prevent university teachers from commenting unfavourably on government policy. The economic situation was farcical. In the 1960 Budget there was a deficit of 500 million *liras*, making a cumulative deficit for the ten years of Democrat rule of 2,141 million. The Treasury owed the Central Bank 1,350 million, and civil servants were being paid with the soiled notes sent in by the banks to be destroyed. The total foreign indebtedness was 12,191 million *liras*, in spite of American gifts totalling $900 million and military aid totalling $1,650 million.

On 18 April the GNA voted the establishment of a fifteen-man Commission 'to investigate the opposition which, in co-operation with a section of the Press, is trying to set up illegal and secret columns and armed political gangs composed of ruffians and ex-convicts'. Only one Democrat, Sıtkı Yırcalı, voted against the motion. The Commission, 'to facilitate its investigations', at once banned all political activity and any published reference to the debates of the Assembly. On 27 April the Commission was voted dictatorial powers of search, arrest, and detention. In spite of the ban, some newspapers printed this news the next day, with statements by members of the Law faculties of the universities about the unconstitutionality of the measure. They also printed as their main news story the report from South Korea that Syngman Rhee had been forced to resign the Presidency after large-scale rioting triggered off by student demonstrations.

Turkey's student demonstrations began after a professor at Istanbul University had told his class that he did not propose to lecture on constitutional law that day (28 April) as there was no such thing in Turkey. Police riot-squads had been watching the universities for some days, as events in Korea had not escaped the notice of the Turkish authorities. The police invaded the university precincts and dragged away nine of the demonstrators. For the sake of the reader who has seen accounts *ad nauseam* of 'student riots' in one country after another, it should be said that these demonstrators really were students and not schoolchildren. Nor had there been any notable student intervention in national politics since the days of Abdülhamid. The Law of Associations of 1908 said uncompromisingly 'Student organizations may not engage in politics'. Part of the brief given to the Ottoman delegates to the armistice talks at Mudros in 1918 was that they should reject any proposal for repatriating subjects of the Central Powers residing in Turkey, as this would lead to reciprocal action on the part of Germany and Austria-Hungary; 'the return of Ottoman subjects numbering perhaps more than 15 or 20 thousand, especially students, will absolutely not be possible at this time'. But the Democrats were not so aware of the danger as their Ottoman counterparts had been. The Rector was manhandled when he protested to the police and as the demonstrators grew more incensed the police opened fire. One student was killed, though rumour put the figure at eleven or twelve. As the police could not have missed so large a crowd at such close range, we may take it that they were not shooting to kill. Nevertheless, a most circumstantial story arose that there were many dead whose bodies had not come to light as they had been hidden in the cold-storage lockers of the Meat and Fish Corporation, a government agency. Nonsense though the story was, a kind of shudder went through the crowd attending the student's funeral, at the sight of a wreath from the slandered organization.

On the afternoon of the demonstration, martial law was proclaimed in Ankara and Istanbul. The martial law commander in the latter city was Fahri Özdilek, a general sympathetic to the officers' movement. His opposite number in Ankara, however, was Namık Argüç, who was loyal to Menderes, and a demonstration next day at the Faculty of Political Sciences in Ankara was fired on by the army.

Two Democrat deputies called on President Bayar and begged him to dissolve the Commission. His reply was, 'If we give them our hand they'll take our arm; if we give them our arm they'll take our head'.

In Istanbul, on the other hand, the students fraternized with the army and hailed them as saviours; this points to the fact that the common soldier was neutral in the struggle but, as ever in Turkey, did what his superior officers told him to do. On 29 April all universities and institutions of higher education were closed. For the next few weeks Istanbul saw sporadic student demonstrations in which the general public played virtually no part at all; students arrested by the army were taken off to barracks, fed on steak and beer until they could barely stagger to bed, and then sent home the next day. For a little while the undergraduate catchphrase was 'Where did you have dinner on Wednesday?'

The leave which General Gürsel had requested was granted on 2 May. Before leaving for his home at İzmir, he sent a farewell message to all units, which never reached them, urging that they should not let the honour of the army be sullied by involvement in the ambitions of politicians. To the Minister of Defence he wrote a long memorandum deploring 'the unintelligent use of troops against the students'. It was essential that the President resign, 'because there is a general conviction in the country that all evils stem from him'. The governors and police-chiefs of Ankara and Istanbul and the martial law commander of Ankara must be replaced; the Commission must be dissolved; the imprisoned journalists must be amnestied and the arrested students released; the exploitation of religion for political purposes must end. The memorandum was ignored.

On 21 May, cadets of the War College in Ankara staged a silent protest-march. This caused a panic among the government as it was the first demonstration by members of the armed forces, however junior. Some ministers were reportedly ready 'to abolish the military schools', by which they did not mean closing them but rather subjecting them to the sort of treatment the Janissaries had received in 1826.

After that, things moved very fast. At 12.26 a.m. on 27 May, the Istanbul end of the conspiracy received this telephoned message from Ankara:

> I've got the 2,740 *liras* you wanted from the Pensions Fund. They've docked 10, which leaves 2,730. I've got the money for our aviator chum at Eskişehir too, but I can't get word through. You'll have to see to it.

This was intended to convey that the operation was to be completed by 4 a.m. on the 27th and should be begun at 3 a.m. The 'aviator chum' was Menderes, who had unexpectedly flown to Eskişehir and would have to be dealt with by the Istanbul people. That much was clear, but the first part of the message was misunderstood to mean that the operation was to have been started at 4 but had been brought forward by one hour. Consequently, at 3 o'clock in the morning officers and cadets took over every key building and communications centre in Istanbul; the operation was completed by 3.30. Half an hour later, the same thing had happened in the capital. The misunderstanding did not affect the success of the *coup*, which was otherwise beautifully planned and executed. All the ministers and Democrat deputies were arrested. It was just after 6 a.m. when Celâl Bayar was locked up in a room at the War College. Two hours later Adnan Menderes, who had been pursued from Eskişehir to Kütahya, was also in custody. There was no bloodshed except that one army lieutenant was shot dead by an auxiliary policeman during the takeover of a post office in Ankara. Of the part played by the ordinary citizen, the street-sweeper outside the British embassy is perhaps typical. When the tanks roared down the Çankaya hill, bringing the President of the Republic in handcuffs, he was busy with his broom and never raised his head.

NOTE

[1] To this period belongs the use by restaurant and nightclub waiters of the term *gazozcu*, 'fizzy lemonade merchants', for officers, who were no longer of the champagne-drinking class. (Verbal communication from Mr Kasım Yargıcı, April 1973.)

CHAPTER 17

Constitutions and Coalitions

GENERAL GÜRSEL HAD not been told the final details of the *coup* because his house at İzmir was known to be under surveillance. But on 26 May he had a laconic telephone-message asking him to be ready for a journey early next morning. By 4 a.m. he was up and dressed and watering his garden. By 10.20 a.m. an air force jet had brought him to Ankara, where he was proclaimed President of the National Unity Committee (hereafter referred to as NUC), a group of thirty-eight officers who had played leading parts in the revolution and who now declared that the powers of the GNA were vested in themselves. That same morning another air force machine brought to the capital five professors from Istanbul to help draw up a new constitution. Now there was a new cocktail-party joke: that the first two clauses of the constitution were to be amended to read, 'The Turkish State is a Republic. Its official language is Turkish. Its capital is the University of Istanbul'.

The next day, the General formed a provisional government, with himself as Head of State, Prime Minister, and Minister of Defence, and two other generals as Ministers of the Interior and Communications. The remaining fifteen members were all civilians; professional men and civil servants, except for Ekrem Alican, a politician. A founder-member of the Democrat Party, he was one of those who left it in 1955 to found the Freedom Party and had not been re-elected to the Assembly in 1957. The General wanted a government of men above party, but he had not allowed for the enthusiasm with which the NUC plunged into the task of putting the country to rights. The Minister of Agriculture complained that the officers who were planning a drastic land reform did not take him into their confidence; the Minister of Health was similarly ignored by those planning a national health service.

On 9 June, Gürsel made his position clear to a gathering of officers at the Ministry of Defence:

> The army today has taken on a number of tasks all over the country. This is a matter of duty. But to continue it would be weakness . . . We must all be eager and anxious to slip away from this duty as soon as possible and return to our real jobs. Our highest ideal must be to get back to soldiering. Because our present duties involve a little less discipline, are a bit more fancy than we're used to, people may be unwilling to leave them. That's human nature. But we aren't going to give in to it . . . The world will see that the moment our task is done we shall return to our own honourable ranks, our own units, our own duties.

On 12 June the NUC promulgated a provisional law amending the constitution retrospectively from 27 May, in order to provide a legal basis for its own existence and its assumption of the authority which, constitutionally, was delegated by the nation to the Grand National Assembly. Its most interesting provisions are here summarized.

The 'General Provisions' explain that the GNA had lost its legality as a result of violation of the constitution by the leaders of the party in power. The Turkish army, in accordance with its statutory duty to protect the country and the Republic, acted on behalf of the nation, dissolved the Assembly, and provisionally entrusted power to the NUC.

> *Article 1.* The NUC exercises the right of sovereignty on behalf of the Turkish nation until the date on which it will hand over the administration to the GNA, which will be re-established by elections to be held as soon as possible and when the new constitution and electoral law have been approved according to democratic methods. During this period all rights and powers given by the constitution to the GNA belong to the NUC.
>
> *Article 2* laid down the form of oath taken by members of the NUC: 'I devote myself to the Turkish nation without expecting any return . . . I will not pursue any aim contrary to the sanctity of the fatherland and nation and the sovereignty of the nation. I will not depart from loyalty to organizing the democratic community in accordance with the new constitution, and to the aim of handing over power to the new Assembly. I swear this on my honour and on all things held sacred'.
>
> *Article 3* gave the legislative power to the NUC, and executive power to the Council of Ministers appointed by the Head of State.

Article 6 instituted a High Court of Justice to try 'the fallen President, premier, ministers, and deputies of the former administration and those who participated in their offences'. It would consist of a president, eight regular members, and six reserve members, elected by the NUC from the judges of the judicial, administrative, and military courts. The prosecutors would be elected by the NUC from the members of a High Investigation Committee that would look into the responsibility of the accused and decide whether to bring them to trial. Members of the NUC could not serve on either of these new bodies.

Article 8. The NUC will cease to exist upon the re-establishment of the Grand National Assembly of Turkey, which will come into existence after general elections. The Committee will dissolve itself or will be automatically dissolved.

Article 24 abrogated a number of Articles of 'the Law of Fundamental Organization No. 491 of 1924'. These included the prohibition of confiscation (as the NUC were determined to deprive the Democrats of whatever profits they had corruptly made in their period of office) and the provision absolving the President of the Republic from responsibility for decrees he had signed; he was to share the guilt, if any, with Menderes and his ministers.

Over-haste in drafting this provisional constitution led to one curious consequence, of academic interest only, since no one noticed it and therefore no one sought to take advantage of it. As Article 24 abrogated parts of 'Law No. 491 of 1924' and not 'Law No. 491 as subsequently amended', and left the remainder of that law in force, it could be held that between 27 May 1960 and 9 July 1961 the original Article 2 of the 1924 Constitution was once again operating, so that during that period the religion of the Turkish state was Islam.

Not all the NUC were of the same mind as General Gürsel. A powerful group believed that İnönü had acted prematurely in holding free elections in 1950, a view which İnönü never held even in the darkest days. They resented the way in which Gürsel had let civilians into 'their' government and they did not propose to hold free elections and start the whole miserable process over again. They were great believers in purging. They began with the armed services. Of the 260 generals and admirals, 235 were placed on the retired list on 3 August, and 5,000 colonels and majors followed them three days later.

Then came the universities' turn. On 27 October the NUC decreed the dismissal of 147 university teachers on grounds of incompetence, absenteeism, homosexuality, and communist sympathies. The 147 included two members of the Constitutional Commission and a large proportion of those whose scholarly reputation was known beyond the walls of their own universities. It is true that some of the reasons offered for the dismissals could be held to apply to some of the 147, but they also applied to some university teachers who were not on the list. One motive which seemed to have been at work was a desire to get rid of any teacher capable of influencing his pupils. The one factor common to all the 147 was that they had been denounced. The NUC were surprised by the violent reaction of the universities, both faculty and students, an important element in which was the detestation of informers that has been innate in the Turk since the time of Abdülhamid. The author of a manual of civil law writes, apropos of grounds for divorce:

> Our law has had the courage to place, very logically, the leading of an indecent mode of life on the same level as committing a shameful crime. As examples of an indecent mode of life we may cite the occupations of brothel-keeper, *agent provocateur*, and informer.[1]

Protests continued until the end of March 1962, when the NUC rescinded its decision.

The judiciary and the civil service were to have been purged too, but General Gürsel beat the purgers at their own game. They proposed a decree perpetuating their rule for four years. This was defeated by 19 votes to 18, Gürsel having used his casting vote. (One member of the NUC, General İrfan Baştuğ, had been killed in a road accident on 12 September.) On the Committee's agenda for 14 November was another decree, which Gürsel feared would be carried. It established a National Union of Ideals and Culture, into which the Ministry of Education would be absorbed, with a regional countrywide organization and an immovable head. The day before this was due to be voted on, Gürsel announced in a broadcast that he had dissolved the NUC 'as its functioning was endangering the country's interests', and had created a new Committee consisting of twenty-three members of the old one. The explanation of this tortuous procedure was that the provisional constitution, which had been promulgated on 12 June, made it impossible to dismiss a member of the NUC unless a court found that he had broken his oath to hand over power as soon as possible to a freely elected Assembly. But no member could be put on trial except by vote of four-fifths of those present at a meeting attended by six-sevenths of the Committee, a majority which Gürsel knew he could not secure.

The fourteen thus dropped, who included Colonel Türkeş, were sent into a novel form of exile, being posted to widely dispersed missions abroad as 'attachés' with no specific duties. Gürsel's prompt action had protected the honour of the army and saved Turkey from a fascist dictatorship.

On 31 August, an Ankara court ordered the suspension of all activities of the DP and placed all its assets and property in custody, pending a decision by the High Investigation Committee of its alleged infringements of the constitution. On 29 September the court ordered the party to be dissolved.

On 6 January 1961, the Constituent Assembly met for the first time. It consisted of the NUC as an upper house, with a House of Representatives of 272 members, including 49 representatives of the RPP and 25 of the RPNP. There were also representatives of the professions, the universities, the trade unions, and the sixty-seven provinces. Its task was to prepare a new constitution and electoral law. While the constitution-making committee created by the NUC on 27 May had been at work, a group at the Faculty of Political Sciences in Ankara were devoting themselves independently to the same end, and the Constituent Assembly was their idea.

The ban on political activity, imposed immediately after the *coup*, was lifted on 13 January. Eleven new parties were formed, the most important being the Justice (*Adalet*) Party (JP) of General Ragıp Gümüşpala, whose avowed aim was to secure justice for the officers who, like himself, had been compulsorily retired the previous August. There is no reason to doubt his sincerity, but his vice-chairman, Mehmet Yorgancıoğlu, was arrested for declaring that the Party was a continuation of the outlawed Democrat Party, and thus it proved to be. The New Turkey (*Yeni Türkiye*) Party (NTP), under Ekrem Alican, sought the support of those who had left the DP before the end; it had planned to call itself the Free Democratic Party, but was forbidden to do so. A group of Istanbul trade unionists led by Avni Erakalın founded the Turkish Labour (*İşçi*) Party (TLP).

The new constitution was published on 31 May 1961. It began with a long and somewhat woolly preamble:

Having enjoyed independence and having fought for its rights and liberties throughout history, and having brought about the Revolution of 27 May 1960 in the exercise of its right to resist a regime which had lost its legality through its unconstitutional and unlawful attitude and actions, the Turkish nation . . . in order to set up a democratic rule of law based on juridical and social foundations, which will make possible the realization and guaranteeing of human rights and liberties, national solidarity and social justice, and the wellbeing and prosperity of the individual and society, accepts and proclaims the constitution prepared by the Constituent Assembly . . . and, with the conviction that its basic guarantee lies in the hearts and wills of the citizens, entrusts it to the vigilance of its children, who love freedom, justice, and integrity.

As certain of the Kemalist reforms, notably the Hat Law, could be held to contravene the spirit of human rights and liberties, special provision was made to safeguard them by Article 153:

No provision of this Constitution shall be construed as rendering unconstitutional the following Reform Laws which aim at raising Turkish society to the level of contemporary civilization and at protecting the secular nature of the Republic . . .

The other most noteworthy provisions were these.

Article 14 lays down that no one shall be subjected to ill-treatment or torture. No punishment incompatible with human dignity shall be imposed. Article 19 permits every individual to follow freely the dictates of his conscience, to choose his own religious faith, and to have his own opinions. No person shall be compelled to worship, or to reveal his religious faith and belief. The exploitation of religion for political or personal advantage is prohibited.

Article 22 establishes the principle that the Press is free and not subject to censorship.

Article 39: 'Where it is deemed necessary in the public interest, private enterprises which bear the characteristics of a public service may be nationalized, provided that the true equivalent value thereof is paid as indicated by law . . .'

Article 45: 'The state shall adopt the necessary measures so that workers may earn decent wages commensurate with the work they perform and sufficient to enable them to maintain a standard of living befitting human dignity'.

Article 46 entitles employees and employers to establish unions (*sendika*) and federations of unions without having to obtain prior permission, and to become members or to cease to be members of them freely. *Article 47* recognizes the worker's right to engage in collective bargaining and to strike 'to protect or correct' his economic and social position.

Article 49: 'It is the responsibility of the state to ensure that everyone leads a healthy life both physically and mentally and receives medical attention. The state shall take steps to provide destitute or poor families with housing that conforms to sanitary requirements'.

Article 54: 'Every individual who is bound to the Turkish state by ties of citizenship is a Turk . . .'

Article 57, on political parties, obliges them to conform to the principles of a democratic and secular republic and to account for their income and expenditure to the Constitutional Court. This is set up in *Articles 145–152* and is empowered to review the constitutionality of laws and to try the President of the Republic, ministers, the chief law officers of the state and members of all high courts, including itself.

Articles 63–94 deal with the GNA, which consists of the National Assembly (*Millet Meclisi*) and the Senate of the Republic (*Cumhuriyet Senatosu*). The National Assembly is composed of 450 deputies elected by general ballot; candidates must have completed their thirtieth year, have done their military service, be literate, and have never been sentenced to penal servitude or five years' imprisonment or have been convicted of such disgraceful offences as breach of trust and fraudulent bankruptcy. Judges, officers, military officials, and non-commissioned officers cannot be candidates or deputies unless they first resign their position. Elections to the Assembly are held every four years, but the Assembly may decide to hold them earlier.

The Senate is composed of 150 elected members and fifteen appointed by the President of the Republic. The chairman and members of the NUC as reconstituted in November 1960 and former Presidents of the Republic are *ex officio* members of the Senate, but *ex officio* members who join a political party shall lose their status as Senators on the date of the first senatorial election held thereafter. Elected Senators must be over forty and have received a higher education. The President's nominees shall be selected from among people distinguished for their service in various fields and must also be over forty. At least ten of them must be members of no political party. The term of office is six years, one-third of the elected members and the President's nominees being rotated every two years. *Ex officio* members are exempted from this provision.

By-elections to both houses shall be held every two years at the same time as the senatorial elections. Members represent neither their constituencies nor their constituents but the nation as a whole.

Bills and proposals are debated first in the Assembly and then referred to the Senate. If accepted there they become law. If a measure rejected by the Assembly is passed by the Senate, the Assembly reviews the draft approved by the Senate and can reject or approve it. A measure rejected by a two-thirds majority vote of a plenary session of the Senate can become law only if approved by a two-thirds majority vote of a plenary session of the Assembly. Laws must be promulgated by the President within ten days or returned by him to the Assembly for reconsideration. If re-enacted there, the law must be promulgated by the President within ten days.

Article 95 lays down the rules for the election of the President of the Republic: he is elected by secret ballot, at a plenary session of both houses, from among those members who are over forty and have had a higher education. His term of office is seven years and he is not re-eligible. He must dissociate himself from his party. He is not accountable for his actions connected with his duties. (*Art. 98*), but may be impeached for high treason on the proposal of one-third of the plenary session of both houses (*Art. 99*). In his absence abroad or through illness, the chairman of the Senate acts for him, as he does in the event of the President's death (*Art. 100*).

The Prime Minister is designated by the President from among the members of the GNA (i.e., of both houses). The Prime Minister nominates ministers from among the members of the GNA or from among those qualified for election as deputies.

The members of the Council of Ministers are jointly responsible for the manner in which government policy is implemented.

The office of Commander-in-Chief is 'inseparable from the spiritual being of the GNA and is represented by the President of the Republic' (*Art. 110*).

No act of the administration is immune from the review of the courts. The administration is liable for damages resulting from its acts (*Art. 114*).

Article 120 relates to universities; they may be established only by the state and are public corporate bodies enjoying academic and administrative autonomy. They are administered and supervised by bodies consisting of qualified members of the teaching staff elected from among themselves. Neither these bodies nor any member of the teaching staff may be removed from office by authorities other than the universities. University teachers may join political parties but may not assume executive functions outside the central organizations of political parties.

Article 121: 'The administration of broadcasting and television stations shall be regulated by law as an autonomous public corporate body . . . A basic requisite for news agencies established or subsidised by the state is impartiality'.

Persons employed in public services shall not carry out any order of a superior if the person receiving the order thinks it unconstitutional or illegal. If the superior insists on the performance of the order he must put it in writing and the subordinate who carries it out is not responsible; but no one can be absolved from responsibility if he carries out an order which by its nature constitutes a crime (*Art. 125*).

Article 131: 'All forests shall be under state supervision . . . No activity likely to harm forests shall be allowed . . . No amnesty shall be granted for offences involving forests . . .'

Judges are independent in the discharge of their duties and no one may make recommendations or suggestions to a judge. They may not be dismissed or retired before the age limit of sixty-five years unless they so desire (*Articles 132, 133*). Court proceedings are open to all. Cases may be heard in secret only if 'definitely required by public morality or public security' (*Art. 135*).

A referendum on this new constitution was held on 9 July 1961. The results were:

Electorate	12,735,009
Votes cast	10,322,169
Abstentions	2,412,840
'Yes'	6,348,191
'No'	3,934,370
Invalid votes	39,608

With the 3.9 million 'No' votes may be compared the votes cast for the DP in the 1950, 1954, and 1957 elections, respectively 4.2 million, 5.2 million, and 4.4 million.

The trials of the former administration had begun in October 1960, on Yassıada, the bleak 'Flat Island' in the Sea of Marmara, before the specially created High Court of Justice, consisting of nine regular judges. The charges were all brought under the existing Penal Code; there was no *ad hoc* legislation. The gravest charge, which carried the death penalty, was of 'forcibly changing, modifying, and abrogating the constitution' (that is, of course, the 1924 Constitution), with especial reference to the establishment of the fifteen-man Commission, which was regarded by the prosecution as violating the fundamental provisions of the constitution, particularly Articles 6, 7, and 8:

> *Article 1*: The Turkish State is a Republic.
>
> *Article 2*: The Turkish State is republican, nationalist, populist, etatist, secular, and reformist. Its official language is Turkish. Its capital is the city of Ankara.
>
> *Article 3*: Sovereignty belongs unconditionally to the nation.
>
> *Article 4*: The Grand National Assembly of Turkey is the sole rightful representative of the nation and exercises the right of sovereignty in its name.
>
> *Article 5*: Legislative authority and executive power are manifested and concentrated in the Grand National Assembly.
>
> *Article 6*: The Grand National Assembly exercises its legislative authority directly.
>
> *Article 7*: The Grand National Assembly exercises its executive authority through the person of the President of the Republic elected by it, and through a Council of Ministers chosen by the President.
>
> The Assembly may at any time scrutinize the acts of the government and overthrow it.
>
> *Article 8*: Judicial authority is exercised by independent courts in the name of the nation, in accordance with the laws and regulations in force.

The defence argued that if the GNA chose to vote its sovereign power over to a smaller body, that was its own affair, but this view was held to be inconsistent with Articles 6 and 8. The argument that the Democrats had had a sufficient majority in the Assembly to amend the constitution under Article 102 ('Amendments can be adopted only by the vote of a majority numbering two-thirds of the total membership of the Assembly') was met by the short answer 'Well, why didn't they?' The argument that the NUC and the provisional government were no less guilty, in that they had themselves first usurped the sovereign power and then changed the constitution, was foredoomed; the NUC and the provisional government were not on trial. Other charges included organizing the riots of 6–7 September 1955, misuse of public funds, and various acts of corruption.

The former Prime Minister was charged, for example, with misappropriating the equivalent of half a million sterling from the secret funds placed at his disposal for purposes of state security. He was said to have used some for household and personal expenses, some to make an ostentatious gift to charity as a thankoffering for his escape from death at Gatwick, some to help a colleague to pay his alimony. The only charge on which he was acquitted was of procuring the death of his illegitimate child by an opera singer. Celâl Bayar was accused of compelling the Ankara Zoo to buy from him a valuable Afghan hound which the King of Afghanistan had presented to him as Head of State. The 'baby charge' and the 'dog charge', as they were currently referred to, aroused a good deal of amusement in the foreign Press, as not being on a par with the high crimes on the indictment. But the accusers were determined to punish the fallen government for every misdeed, in order to show that no man could set himself above the law. Puritans that they were, they were genuinely shocked at some of the results of their investigations, and were then surprised and hurt that many people at home and abroad thought the court should never have bothered with such trivial matters. The sad fact was that the misuse of state funds and the begetting, if not the killing, of illegitimate children were precisely the sort of conduct many Turks expected of their rulers at that time.

It may be wondered why there was not the slightest attempt by Menderes's supporters to save him from arrest or trial or execution. It is not unknown in Turkey for a football crowd to attack a gendarmerie post in order to rescue one of their number who has been arrested; true, it would have taken a foolhardy man to defy the extraordinary security precautions which surrounded Menderes and the other prisoners, but one might have expected there to be enough foolhardy men, among the millions who idolized him, to try a forlorn hope. The explanation lies in the deep-rooted reluctance of the peasantry to interfere in the affairs of *büyükler*, 'the great'.

The efforts made by Mustafa Kemal, by İnönü, and by Menderes himself, to arouse the electorate to an awareness of its political power and responsibilities had not been fruitless; people were certainly ready to vote for the party of their choice, but they were not prepared to stick their necks out in a quarrel among their 'betters'. During the trials, stories circulated of how Menderes flew from his prison every night on a winged white horse to pray in his favourite mosque at Eyüb; of how he had appeared in full view of this or that congregation. It was precisely this superstitious adoration of him which prevented – a psychologist might say 'excused' – even his most fanatical adherents from trying to rescue him; he was a saint, a prophet, *ergo* he was not one of them. If he could save himself, good luck to him; if not, what could human help achieve?

The proceedings were conducted scrupulously. Some foreign correspondents took the contrary view, but the author's impression at the time was that the defence was being given more latitude than is usual in Turkish trials. Fifteen of the accused were sentenced to death, thirty-one to life imprisonment, 418 to lesser terms and fines, 123 being acquitted. The NUC, by 13 votes to 9, commuted eleven of the death sentences, but confirmed those on Celâl Bayar, Adnan Menderes, the former Foreign Secretary Fatin Rüştü Zorlu, and the former Finance Minister Hasan Polatkan. The feeling in the country had been that there would be no executions; everyone remembered how on 27 May the radio stations had broadcast appeals to all members of the Menderes government to 'place themselves under the protection of the armed forces'. There is some reason to believe that the judges themselves, when they duly passed the sentences laid down by the penal code for the crimes they found proved, had expected the NUC to exercise its prerogative of mercy.

At the time of the referendum, Democrat canvassers had been telling the peasants 'If you vote "Yes" they will hang Adnan Menderes'. This was the reverse of the truth; it was the size of the 'No' vote that scared a group of officers, whose identities are still unclear, into insisting that the confirmed death sentences must be carried out. Celâl Bayar was reprieved because of his age, but Zorlu and Polatkan were hanged on 16 September and Menderes the next day, in spite of appeals for clemency from İsmet İnönü, the British, French, and American governments, and Pope John XXIII. Why Zorlu and Polatkan were singled out for death is not immediately apparent. Of the former, Lord Caradon has this to say in his autobiography:

> Zorlu . . . was, I think, the rudest man I have ever met . . . On another visit to Ankara we were on the point of agreement when Prime Minister Macmillan, infuriated by Zorlu's intolerably insulting behaviour, got up and left the conference room . . .[2]

He was certainly hated in his own country for his arrogance. Polatkan seemed to be a much weaker character. The revolutionary officers' name for him was 'the Treasury rat'; his lack of financial integrity was a matter of common gossip. The conclusion one is forced to is that whereas Menderes was hanged because some of those who had overthrown him were scared of his vengeance, the other two were hanged because they were unpopular. Such was the grim background to the general election of 15 October 1961.

Only four parties contested, as the new electoral law debarred parties with a provincial organization in fewer than fifteen of the sixty-seven provinces. The elections to the Senate were by majority vote, to the Assembly by proportional representation. There was an 81 per cent poll.

Name of party	*Percentage of votes*	*Seats won*	*Percentage of seats*
	Assembly		
JP	34.8	158	35.1
RPP	36.7	173	38.4
RPNP	14.0	54	12.0
NTP	13.7	65	14.4
Independents	0.8	0	—
	Senate		
JP	35.5	70	46.7
RPP	37.2	36	24.0
RPNP	13.4	16	10.7
NTP	13.9	28	18.7

These results were described by many foreign journalists as 'a shock to the military junta', a verdict which exaggerated the naïvety of the junta, who were relieved, if anything, that the whole of the old Democrat vote had not gone to the Justice Party.

A joint session of both houses on 26 October elected General Gürsel as President of the Republic, by 434 votes to 173. The only other candidate was Professor Ali Fuad Başgil, leader of the extreme right wing of the JP, who was opposed to secularism. The news of his candidature had prompted Ragıp Gümüşpala, the chairman of the Party, to disown him and had also occasioned protests from officers and cadets. Başgil was intimidated into leaving Ankara before the joint session and he telegraphed from Istanbul his resignation from the Senate, thereby abandoning his candidature.

A fortnight later, after fruitless discussions among the party leaders about the possibility of a coalition, Gürsel appointed İnönü Prime Minister, an office he had last held in 1937. The JP were prepared to enter a coalition on their own terms, which included İnönü's resignation from the RPP and an amnesty for the imprisoned Democrats. The army lost patience; the *ex officio* Senators met in the Assembly building and there was much coming and going between there and the General Staff headquarters. Eventually, in what the newspapers realistically termed 'a triumph for Messrs Thompson and Sten', the JP were persuaded to agree to join a coalition with the RPP. A twenty-two-man Cabinet was formed, half from each party, which began work on 20 November.

For many months the coalition did nothing but quarrel about an amnesty and vote an increase in deputies' salaries. The Justice Party Press poured forth abuse on the revolution and its makers. Though some of the JP had the sense to see that their first concern ought to be not to provoke a further army intervention, most seemed to think that they had a mandate from the electors to take vengeance on the RPP which had opposed Menderes and on the officers who had brought about his downfall and death. On 22 February 1962, the Commandant of the Ankara War College, Talât Aydemir, led his cadets and some armoured units in an abortive *coup d'état*. The immediate cause was that he had learned that he was about to be deprived of his post, as he was known to deplore the army's quixotic honesty in handing back power to the politicians. The rising was put down, mainly by the air force, without bloodshed. İnönü broadcast to the nation on 26 February, saying that the officers responsible had lost confidence in democracy, under provocation. In a later statement he reminded the country how the army had honoured its pledge to restore civilian government and how infuriating it was for them to be exposed to insult and threats of vengeance. Aydemir and three other colonels were retired and a number of other officers transferred from the capital.

The debate on the amnesty continued to absorb most of the working time of the Assembly. In an attempt to heal the breach, İnönü agreed in May to a reduction in the sentences of the imprisoned members of the former regime. The JP were not satisfied with his terms and he resigned. Gürsel told him to try again and in June a new coalition took office, composed of the RPP and the two smaller parties, with the JP in opposition. The coalition agreed on an amnesty to be proclaimed in October, whereby those serving sentences of up to six years would be released and longer sentences would be reduced by four years.

On 22 March 1963, Celâl Bayar was released for six months on medical grounds. Such were the scenes on his way to Ankara, and so triumphant a welcome was he given there, that the Army Council demanded action. There were demonstrations and counter-demonstrations, in which the JP headquarters was stoned and their newspaper buildings attacked. Four days later troops had to intervene in Istanbul to keep 30,000 students away from 5,000 JP supporters, and the JP headquarters in Ankara was totally wrecked. After midnight, at the end of a seven-hour cabinet meeting, Bayar's release was revoked and he was taken to hospital under guard. Some JP members nervously proposed that the Party dissolve itself; this did not happen, but there were several resignations from its central committee.

On the evening of 20 May, cadets of the Ankara War College again followed their brave but imprudent ex-Commandant, Talât Aydemir, in an ill-fated *coup d'état*. Twice during the night they gained control of Ankara Radio and broadcast announcements that the armed forces had seized power. Two cadets and five loyal soldiers were killed and twenty-six people wounded, one of whom died the next day. Aydemir was tried and sentenced to death; he was executed in July 1964. Colonel Türkeş and three others of the fourteen ex-members of the NUC, who had been permitted to return home in February, were tried on a charge of having been preparing an independent *coup*, but were acquitted. On 31 May, nine deputies and three senators resigned from the Justice Party to sit as Independents, having found the pace too hot.

Meanwhile, some of the leaders of the two smaller parties in the coalition had been looking for an excuse to walk out. To help finance the Five-Year Development Plan, which came into operation on 1 January 1963, the coalition government had bravely taken the step no previous government had dared to take: on 10 February it introduced an agricultural income-tax. It was to be levied only on farms with a gross annual profit of over £1,600, i.e., 1 per cent of the country's 2 million farms; nevertheless, it did nothing to increase the government's popularity, as it was followed by increases in the prices of products of the State Monopolies, including cigarettes, spirits, beer, wine, and petrol. It was because of their unwillingness to share in the government's consequent unpopularity that the NTP and RPNP were anxious to quit the coalition. They were on the verge of doing so in August, but kept going on the insistence of President Gürsel. They found the excuse they were seeking when the results were declared of the local elections held on 10 November. These were to elect mayors and provincial, municipal, and village councils. The more reputable commentators seemed to be agreed that the RPP had a better set of candidates, but that people do not vote for candidates but for parties; it had not taken the young Turkish democracy long to learn this sad truth.

The rising cost of living, principally due to higher taxation, had polarized political sympathies. Regularly one heard, 'We were better off under Menderes'. It was no good replying that their comparative prosperity in the old days was at the expense of their Western allies; this they considered no more than their just reward for standing between Russia and the West. Even people who detested Menderes, however, were saying, 'It wasn't worth hanging him for this'. The JP announced that it expected to win most of the votes which in the general election had gone to the two smaller parties, and this prognostication was correct. JP candidates were elected mayor in forty-two provincial capitals, RPP in twenty-three, NTP in one, an independent candidate in one.

By the time the results were known, İnönü had left for the United States to attend President Kennedy's funeral. In his absence the RPNP and NTP decided to leave the government. On 2 December İnönü saw Gürsel and offered his resignation. As before, the President asked him to stay on. Now in his eightieth year, İnönü had had enough, and the collapse of his coalition while he was abroad had been a heavy blow. A few months before, a journalist had asked him, 'Pasha, what will happen after you leave politics?' His reply was 'After me? After me the deluge'. But on 14 December it became known that Gümüşpala had failed to form a government – to no one's surprise, because sitting in opposition and sneering at the Five-Year Plan was one thing, whereas having to administer it or find an alternative was quite another – and on 25 December İnönü announced his new Cabinet, of twenty men of his own party and three independents.

He got his vote of confidence on 4 January 1964: 177 RPP, 29

NTP, and 19 independents; 225 votes against 175. The next test came on 7 June, when one-third of the Senate places came up for election. On 31 March the Assembly had decided by 214 votes to 128 that senators as well as members of the Lower House should henceforth be elected by proportional representation. The smallness of the poll (60.2 per cent) suggested that the country was as weary of politics as was the Prime Minister.

Name of party	*Percentage of votes*	*Seats won*
JP	50.3	30
RPP	40.8	20
RPNP	3.0	0
NTP	3.5	0
Independents	2.3	1

The strength of the parties in the Senate was now: JP 81, RPP 35, RPNP, NTP, and independents together 34.

As the Prime Minister was about to leave for the United States to discuss Cyprus with President Johnson, he decided to ask for another vote of confidence, not wishing to find himself again sitting on top of a non-existent tree. The constitutional requirement for defeating a vote of confidence was a majority of the votes of all 450 members of the Assembly, i.e., 226 votes. İnönü went further, however, and declared that he would resign unless he secured an absolute majority of all the votes cast, which he did. Fifteen of the JP, three of the NTP, and two of the RPNP defied their parties' decision to vote against the government; the three NTP members voted for it and the others did not vote at all. Of the 396 members who voted, 200 were for, 194 against, the other two registering a *çekimser*, 'abstaining', vote.

So the Prime Minister left for Washington. One of the old Bosphorus paddle-steamers had recently been refitted and put back into service. It was affectionately suggested that it ought to have been renamed *İsmet İnönü*.

In November 1964, the Justice Party elected Süleyman Demirel as its chairman in succession to General Gümüşpala, who had died in June. Demirel, then in his fortieth year, was an engineer, the son of a peasant. Under Menderes, he had been head of the state hydrological service.

On 13 February 1965, the government resigned after a vote of 225 to 197 against its budget proposals. A Cabinet was formed of members of the JP, RPNP, NTP, and the National Party (NP), a splinter party which broke away from the RPNP in June 1962. The new Prime Minister was Suat Hayri Ürgüplü, an independent deputy and former ambassador.

The countless millions of words spoken and written in praise of liberty after the 1960 revolution, had given hope to three groups whose voices had been seldom heard during the previous forty years : the Kurds, the Shi'ites, and the Left. Nationalism among the Kurds in Turkey, though only a minority movement, had been increasing because of sympathy with the endless struggle of their brethren in Iraq, where the Barzani tribe in particular had been at war with successive governments on and off since 1931. Further impetus to separatist feelings had been provided by the Turks' short-sighted refusal to allow their state radio to broadcast in Kurdish, thus giving the Soviet radio, which suffered from no such inhibitions, a clear field in eastern Anatolia. With the chronic instability of government in Iraq since 1958, it is always on the cards that the Iraqi Kurds may some day achieve their independence, and as this would obviously entail an upsurge of nationalist feeling among the other Kurds, the Turkish authorities do not look kindly on *Kürtçülük*, Kurdish nationalism. But the movement does not as yet command large-scale support, and the majority of indigenous Kurds would probably be well content if only a little flexibility were shown in the matter of their language. President Gürsel could not believe that anyone would choose to be a Kurd if it were open to him to be a Turk, so having assured his 'eastern compatriots' that they were as Turkish as the next man, he said, in his bluff paternal fashion, 'If anyone calls you a Kurd, spit in his eye'. In November 1963, the New Turkey Party, with its eye on the Kurdish vote, blazoned these words, duly attributed, on a banner they displayed at an open-air meeting in Diyarbakır, which has the largest Kurdish population of any city, some 22,000. It was probably no coincidence that in the 1965 election they shared the six seats for the province equally with the two big parties.

General recognition of the Shi'ites' existence began not long after the revolution. In May 1963, Istanbul newspapers carried an announcement of a public debate on the theme of Sunnism and Shi'ism, and a subject which had been tabu was suddenly out in the open. In October 1966, the Unity (*Birlik*) Party was created with the intention of representing Shi'ite interests; one might therefore have expected the authorities to clamp down on it, but they did not, and in the 1969 elections it won eight seats, with 2.8 per cent of the poll. In November 1971, it changed its name to Unity Party of Turkey.

As for the Left; in 1961 the author asked the Istanbul Chief of Police how many communists there were in Turkey. The reply was 'Do you mean "communists", or real communists?' 'Real communists'. 'Eleven', said the Chief of Police, 'perhaps twelve'. But this situation, like so much else in the Turkey of the sixties, was to change rapidly. In the early years of industrialization the policy towards industrial workers had been to keep them on a tight rein. In fact they did not represent a danger to the state because they were few and unorganized. It was hard to keep a permanent labour force in the factories because of the arduousness of agricultural life; no Turk worth his salt is going to keep on working at the bench when he knows his old Dad is breaking his back in the fields. So at ploughing and harvest there would be a mass exodus from the cities, and to a lesser extent this is true even now. With the expansion of industry and the three events which gave hope that men's desire for more freedom might be fulfilled – the end of the Second World War in 1945, the rise to power of the Democrats in 1950 and their fall in 1960 – it became harder and harder to deny workers their basic rights. In 1947, by the Law on Employees' and Employers' Syndicates, the RPP had allowed the formation of 'occupational organizations for the purpose of mutual aid and protection and to represent the common interests of their members', but not to engage in collective bargaining, which was not sanctioned until January 1950. The right to strike was built into the 1961 Constitution, but the special law implementing the principle was enacted only in April 1963, although there had been occasional strikes before that, towards which the authorities generally behaved in a restrained and sensible fashion.

The most acrimonious debates over the 1961 Constitution had concerned the use of the words 'social justice' in the preamble, which were widely regarded as opening the door to communism. For most people, 'social justice' was synonymous with 'justice, Russian-style'. This is not a matter of paranoia, as the outsider might exasperatedly think, but of semantics. An analogy may help. In Turkish, *ortodoks* means 'belonging to the Greek Church'. Most Turks, however flawless their English may be, still feel a quiver as at an essential wrongness if they hear a foreigner talking about 'orthodox Muslims'. 'Socialist' is what the ancient enemy Moscow now calls itself; 'Union of Socialist Soviet Republics'. How then can one expect ordinary people, in a country where accurate information about the doctrines of socialism and communism has been generally hard to come by, to listen calmly to alien expressions such as 'We are all socialists now', or 'a reasonable measure of socialization'? One might as well talk about being slightly dead.

In an attempt to capture the left-wing voters, who might otherwise support the Labour Party (although most of that party's efforts had been directed towards trade unionists, not intellectuals), İsmet İnönü declared, in a speech at Trabzon a week before the 1965 elections, that the RPP was 'left of centre'. This announcement did the Party no good at all; indeed, the TLP too did not do as well as it had hoped, partly because of a general awareness that the government was going to clamp down on the Left and partly because many of the more wide-awake workers had emigrated to western Europe. The beginning of this movement can be dated to 1957, when President Theodor Heuss invited 150 graduates of Turkish technical institutes to work in West German industry. By 1960 there were 2,700 Turks there. Under a bilateral agreement signed on 30 October 1961, a German liaison office was opened in Istanbul, and in September 1963 another was opened in Ankara, to organize the recruitment and medical and other tests. By 1963 the number of Turks employed in West Germany had risen to 27,500. Of the 112,000 Turks who left to seek employment abroad in 1965, 108,250 went to West Germany.

For the elections of 10 October 1965 a modification of the system of proportional representation was introduced, the 'national remainder'; the additional seats thereby allocated to the parties appear after the plus signs in the table below. As it was found to favour the smaller parties, the experiment was abandoned in 1968.

Name of party	*Percentage of votes*	*Seats won*	*Percentage of seats*
JP	52.9	204+36	53.3
RPP	28.7	102+32	29.8
RPNP	2.2	0+11	2.4
NTP	3.7	3+16	4.2
NP	6.3	6+25	6.9
TLP	3.0	2+13	3.3
Independents	3.2	0+0	—

One of the eleven RPNP candidates who were given seats from the national remainder was Alpaslan Türkeş. In the previous October he had announced the formation of a new party, to be called the Popular Socialist Movement, but nothing more was heard of this and he was elected chairman of the RPNP in August 1965. Within a matter of days nine of its leading members resigned in protest against the 'totalitarian and adventurist character' he was imposing on the Party. In 1969 he changed its name to National Action (*Millî Hareket*) Party. Meanwhile, he had been busy organizing his personal youth movement, the Grey Wolves. He dropped his attempts to give them weapon-training after a quiet warning from the army, and complaints from the neighbours put an end to another of his ploys: to lull him to sleep, he had a number of his lads howling like wolves outside his house every night.

Early in March 1966, President Gürsel, who had suffered a number of strokes, was declared by his doctors to be unable ever to resume his duties. On 28 March the former Chief of the General Staff, Cevdet Sunay, was elected in his stead, with 461 votes. The only other candidate was Türkeş, who received 11 votes.

At the Republican People's Party's post-election inquest, the left-of-centre policy was bitterly attacked; it was pointed out that for most Turks 'left' was synonymous with 'communist' and that İnönü ought never to have put such a weapon into the hands of the right-wing parties. A former General Secretary of the Party, Kasım Gülek, was ever more explicit in his cricitism: 'Terms like "left" and "left of centre" in the West imply democratic socialism, which is legitimate there. Here they shake people's confidence. Our business is politics in Turkey, not in Europe'. The Pasha was unrepentant; he thought the Party needed a new dynamism, which this new slogan would eventually provide. Nevertheless, the central committee decided not to emphasize it for the Senate elections of June 1966. These gave the RPP a net gain of two seats, but the JP gained eight, making the state of the parties as follows:

	Senate	*Assembly*
JP	92	242
RPP	50	134
RPNP	1	9
NTP	1	18
NP	2	27
TLP	1	14
Independents	3	6
Life Senators	20	—
Presidentially appointed Senators	15	—

Turhan Feyzioğlu, one of the RPP's leading intellectuals, renewed the accusation that the slogan had cost the Party many votes. At the Party's conference in October the General Secretary, Bülent Ecevit, strongly defended the new policy, of which he was generally thought to have been the architect, and in the upshot the conference went on record as being 'a left-of-centre party working for the betterment of the masses and against the exploiters, in accordance with its principle of populism'. There were those who argued quite seriously that this was a radical new departure, since 'populism' embraced all the people, exploiters as well as exploited. Feyzioğlu put it a little more diplomatically: 'Once you make the Party discriminate between bourgeois and proletarian it will disintegrate'. Efforts to heal the breach failed, and on 30 April 1967, Feyzioğlu and some fifty others resigned from the Party, reducing its strength in the Assembly to 102 and in the Senate to 32. Two weeks later the rebels founded the Reliance (*Güven*) Party.

NOTES

[1] H. A. Göktürk, *Medenî Hukuk* (Ankara, 1943), II, 41.

[2] Sir Hugh Foot, *A Start in Freedom* (London; Hodder and Stoughton, 1964), 150.

CHAPTER 18

The Light at the End of the Tunnel

THE 1965 ELECTIONS had given the Justice Party an absolute majority, and the question may be asked : leaving aside those who voted for it because of its policy of encouraging private enterprise, what was in it for the mass of the electorate? The short answer is self-respect.[1] They believed that the Justice Party would give them what the Democrat Party had given them : surcease from the RPP line that they were primitive, brutish, and superstitious blots on the new Turkey, who needed to be civilized, i.e., westernized. They were tired of being told that their ancestral values were outmoded; they were tired of feeling '. . . a stranger and afraid/ In a world I never made'. So they cast their votes for 'Islam' in the sense of the idealized world of their grandfathers; they voted for the JP because they hoped it would bring them peace and quiet and an end of nagging.

Demirel soon proved to have the makings of a good Prime Minister, to the surprise of those cynics who had described him as the first head of government whose only policy was to avoid being hanged. But such indeed was the policy of some members of his government, whereas others wanted nothing except to avenge the downfall of the Democrats and the death of Menderes. What Demirel hoped to do was to achieve a compromise between the wishes of Atatürk and the wishes of the majority of the electorate; to give the country economic prosperity and the appurtenances of civilized living and, at the same time, to let the peasant and the small urban tradesman feel that the principles of his religion were respected and that he was free to observe them; all this without goading the intellectuals beyond endurance. A measure of his sophistication is to be seen in his remarks to the opposition during a speech in the Assembly in February 1967 : 'You are the protectors of the poor and needy. All right, but what about those who aren't poor and needy? Aren't they citizens too?' This question puzzled even some editorial writers in the opposition Press, who thought it would have been more reasonable to ask whether the poor and needy weren't citizens too. Western readers, however, will recognize Demirel's words as the authentic voice of a by no means unthinking conservatism. But too much of his time and energy were spent on trying to keep his ill-matched team pulling together, or at least to prevent them from tearing him to pieces. As he did not have much confidence in his Cabinet, increasingly he let decisions be made by the National Security Council, a body under the chairmanship of the President or Prime Minister and consisting of ministers, the Chief of the General Staff, and representatives of the armed services. Its duties, as laid down in Article 111 of the 1961 Constitution, are 'to communicate the requisite basic views to the Council of Ministers in order to assist in the taking of decisions relating to national security and to ensure co-ordination'. This body met more and more frequently, while cabinet meetings grew rarer. And then, by an evil chance, Demirel was confronted with a serious breakdown of public order.

It is debatable how much the agitation of the last years of the decade was a reaction against repression in the middle years; the correct answer is probably not very much. That is, the agitation would have happened anyway, though perhaps it might have been nipped in the bud if the authorities had not wasted their time hunting bogymen instead of concentrating on the real danger. There was, for example, a witch-hunt over Atatürk's Bursa Speech. The former chairman of a left-wing student society at the Aegean University was prosecuted on a charge of sedition for having quoted the speech in a manifesto published in 1966 on the anniversary of the Istanbul University demonstration which triggered off the 1960 revolution. The public prosecutor, who demanded a four-year sentence, asserted that the speech was not by Atatürk at all but was cribbed from Stalin. A committee of historians declared that it was indeed by Atatürk, with one dissentient, who would not say that it was not by Atatürk but agreed with the prosecutor that it was subversive. The prisoner was acquitted, on 25 February 1966.

The following month a fifteen-year-old schoolboy was denounced by his history teacher as a communist. She had asked the class to write an essay comparing Atatürk with any other world figure, and this boy had chosen Lenin, whom he compared unfavourably with Atatürk. Released after five days at police headquarters, he told the waiting reporters what he had written, for example, that Lenin 'had created an anti-aircraft unit'. And what was the significance of that? He didn't really know, but he had read it in a newspaper article about Lenin the previous August, when Prime Minister Ürgüplü was visiting Russia, and it had stuck in his mind. He said that the police had treated him kindly and that the prosecutor who took a statement from him was crying.

In 1966 and 1967, over 200 educational administrators and teachers were transferred or dismissed for socialist and communist propaganda, for insulting the Justice Party, for recommending their pupils to read certain newspaper articles, arranging 'Atatürk Days' or reading the Bursa Speech, or not letting children go to mosques in school hours. One teacher was suspended for using a fountain-pen bearing the initials of the Turkish Labour Party. At the end of January 1967, thirteen members of the Ministry of Education's Translation Bureau resigned, as their chairman had done in December, in protest against governmental interference in the choice of books for translation. A new version of Tolstoy's *Anna Karenina* (there were earlier Turkish translations, one under Abdülhamid, one under Atatürk) had left the Bureau in October 1965 to be sent to the printer by the ministry, but had sunk without trace. And so on; the story would fill several volumes. The Istanbul municipality's budget for 1967 included a sum of 220,000 *liras* (say £70,000) for subsidies to anti-communist organizations. The Chief of the General Staff took a hand, issuing an order informing all ranks that the communists were trying to make Turkey a nation of 32 million alcoholic degenerates and that the cinema and threatre, as well as the student societies, were all instruments of communist propaganda. It was at this time that the housekeeper of a friend of the author's took fright at a small statue of an athlete which had long graced his garden in Istanbul. As its right arm was raised in what she thought was a communist salute, she loyally broke it off and threw it away so that her employer should not get into trouble.

Meanwhile, the real disrupters were busy. The first major incident was in February 1968, when fighting broke out between leftist and rightist students at Ankara, in sympathy with a fight between JP and TLP deputies in the Assembly. This set the pattern for the next two years, with a marked increase in tempo after the French university disorders of May–June 1968. In July 1968, when the US Sixth Fleet visited Istanbul, a number of people were injured in left-wing demonstrations and right-wing counter-demonstrations. On the Fleet's next visit, in February 1969, a pitched battle in Istanbul cost three lives. The government introduced legislation designed to impose tougher penalties on extremists, to ensure, as the Prime Minister put it, that the Republic was not replaced by communism, anarchism, fascism, or theocracy. But he did not have the full support even of his own party, and the legislation was dropped and the fighting continued. Sometimes the issue was university reform, sometimes national policies, but week by week the number of brutal murders and maimings increased. The work of the universities was at a standstill more often than not. It is no exaggeration to say that the purpose of all the militants was to overthrow the Republic. There were the avowed Marxist-Leninists, Trotskyites, and Maoists, often fighting each other but usually ready to combine against Türkeş's fascists and those whose aim was to re-establish Islamic law as the law of the land and even to restore the Caliphate. Both sides were receiving subsidies from outside the country, the Right from Arab sources, the Left from Russia. How the Arab money arrived is not clear; the Russian funds were brought by workers coming home on leave from Germany, while the Russian ambassador to Turkey sat with his arms folded and his hands clean. And why did the government not take strong measures against the students? One heard of three reasons. The first was that Demirel was too civilized and humane to get as tough as the situation required. The second was that he never had the backing of the judiciary, few of whom were admirers of the old Democrat Party or the new Justice Party, so that a minimal sentence or an acquittal on technical grounds was often given to people arrested for flagrant breaches of the law. The third reason suggested was that Articles 120 and 121 of the constitution made the universities and TRT, the radio and television service, autonomous. TRT was accused of left-wing bias, an accusation in which there was a modicum of truth. More to the point was that the police had no right to enter university premises without an express invitation from the university authorities. With the events of 1960 fresh in most memories, neither they nor the police were eager for this. Demirel had undertaken to amend the constitution as necessary, but even with his increased strength in both houses after the 1969 elections he never had the requisite two-thirds majority, and the opposition parties were not about to make things easier for him. He cannot be absolved from blame, however; it was always open to him to declare a state of emergency, and it is hard to believe that universities would willingly see their campuses turned into battlefields. So while conceding that there was some validity in all three reasons, especially the second, one cannot help thinking that the government was not averse to letting the right-wing students suppress the left-wing students.

But the students were not alone in resorting to violence. In 1967 the TLP founded its own left-wing union organization, with some 70,000 members, in competition with the Confederation of Workers' Unions, which had the lion's share of the country's million-odd manual workers. The new organization regarded the Confederation as part of the establishment, pointing to its having opposed the TLP demand that employers should be legally deprived of the right of lock-out. The left-wing unions were poaching members from the Confederation by promising to secure bigger pay increases and better conditions than the Confederation could or would. The Confederation therefore persuaded the government to promote legislation forbidding any union to engage in collective bargaining unless its members numbered at least one-third of the total insured labour force in any given industry. This would have meant the virtual end of the left-wing unions, so on 15 June 1970, they came out on the streets of Kadıköy, part of the city of Istanbul on the Asian side of the Bosphorus. They were joined by large numbers of students. The ensuing battle with the police went on for two days and took three lives. Martial law was proclaimed in Istanbul and the province adjoining it on the east, Kocaeli, and was maintained until September. By the end of 1970 the Istanbul riot police were demanding higher pay, and a good many people thought they deserved it.

Reference has already been made to the 1969 elections. These took place on 12 October and returned the JP to power with an enlarged majority. The poll was down: 64.35 per cent as against 71.3 per cent in 1965. In the following table, 'NAP' is the National Action Party, 'RP' the Reliance Party, 'UP' the Unity Party.

Name of party	*Percentage of votes*	*Seats won*	*Percentage of seats*
JP	46.53	257	56.89
RPP	27.36	144	31.78
NAP	3.03	1	0.22
NTP	2.18	6	1.33
NP	3.22	6	1.33
TLP	2.68	2	0.44
RP	6.58	15	3.33
UP	2.80	8	1.78
Independents	2.18	11	2.39

The smaller parties' loss of seats (despite, in one case, an increased vote) was due to the new electoral law of March 1968, which abolished the 'national remainder'. The success of most of the independents is explained by the fact that some big landowners, not finding any party's policies to their liking, simply nominated candidates for whom the local tenantry voted if they knew what was good for them. One exception was Necmettin Erbakan, a religious fanatic and former member of the JP, who was returned as an independent for Konya. In January 1970, with two other independents, he founded the National Order (*Millî Nizam*) Party.

Encouraged by the election results, Demirel dropped the right-wing members of his Cabinet. But they and their supporters were still in the parliamentary party, and they gave Demirel no peace. In the debate on the Budget proposals in February 1970 the government was defeated when forty-one of the right-wing faction voted with the opposition. Demirel resigned, but was asked by President Sunay to try again, which he did, receiving a vote of confidence on 15 March. In view of his failure to carry the Assembly the previous month, this may seem surprising. But the explanation is simple if one remembers the background of internal disorder; no one else was eager to assume the thankless task of trying to govern the country at that time, and this was true of the army as well as the politicians. In June 1970, Demirel expelled his implacable enemies from the party and they, together with others who resigned in sympathy, formed the Democratic Party on 18 December 1970. Its Turkish name was *Demokratik*, not quite the same as the outlawed *Demokrat* Party of Menderes, but close enough; that they were allowed to get away with it was due to the government's reluctance to force a showdown with them or with anyone else. The state of the parties at the beginning of 1971 was this (in case the reader is beginning to lose his way among all the initials, the names of the parties are given in full):

	Senate	*Assembly*
Justice Party	89	227
Republican People's Party	34	142
Democratic Party	5	37
Reliance Party	10	13
National Party	1	5
National Order Party	—	3
Unity Party	—	2
Turkish Labour Party	1	2

	Senate	*Assembly*
New Turkey Party	1	1
National Action Party	1	1
Independents	8	13
Life Senators	17	—
Presidentially appointed Senators	14	—
Vacancies	2	4

The chairmen of both Houses, who do not have a vote, were members of the JP.

The beginning of 1971 saw a change in the nature of the prevailing lawlessness. From killing each other and any innocent bystanders who happened to be in the line of fire, the militant students turned their hand to bank-robbery, dynamiting, and kidnapping. When Demirel first became Prime Minister, he said that his party had been duly elected by the people's vote; 'to suggest that it could be overthrown by a military *coup* is to suggest that there is a power superior to people and Parliament'. Now, six years later, the irony of these words could be appreciated. On 12 March, the Chief of the General Staff and the heads of the three services presented to the Press and the chairmen of the Senate and Assembly a 'memorandum', a polite description of what was in fact an ultimatum:

> Parliament and the government, by their sustained attitudes, views, and actions, have plunged our country into anarchy, fratricidal strife, and social and economic disorder. They have made the public despair of attaining the level of contemporary civilization which Atatürk set as our target, and have failed to bring about the reforms envisaged in the constitution; the future of the Republic has been gravely imperilled . . . It is seen as essential to form a strong and credible government that will end the present anarchic situation and take in hand the reforms, with an Atatürkist outlook. If this does not speedily occur, the armed forces, in pursuance of the duty laid on them by law of defending and watching over the Republic, are determined to assume direct rule.

Demirel resigned and the President nominated Dr Nihat Erim, a distinguished international and constitutional lawyer, as Prime Minister. He resigned his membership of the RPP and on 26 March announced the names of his Cabinet. Five belonged to the JP, three to the RPP, one to the Reliance Party, and one was a Life Senator. The other fourteen were chosen from outside the GNA. The news, released on 16 March, that four generals and an admiral had been retired and a number of other officers transferred, lent support to rumours that the 'memorandum' had come when it did in order to forestall another *coup d'état*.

On 21 March Bülent Ecevit resigned as General Secretary of the RPP, in protest against its decision to support the Erim government, but remained a member of the central committee. There were increasing signs of a serious conflict between him and İnönü. The Pasha held that the party's parliamentary group should be free to make their own decisions on how to vote in the Assembly, whereas Ecevit wanted them to be under the control of the central committee. On 7 May 1972, he defeated İnönü in a vote of confidence. The next day, İnönü resigned the chairmanship of the party, an office he had held since he took it over from Atatürk in 1938. On 14 May, Ecevit was elected in his place. But there was worse to come, for on 4 November the central committee decided that such of its members as had accepted ministries under Melen (who by then, as we shall see, had succeeded Erim) must quit the government, and İnönü resigned from the party which he had helped to found forty-nine years before. He also resigned his seat in the Assembly, but let it be known that he would like to become a Senator, which was at once arranged; this was his constitutional right as an ex-President of the Republic. Afterwards (on 12 January 1973) he said something which confirmed the impression that Ecevit and not he was responsible for the 'left of centre' policy; it was that Turkey could not become a socialist country and retain her independence, given the proximity of Russia, 'the leader of the socialist powers'.

Other parties had their troubles too. The Turkish Labour Party had never been free from internal dissensions since its foundation in 1961, and these came to a head after the Russian invasion of Czechoslovakia. The chairman, Mehmet Ali Aybar, who was far too moderate for most of his colleagues, resigned from the party in November 1969. Most of its votes in 1965 had come from the industrial regions and the big cities. In 1969 its vote dropped in these places but rose in the east; it thereupon began to set up 'Revolutionary Cultural Centres' in the Kurdish areas. In March 1971, it was made known that the public prosecutor in Ankara had begun to prepare a case against the party 'for communist propaganda and separatist activities'. Next month its Centres were closed and on 20 July the Constitutional Court dissolved the Party itself 'for having sought to perpetuate differences among the various ethnic minorities'. Erbakan's National Order Party had been similarly dissolved two months earlier, 'for seeking to restore a theocratic order'. On 12 October 1972, he founded the National Salvation (*Selâmet*) Party.

The Erim government made some headway with constitutional amendments. Among those passed in September 1971 was one depriving the universities of their administrative autonomy while retaining their 'academic autonomy'. The state broadcasting organization too ceased to be fully autonomous, and its director was replaced by a retired general. The programme of economic and social reform, however, did not get very far, and for this most of the blame went to Demirel, who was determined not to co-operate with the man who had usurped his position. One cabinet crisis followed another, and on 17 April 1972, the President finally accepted Erim's resignation. On 28 April of the previous year martial law had been imposed in eleven provinces: those containing the principal cities, the mining and industrial regions, and the Kurdish areas, and including Adana and Hatay, the two coastal provinces nearest to Syria. The number of terrorist acts was consequently reduced; unfortunately those that did occur were of a particularly shocking nature. In May 1971 the Israeli Consul-General in Istanbul was kidnapped and murdered by members of the 'Turkish People's Liberation Army', a manifestation or offshoot of the 'Revolutionary Youth' organization. The same befell a Canadian and two British civilian radar technicians in March 1972. The newspapers seem to have missed one tragic circumstance of this latter incident, namely that it was not premeditated. Eleven terrorists, on the run from the massive security operations that were going on in the principal cities, arrived at Ünye on the Black Sea coast where a sympathizer owned an apartment block. They took refuge in his flat and he suggested that if they wanted some hostages there were some foreigners upstairs. It was as simple and as terrible as that. Ten of the terrorists were killed in a gun battle, one of them a suspect in the murder of the Israeli Consul-General.

On 29 April 1972, President Sunay invited Senator Ürgüplü to form a new government, but rejected his proposed Cabinet as it 'did not conform to the spirit of the 12 March memorandum'. On 3 May four terrorists hijacked an aircraft of Turkish Airlines to Sofia. Their demands included the release of three of their friends under sentence of death, and the cancellation of small debts owed by peasants to the Agricultural Bank. The Acting Prime Minister, Ferit Melen of the Reliance Party, who had been Erim's Minister of Defence, refused to parley with them and they surrendered the next day. As this was evidently the sort of strong-minded behaviour the armed forces favoured, Melen was invited to become Prime Minister. His cabinet list was approved by the President on 22 May. It included another member of the RP, eight of the JP, five of the RPP, one presidentially appointed Senator, and nine 'outsider technocrats'.

From 2 December 1972, all student organizations were dissolved and henceforth there could be no more than one students' society in any educational establishment. The beginning of 1973 saw the Melen government in firm control of affairs, but martial law was still in force and many teachers, students, writers, and journalists were in jail or awaiting trial. The Press was free, but sometimes it looked as if freedom meant one could print what one liked if one didn't mind being arrested. That the majority of those in jail on political charges were of the left wing does not necessarily imply that the authorities were soft on fascism; it might only reflect the fact that there are more intellectuals on the left than on the right. Nor, while feeling indignation at a scholar's having to stand trial for making a translation of an eighteenth-century French political tract, should we blind ourselves to the fact that some of those arrested really did represent a danger both to the established order and to life and limb.

On 3 May 1972, the trial concluded in Istanbul of eighty-four people accused of attempting the violent overthrow of the constitution and trying to set up a Marxist-Leninist system. It is perhaps an indication of the integrity of the judiciary in difficult circumstances that while fourteen of the accused were given sentences ranging between six months and thirty-six years, the remaining seventy were acquitted.

Figures published on 24 May 1972 showed that 2,050 people had been arrested in the previous thirteen months, of whom 687 had been convicted, 111 were awaiting trial, and 807 were being tried, the other 445 having been released. Two days later another sixty-eight arrests were announced, this time of members of a new organization, the Revolutionary Workers' and Peasants' Party. By the time they came to trial, on 10 January 1973, their numbers had risen to 267. When the judge asked them their occupations, twenty-eight replied 'revolutionary communist', two said 'Kurdish communist', and two others 'Marxist-Leninist communist'. Later that month another mass trial began, this time of some thirty people accused of 'conspiring to change the constitution and overthrow the GNA by insurrection'. They included two members of the 1960 National Unity Committee, Lieutenant-General (rtd) Cemal Madanoğlu and Colonel (rtd) Osman Köksal, together with eleven colonels and a major, half of them on the active list, four writers and journalists, and several professional men. This was the first time that senior military men had been charged with being implicated in a left-wing conspiracy.

On 17 October 1972, a military court in Ankara passed sentence on officers of the banned Turkish Labour Party. The finding of the court was that the accused had led the party astray from the road of legality and had chosen to run it in accordance with Marxist-Leninist principles; it had been turned into an association aimed at creating the domination of one social class over others, at abolishing one social class, and at overthrowing the established economic and social order. To achieve its secret aims, it had tried systematically to destroy the administrative order; to shake the citizen's confidence in the laws and their application; to incite the people, by talk of poverty and exploitation, to rise against the democratic constitutional order. Such intensive activities, aimed at bringing about an anarchic situation, had dragged the country into great difficulties that would be hard to remedy; had caused the deaths of many of our young people, who were our chief weapon and our hope in the struggle against backwardness. Thousands of them had abandoned their education for the sake of revolution. Intolerable rifts had been created in many homes and a number of families had been destroyed. The seriousness of the crime justified real severity towards the accused.

The party chairman, Mrs Behice Boran, and seven other members of the central committee were given fifteen years, thirteen others receiving sentences ranging from six years ten months to twelve years six months. All those sentenced would also have to spend four or five years, after their release from prison, in 'exile', residing in various designated provincial centres under police supervision.

Something which exercised the authorities at this time was that allegations were being made in the foreign Press that people in custody had been subjected to torture. Official statements tended to be on the lines that nothing happened in Turkey which did not happen in some of the Western democracies; though probably true, this did not constitute a denial. That some of the allegations were demonstrably exaggerated did not alter the fact that some people had been the victims of gross brutality. The bastinado, beating on the soles of the feet, was a regular police practice in Ottoman times, and though it is now illegal one hears rumours that it persists. Where Turkey differs from other countries whose police methods have been criticized abroad is that Turks are sensitive to criticism. Publicity in the foreign and domestic Press has begun to effect an improvement. There had already been an improvement since the Menderes era, when to say that so-and-so had received citizen's treatment, *vatandaş muamelesi*, was the current way of expressing that he had been arrested and beaten up. But many Turks, who deplore police brutality and want to see it eliminated, will tell you that it is a curious fact that whereas no foreign writer ever made a fuss when pickpockets and burglars were being bastinadoed, there is loud indignation abroad when terrorists suffer.

Meanwhile, President Sunay's seven-year term was drawing to a close; it was due to end on 28 March 1973. In mid-February, Demirel was reported to have refused to confer with the generals over the choice of a successor. Nevertheless, in the first week of March the foreign Press was confidently predicting that the next President would be the Chief of the General Staff, Faruk Gürler, on the basis of a statement to this effect by President Sunay. But the choice was not Sunay's, and no one would have thought otherwise who had grasped the extent of the resentment aroused in Turkish parliamentarians by the 'memorandum' of March 1971.

The following table, which shows the state of the parties at this time, includes a new name. In May 1972 the RPP had suffered another split, when Dr Kemal Satır led the right-wing members, including ten deputies, into a new Republican (*Cumhuriyetçi*) Party. Ten is the minimum number of deputies required to constitute a recognized parliamentary group. In December one member resigned his seat. Having thus lost its group status, on 3 March 1973 the party merged with the Reliance Party and some independents to form the Republican Reliance (*Cumhuriyetçi Güven*) Party.

	Senate	*Assembly*
Justice Party	90	227
Republican People's Party	19	96
Republican Reliance Party	20	43
Democratic Party	7	41
National Party	—	4
Independents	11	22

	Senate	*Assembly*
Life Senators	9	—
Presidentially appointed Senators	15	—
Vacancies	3	14

On 5 March the wheels began to turn in Ankara. The Minister of Defence, Mehmet İzmet, resigned his place in the Senate, thus creating a vacancy in the quota of fifteen presidential appointees (he was not thereby resigning his portfolio, as ministers need not belong to either house), and General Gürler resigned as CGS, his place being taken the next day by General Semih Sancar, Commander of Land Forces. The day after that, 7 March, Gürler took the oath as a presidentially appointed Senator. As a member of the GNA he was now eligible for the Presidency. But on 13 March, when the election began, there were two additional candidates: Tekin Arıburun, the JP chairman of the Senate, and Ferruh Bozbeyli, leader of the Democratic Party. The constitutional requirement for election was a two-thirds majority of a plenary session of both houses (423 votes). If two ballots failed to produce this, a simple majority (318 votes) would suffice. In the first ballot Gürler received 175 votes, Arıburun 282, Bozbeyli 45. In the second their respective scores were 176, 284, and 47; in the third, 186, 285, 47. On 21 March Gürler and Arıburun withdrew their candidacies, but votes continued to be cast for them in the balloting, which carried on. The next day, a proposal in the Assembly for a constitutional amendment to extend Sunay's term by two years failed by one vote. On 25 March a similar proposal failed in the Senate by 19 votes. Then, when people abroad were again talking darkly of the imminence of a military *coup*, there came the first sign of hope for Turkish democracy since that day in 1964 when the JP had elected as its chairman the cool Süleyman Demirel and not the hot-headed Sadettin Bilgiç. The Republican People's, Justice, and Republican Reliance Parties agreed on a candidate, Muhittin Taylan, the chairman of the Constitutional Court. President Sunay was unwilling to be rushed into appointing him to the Senate, and the idea was dropped, but the very fact that the three parties had agreed in a matter of importance brought a wave of optimism.

The fateful 28 March came and went. Cevdet Sunay took the oath as an *ex officio* Senator, while Tekin Arıburun, as chairman of the Senate, became Acting President of the Republic. But what the parties had done once they could do again. On 6 April, just in time for the fifteenth ballot, they agreed on another candidate, already a member of the Senate; he was the seventy-year-old Admiral (rtd) Fahrî Korutürk, who, having left the navy after the 1960 revolution at his own request, had then served as ambassador in Moscow and later in Madrid. In the fifteenth ballot he and Bozbeyli were the only candidates, receiving 365 and 51 votes respectively. Votes were also cast for Arıburun (17), Gürler (87), and İnönü (3). Turkey had democratically chosen her sixth President.

For this happy outcome much credit is due to the Turkish Press; throughout the crisis it continued to emphasize how ridiculous the politicians appeared in the eyes of people both at home and abroad. Having struck a blow for democracy by refusing to accept the military nominee, would they then leave the highest office in the state unfilled because they could not subordinate their party interests and personal pride to the public good? And, wonderful to relate, the politicians had taken heed. As for the officers, why they had tamely swallowed the insult of Gürler's rejection by the GNA is a problem only for those who will not give them credit for saying what they mean. On both occasions when they overthrew a civilian government, in May 1960 and again in March 1971, there was arguably a threat to the constitution or to the state. This time there was no such threat and consequently no grounds for the military to invoke its statutory duty of protecting the Republic.

On 7 April, the new President having taken office, Prime Minister Melen offered his government's resignation, 'so that the President may be free to exercise his constitutional authority, this being a requirement of the democratic regime'. Whatever the future might hold, there could be no denying that in the space of just over three weeks that democratic regime had shown some evidence of an ability to survive.

On 12 April, the new President 'exercised his constitutional authority'; that is to say, he designated a new Prime Minister, Senator Naim Talû. Talû, formerly Governor of the Central Bank, had served as Minister of Commerce in the previous government. His name had been put forward to the President on the basis of an agreement between the Justice Party and the Republican Reliance Party. His Cabinet comprised thirteen members of the former, five of the latter, and seven independents. It was understood that this was to be a caretaker government, general elections being due on 14 October.

The end of June saw a demonstration of commonsense over what became known as the *Homongolos* case. Kemal Bıyıkoğlu, Rector of Atatürk University at Erzurum, denounced ten of his students to the public prosecutor and demanded that they be put on trial for publishing communist propaganda and indecent material in a rag-week magazine they had produced under the title of *Homongolos*, a turkicized form of *homunculus.* He pointed out that if the last syllable of the word was spelled backwards it became *sol*, 'left', and this was clearly communist propaganda, as was the fact that the date of publication of the magazine was 22 April 1973, which was Lenin's birthday. Moreover, the Erzurum police had seen fit to confiscate all the copies of the magazine from the newsagents. The public prosecutor, in his *nolle prosequi*, was fairly sharp: there was nothing indecent in the magazine, which had been written by medical students to amuse medical students; the date 22 April did not appear anywhere in it; if anyone arbitrarily chose to read the syllable *los* backwards that did not establish any intrinsic illegality; the police had not confiscated the magazine from the newsagents, because it was printed and circulated inside the university and had never reached the newsagents. One might cynically conjecture that if it occurred to the Rector to invert a syllable to make a naughty word, the same thought could have occurred to the students, but that does not excuse his silliness in letting himself be drawn in this way.

A far sadder instance of the *trahison des clercs* was seen in the prolonged agony of Mümtaz Soysal, Dean of the Ankara Faculty of Political Sciences. A socialist, but a man who belonged to no party and hated violence, he had helped draft the 1961 Constitution and had acted as consultant to the government on constitutional problems. He was among the left-wing intellectuals rounded up in May 1971 after the murder of the Israeli Consul-General. On 14 June of the same year he was remanded in custody on a charge of advocating the violent overthrow of the established political and social order. On 3 December he was sentenced by a martial-law court to six years and eight months' imprisonment for making communist propaganda in his book *Introduction to the Constitution.* On 22 February 1972, a military court of appeal quashed the sentence on the grounds that the academic 'committee of experts' which had scrutinized the book was manifestly biased, its members being known in university circles for their right-wing sympathies and for contributing articles exclusively to right-wing journals. This is a fact to ponder over. Many Western liberals would naturally see any military court as an organ of fascist oppression, and the incident tells us something heartening about some Turkish military men as well as something depressing about some Turkish academics. But unfortunately this was not the end of the story. Professor Soysal, who had spent fourteen months in jail, was released, but on 26 April the lower court reiterated its verdict and sentence. On 26 February 1973, the court of appeal ordered a retrial, but on 29 March the lower court again found him guilty. Twice more the process was repeated. In January 1974, the lower court sentenced him for the fifth time, and he was released pending another appeal.

The elections on 14 October 1973 proved a bitter blow to Süleyman Demirel, leader of the Justice Party. He seems to have believed that as the lawfully elected Prime Minister who had been ousted by the military intervention in March 1971 he was bound to be returned to office at the next election. But much of his support had withered away; apart from those who had decided in the meanwhile that the programme of one or other of the rival parties offered them more, some of his former supporters saw no point in giving high office to a man who let himself be dispossessed of it. The Justice Party ended up with 1,031,185 fewer votes than in 1969, in a 66.82 per cent poll as against 64.35. But that was not the only surprise.

In the following table, the second column gives the percentage of votes won in the election to the Assembly. The last column shows the result of the elections to the Senate that were held on the same day in twenty-seven of the sixty-seven provinces.

Name of party	*Percentage of votes*	*Assembly seats won*	*Senate seats won*
Republican People's	33.3	185	25
Justice	29.82	149	22
National Salvation	11.8	48	3
Democratic	11.89	45	—
Republican Reliance	5.27	13	1
National Action	3.38	3	—
Unity	1.14	1	—
National	0.58	—	—
Independents	2.82	6	1

The RPP had the advantage of being the only surviving party that was avowedly of the left, and it had clearly not suffered from the schisms it had undergone. Another advantage it had was in its chairman, Bülent Ecevit. The term 'intellectual' is not infrequently used in Turkey to denote somebody with a lycée diploma. Ecevit was an intellectual by any standards. Born in Istanbul in 1925, he graduated from the American College there in 1944. During the four years he spent in the Press Counsellor's office of the Turkish embassy in London, he found time to study Sanskrit and art history. On his return home in 1950 he worked on the RPP newspaper *Ulus* as art critic and translator. In 1957 he was elected deputy for Ankara. From 1962 to 1965 he served as Minister of Labour in İnönü's various coalitions. He was General Secretary of the RPP from 1966 to 1971 and, as we have seen, was elected to its chairmanship in 1972. An excellent public speaker, his written Turkish too was vigorous and lucid. His campaign speeches attracted large crowds. Some of his audiences were heard to describe him as a second Menderes, which was a tribute to his charisma rather than a comment on his politics.

Even more remarkable was the success of the NSP. In open defiance of the law prohibiting the exploitation of religious sentiments for political ends, it appealed for the votes of those to whom secularism was anathema. Students of Turkish affairs had long wondered just how large a section of the population such people constituted. A clear indication was at last forthcoming: the NSP won 1,265,771 of the 11,223,843 votes cast. As its chairman, Necmettin Erbakan, could be a force to reckon with in the future, a quotation from a speech he made in the Assembly on 11 December 1970 may be of interest. The theme was that Turkey should have nothing to do with the European Common Market but should join in an Islamic common market. He then explained why the Zionists wanted to push Turkey into Europe.

> Turkey, with its population of 36 million, is the head of the Muslim world, whose numbers today approach a thousand million. The Zionists want to take Turkey and melt it in the crucible of a Catholic union at present numbering 200 million but which, with the subsequent addition of 200 million Protestants, will be a Christian union 400 million strong... The Common Market is a three-storeyed house. On the top floor live the Zionist capitalists. On the middle floor are the Europeans, officials in the service of their capital. For the bottom storey, lackeys and labourers are needed. That is why Turkey is being dragged in, to the bottom storey.

During the election campaign one heard a new riddle: why is the NSP like a water-melon? Answer: because it's green (the

Prophet's colour) outside and red inside. What Erbakan was preaching was indeed a kind of Islamic socialism. The importance of this will be apparent if we look at the state of the parties after the 1973 elections (one independent member having joined the RPP).

Name of party	*Senate*	*Assembly*
Republican People's	42	186
Justice	80	149
National Salvation	3	48
Democratic	6	45
Republican Reliance	9	13
National Action	—	3
Unity	—	1
Independents	10	5
Life Senators	20	—
Presidentially appointed Senators	15	—

As the RPP had topped the poll, Ecevit was asked to form a government. This did not prove easy. A coalition was obviously called for, as the RPP did not have a majority in the Assembly, while the strength in the Senate of its chief rival, the JP, would ensure a very difficult passage for any legislation it might introduce. Ecevit approached Erbakan. The wits had a great time over this. A newspaper cartoon symbolized the proposed coalition as a girl wearing a veil and a bikini; it was suggested that the slogan of the new government might be *Ortanın solu şeriat yolu*, 'Left of centre is the way of the sacred law'. But the proposal was not as incongruous as all that; the NSP did believe in socialism of a kind, and both parties believed in the need for an amnesty for political prisoners. Erbakan eventually refused, however, and the President then asked Demirel to try. He made overtures to the DP, which must have taken a good deal of courage, as that party had split away from the JP largely because of personal differences with Demirel. The DP, not surprisingly, gave him a dusty answer.

So the weeks passed. On 25 December, İsmet İnönü died. Few men had served their country so well.

There were those who feared that too long a delay in forming a new government might provoke another military intervention. There were indeed rumblings from some senior officers, but by this time all those who had signed the March memorandum had gone into retirement, and their successors seemed to have a higher threshold of tolerance. The politicians got all the time they wanted in which to make up their minds. On 25 January 1974, Bülent Ecevit at last announced the names of his Cabinet, which took office the next day. Of his twenty-four ministers, seventeen were from his own RPP, the rest from the NSP. Necmettin Erbakan became Deputy Prime Minister. Süleyman Arif Emre, General Secretary of the NSP until the elections, became a Minister of State, and other NSP men were given the portfolios of the Interior, Justice, Industry, Commerce, and Agriculture. So Turkey's new government was after all a coalition between the party of Atatürk in its new left-of-centre aspect and a party dedicated to turning Turkey's face away from Europe. But come what might, it was a civilian government, freely elected, and the future course of Turkish politics promised to be anything but dull.

NOTE

[1] The author is here repeating something he said in the article on Turkey in a number of *The Muslim World* (LVI, 4, October 1966, 235–9) devoted to a symposium on Islam in politics.

CHAPTER 19

Foreign Policy Since 1945

THE END OF the Second World War brought disappointment to those in Turkey who had expected a Russian defeat, and Russia was not slow to crack the whip at her neighbour. On 8 August 1946, a Russian Note declared that wartime events had revealed the inadequacy of the Montreux Convention to guarantee the security of the Black Sea Powers. It proposed a new regime for the Straits, to be confined to these powers. Turkey and the USSR should be jointly responsible for the defence of the Straits, which were to be always open to all merchant ships, but closed to warships other than those of the Black Sea Powers. The Turkish answer was equivocal: it insisted that there had not been 'one case of violation by German warships in which the security of the Soviet government was at stake'. The Turks agreed, however, that the Montreux Convention should be amended, substituting the words 'United Nations' for 'League of Nations'.

This was followed by another Soviet Note refuting the Turkish claim to have adequately guarded the Straits, and indicating that the question of 'the security of the Soviet government' was quite irrelevant; substantial Russian forces had had to be drawn from the battle-fronts to defend the Black Sea coast from the German naval vessels which Turkey had been allowing to come and go through the Straits until June 1944. The exchange of Notes was inconclusive.

On 1 August 1950, Turkey formally applied for admission to the North Atlantic Treaty Organization. At the NATO Council meeting in September, Norway and Denmark strongly opposed the entry of Turkey and Greece. On 4 October, Turkey accepted an invitation 'to be associated with the planning work of the Organization, with regard to Mediterranean defence' – a consolation prize, tantamount to a rejection of her application for full membership. The British and French governments, especially the latter, were opposed to the admission of Turkey, presumably because of their unwillingness to guarantee a country so much on Russia's doorstep, the justification being that Turkey was in no sense a North Atlantic Power. A leader-writer in *The Times* of London, who had presumably been dozing since 1928, saw as another objection the Turks' use of a non-European alphabet.

Turkey's disappointment and chagrin were all the greater since she had loyally and promptly answered the United Nations' call for aid in the Korean War; over 5,000 Turkish troops disembarked at Pusan on 18 October 1950, and the total strength of the Turkish Brigade was subsequently raised to 7,000. The non-communist world paid tribute to the heroic and devoted service rendered by the 25,000 men who at various times formed part of the Brigade. Six hundred and seventeen were killed in action, a hundred died from other causes, and 2,156 were wounded.

Turkey's participation in the Korean War, much though it raised her stock in Western eyes, did nothing to improve her relations with Russia, but as these were already confined to frozenly correct diplomatic exchanges the fact was of no great consequence.

On 18 July 1951, Britain announced that she now favoured Turkey's admission to NATO, Turkey having undertaken to enter a Middle East defence pact. In September the Scandinavian countries also withdrew their objections. The parliaments of all the North Atlantic Powers having formally signified their acceptance, on 18 February 1952 Turkey became a full member.

On 13 October 1951, Britain, France, the United States, and Turkey invited Egypt to join in a proposed Middle East Command. The offer was immediately rejected, and indeed it is difficult to see how any other response could have been expected, as the Egyptian view was well known: no negotiations involving Britain were possible until after the evacuation of the Canal Zone. After this fiasco the scheme for a Middle East Command in that form was quietly dropped, though the idea behind it re-emerged later. Instead, NATO announced the creation of a new South-East European Command on 16 July 1952. A month later İzmir was chosen to be the headquarters of the new Command, which included Turkish and Greek forces and came under the Southern European Command, with headquarters at Naples. This measure did something to assuage the hurt felt by the Turks at the shilly-shallying that had preceded their admission to NATO.

The incident of the stillborn Middle East Command had exacerbated Turkey's relations with Egypt. An Egyptian periodical, *Roz al-Yusuf*, published a cartoon showing a dog dressed in the Turkish flag and having the features of Celâl Bayar, who was at that time President, licking the boots of the British, French, and American representatives. A vigorous Turkish protest elicited an 'apology' in the form of a second cartoon, in which the dog was now seen proudly erect, marching on a leash in front of the three Westerners. A further display of bad feeling occurred in January 1954, when the Egyptians expelled the Turkish ambassador for some undiplomatic remarks he had made about the confiscation of the property of the former Egyptian royal house, of which his wife was a member.

But Turkey's relations with Egypt had never been particularly cordial. Indeed, the common Turkish establishment attitude towards the Arabs in general is one of thinly-veiled contempt; witness the saying 'Neither the sweets of Damascus nor the Arab's face', used when refusing an attractive-seeming offer with unpleasant strings attached. Ask a Turk to explain this and he will speak of the Arabs' poor showing as fighting men and their fatal inability to unite. A senior civil servant in Ankara, with whom the author was discussing the Arab-Israel war of 1967, firmly closed the topic with the words 'We Turks don't like people who start wars and then whine when they're beaten'. An older and deeper reason is probably to be found in the jealousy all non-Arab Muslims feel, to a greater or lesser degree, towards the people amongst whom the Prophet arose and who consequently tend to give themselves airs when dealing with lesser breeds within the Law. The achievements of Arab science and literature, many of which, though the work of non-Arabs, were recorded in Arabic, are another source of Arab pride and non-Arab resentment.

The Arab dislike for Turkey, on the other hand, is based partly on memories of long years of stern Turkish rule and partly on Turkey's recognition of Israel and her continued friendly relations with that state. In the early days of the United Nations, Russian support for the partition of Palestine was enough to swing Turkish opinion towards the Arab side; it was assumed that a Jewish state would be pro-Soviet. But this situation changed with the Western Powers' recognition of Israel. American recognition came *de facto* on 14 March 1947, the day the new state was proclaimed, and *de jure* on 31 January 1949, after its first elections; Turkey followed suit on 28 March 1949. The nomination of Turkey that year to serve with France and the United States on the UN Palestine Conciliation Commission, though it further increased Arab resentment towards her, had a beneficial effect on her self-esteem and her prestige with the rest of the world. A certain modification in the official attitude towards the Arabs was to occur as a result of the Cyprus dispute, as we shall presently see.

Turkey's state of war with Germany ended, so far as concerned the Bonn government, on 24 July 1951. West Germany spared no effort to recapture the unique place Germany had long held in Turkish affections and, from the beginning of the 1960s, as we have seen, encouraged a migration of Turkish workers into the country. Their numbers rose from 2,700 in 1960 to an official 497,000 in January 1973, but unofficial estimates put the real total somewhere over 600,000, with another million on the waiting-list.

In August 1950, to punish the Turks for sending their contingent to Korea, the Bulgarian government began to deport to Turkey a quarter-million Muslims of Turkish origin, many belonging to families that had been living in Bulgaria for generations. Most of these unhappy people were simply pushed across the frontier with only the clothes they stood up in. The Turkish government could hardly refuse to admit them, as the Turkish Press had for some time been criticizing the Bulgars for ill-treating this minority. But the influx of refugees was not to the liking of the Turks, not only because of the difficulty of fitting them into the Turkish economy, but also because of a fear that some of them might be communist agents, availing themselves of the opportunity to infiltrate. In October the Turks closed the frontier and did not reopen it till 2 December, the Bulgars having agreed to take back a number of non-Muslims who had been included among the deportees, and not to put across the border anybody who did not hold a Turkish entry-visa. The frontier was again closed on 8 November 1951, the Turks alleging that the Bulgars had sent across a thousand gypsies 'camouflaged as Turkish emigrants'. On 21 February 1953, when Bulgaria agreed to take them back, the frontier was reopened. Thereafter, however, those Turks still in Bulgaria were not allowed to leave, and this situation persisted until 22 March 1968, when an agreement was signed giving them the right to go to Turkey with all their belongings if they had relatives who had been there before 1952.

In April 1954, Turkey signed an 'Agreement for Friendly Co-operation' with Pakistan, Article 6 of which began thus:

> Any State, whose participation is considered by the contracting parties useful for achieving the purpose of the present agreement, may accede to the present agreement under the same conditions, and with the same obligations, as the contracting parties.

In this Article we see the second attempt to set up a Middle East defensive alliance. The agreement was a product of the new American policy of linking together in a system of alliances those Middle Eastern powers which had not taken the neutralist line. The exclusion of Israel from the scope of this policy was intended to leave the door open for the eventual entry of the Arab states. The Turkish and Pakistani Prime Ministers decided in June 1954 that Staff talks should begin at once to prepare their common defence plans.

The Baghdad Pact grew out of the Treaty of Co-operation signed by Turkey and Iraq on 24 February 1955, with the subsequent accession of Britain (4 April), Pakistan (23 September), and Persia (3 November). The idea behind it was to create a 'Northern Tier' of countries on the southern borders of the USSR. Militarily it added nothing to the strength of its stronger members; politically it was the cause of much trouble for Turkey, and of more than trouble for that well-intentioned and harmless young man, the late King Faisal II of Iraq. The Turks were ready to invade Iraq to suppress the revolution of 14 July 1958, which overthrew him, and they would have done so but for American pressure. After the revolution all Iraqis on the headquarters staff were given indefinite leave with pay 'pending a clarification of the present position'. The headquarters was transferred from Baghdad to Ankara in October 1958, and in August 1960 the organization changed its name to 'the Central Treaty Organization' (CENTO).

In common with other Middle Eastern members of the Baghdad Pact, Turkey condemned the Israeli and Anglo-French attacks on Egypt in October–November 1956, but the feeling in the country, even amongst the officials, was far less critical than its official voice. The Turkish ambassador was recalled from Tel-Aviv and since then diplomatic relations between the two countries have been at *chargé d'affaires* level.

Turkey's most troublesome frontier is the one in the south-east, where smuggling to and from Syria and Iraq is a regular profession. The outgoing commodities are livestock and dairy-produce, tobacco, opium, carpets, guns, and ammunition; the incoming are synthetic fabrics, perfume, paraffin, tea, salt, and sugar. Aware that some Syrians still dream of regaining Hatay, the Turks regard this traffic as due to the connivance of the Syrian authorities through a desire to harm the Turkish economy. In the spring of 1955, Turkish armoured units were moved to the Syrian frontier, and there is some evidence that they were withdrawn only after a blunt warning from

Moscow. In the autumn of 1957 came the 'artificial crisis', when Egyptian forces were landed in Syria to meet an alleged threat from Turkey. King Saud's offer of mediation was accepted by Turkey but rejected, after an initial acceptance, by Syria. On 30 October Syria asked the United Nations to set up a fact-finding commission; and dropped the request two days later. The crisis had fizzled out. Every now and then someone in Turkey notices a Syrian tourist-map showing Hatay inside Syria's borders, and the newspapers make the appropriate indignant noises, but no one takes the matter very seriously.

One of the few pleasant aspects of the immediate post-war scene was the continuance of friendly relations between Turks and Greeks. It was made known in 1952 that Britain and the United States would welcome a defensive alliance of Greece, Turkey, and Yugoslavia, to guard against a possible Russian drive through the Balkans. On 28 February 1953, representatives of the three powers, meeting at Ankara, signed a Tripartite Treaty of Friendship and Co-operation, which was converted into a 'Treaty of Alliance, Political Co-operation, and Mutual Assistance', signed at Bled on 9 August 1954. But it can hardly be considered a potent factor in the politics of the region. The outbreak of rioting in Nicosia and Limassol on 18–19 December 1954, and of terrorism in those two cities, Larnaca, and Famagusta, on 31 March 1955, which differed from previous outbreaks in having the open support of the Greek government and Athens Radio, were seen by the Turks as evidence that Greek protestations of friendship for them were false. Turkey's attitude was widely misinterpreted as due to concern for the Turkish-speaking fifth of the island's population. This concern, though real, was not paramount. Her chief anxiety was for her own security. Looking at the strength of the communist element in Greece at that time, she found reason to doubt the country's internal stability, and feared that, if the demand for *enosis* were granted, a potentially communist Cyprus, some forty miles away, would menace her southern ports, while İzmir and the whole Aegean coast was already boxed in by the Greek-held offshore islands.

When the troubles started, the Turkish view was that so long as Britain retained the island Turkey would be content. The growing support for *enosis* shown by the leaders of the British Labour Party caused the Turks to worry about the likelihood of a Labour government's ceding Cyprus to Greece. They therefore seized on a suggestion (said to have been first made by Walter Elliot, MP, in a letter to *The Times* of 17 July 1956) that the island be partitioned.

Their liking for this solution was increased by the outcome of the Suez landings, which seemed to indicate a diminution of Britain's power, as did the release of Archbishop Makarios from detention in March 1957. By mid-1957 the Turks were going all out for partition, and this was still their official policy on 19 June 1958, when Britain announced her 'Seven-Year Partnership Plan'. The Plan, after modification, was accepted by Turkey on 25 August. Representatives of the Greek and Turkish governments would have a say in the administration, being given the right of direct access to the Governor. During the seven years for which British sovereignty would continue, separate Houses of Representatives would be established for the two communities. Pending elections to these Houses, separate Greek and Turkish municipal councils would be set up where the Governor thought fit. On 1 October 1958, the Turkish Consul-General in Cyprus officially assumed his duties as Turkish representative under the Plan.

The Greek government, however, refused to accept this decision and Archbishop Makarios proposed in September that the island should become independent. This was agreed after discussions in Zürich between the Greek and Turkish Prime Ministers and Foreign Ministers and subsequent discussions in London (February 1959). The Republic of Cyprus was inaugurated on 16 August 1960. Incorporated in its constitution was the Treaty of Guarantee between the new republic on the one hand and Britain, Greece, and Turkey on the other, two articles of which are worth quoting:

> *Article 2.* Greece, the United Kingdom, and Turkey . . . recognize and guarantee the independence, territorial integrity, and security of the Republic of Cyprus, and also the provisions of the basic articles of its Constitution.
>
> They likewise undertake to prohibit, as far as lies within their power, all activity having the object of promoting directly or indirectly either the union of the Republic of Cyprus with any other State, or the partition of the Island.
>
> *Article 3.* In the event of any breach of the provisions of the Treaty, Greece, the United Kingdom, and Turkey undertake to consult together with a view to making representations or taking the necessary steps to ensure observance of these provisions.
>
> In so far as common or concerted action may prove impossible, each of the three guaranteeing Powers reserves the right to take action with the sole aim of re-establishing the state of affairs established by the Treaty.

It was this last paragraph on which Turkey relied, on the several occasions when she was on the verge of armed intervention, and on 9 August 1964 when she carried out air raids on the north-west of Cyprus. Yet from the legal standpoint it appears that the drafters of this paragraph must have been nodding, as it virtually empowers the signatories to go to war against one another, a course which is closed to them as members both of the United Nations and of NATO. Nevertheless, a Turkish invasion was being prepared at the beginning of June 1964, which was averted at the last minute when İsmet İnönü, who was then Prime Minister, received an urgent letter from President Johnson. It warned that a Turkish invasion might involve Russia:

> You will appreciate that your NATO allies have not yet had a chance to discuss whether or not they will feel obliged to defend Turkey against a Soviet invasion resulting from an action undertaken by Turkey without their approval.

Johnson's final and most telling argument was that the United States would not agree to Turkey's using for the projected invasion any military equipment provided by the United States.

It may be that if the letter had been less hurriedly drafted its message could have been phrased more tactfully. As it was, the effect on Turkish feelings towards America was disastrous. It seemed that NATO was an organization designed not for mutual aid but simply to advance American interests; it is from that moment that anti-Americanism in Turkey really dates. While there was no question of quitting NATO, the Turks decided to woo the Arab votes in the United Nations and to introduce a thaw in their relations with Russia, just to warn the United States not to take Turkey for granted. In October the Turkish Foreign Minister, Feridun Cemal Erkin, was reported to be studying the possibility of closer relations with the uncommitted nations as well as with members of 'other blocs', while remaining faithful to existing treaties. The following month, the Minister visited Moscow and secured Russian support for the view that neither community in Cyprus should dominate the other. A cultural agreement was signed, but the Turks refused a proposal for an exchange of students, although the United States had accepted a similar Russian proposal in November 1959. In January 1965, President Podgorny of the USSR addressed the Grand National Assembly in Ankara, but had some difficulty in making himself heard above the barracking. In

March 1967, an agreement was signed whereby the USSR would finance several industrial projects in Turkey, including a glass factory, a vodka distillery, an oil refinery, and a new steel works at İskenderun.

That November, after twenty-four Turkish Cypriots had been killed by Greek Cypriot forces, came another invasion scare. President Makarios, when asked by a foreign diplomat what he proposed to do, wept, saying over and over again 'My poor country!' Pressed for an answer, he said he was going to do nothing at all; there would be no resistance to a Turkish invasion. But there would be a massacre of Turkish Cypriots before the invaders could land; thereafter there would doubtless be a massacre of Greek Cypriots. Hence the tears and hence 'My poor country!'[1] The situation in fact cooled down, thanks largely to United Nations mediation. The saddest aspect is that the Turk minority have strictly confined themselves to their own enclaves, and a generation of young Turkish Cypriots is growing up with no contact at all with Greek Cypriots. But in the summer of 1972 inter-communal talks began, and by the end of the year the prospects of a peaceful settlement looked reasonably bright, with the Turkish and Greek governments equally anxious not to be drawn into conflict.

In January 1971 the *New York Times* gave news of a CIA report to President Nixon that Russian aircraft bound for Egypt had frequently refuelled at Turkish airfields. The matter was raised at NATO and the Turkish reply was that there was only one isolated instance. It is probably safe to consider this as just another move in the campaign not be taken for granted; Turkish military men have not relaxed their centuries-old attitude of extreme caution towards their gigantic neighbour. Nor, incidentally, have American military men; at least once a year they send a war vessel or two into the Black Sea, a practice which they call 'exercising the Montreux Convention'. The Russians make a perfunctory fuss every time, but they know that the Americans are entirely within their rights. If proof is needed of Turkey's fidelity to the Western alliance, we may cite the Defence Co-operation Agreement which she signed with the United States on 3 July 1969. It has become known as the Umbrella Agreement, because it was intended to cover – that is, to consolidate and in some cases to supersede – the fifty-six existing agreements between the two countries. It stressed Turkey's equality with America as NATO partners, and Turkish sovereignty over American installations and bases in the country, for which no rent was envisaged.

Turkey's attempt to win Arab support for her Cyprus policy was unproductive, bringing no perceptible change in Arab voting-patterns in the United Nations. Her Foreign Minister attended the Islamic summit conference held at Rabat on 22–25 September 1969 but, together with the delegates of Persia and the Black African countries, refused to break off diplomatic and commercial relations with Israel. The government had to face much criticism for participating, especially from İsmet İnönü, who took the opportunity of reminding the Assembly that the Arabs had sided against the Ottoman empire during the First World War. Consequently the Foreign Minister did not himself attend the next Islamic conference, which took place at Jedda on 23–26 March 1970; the Secretary-General of the Foreign Ministry went in his stead. As at the previous conference (which the Calcutta *Statesman* referred to as 'the Rabat débâcle'), Turkey committed herself to nothing.

On 31 October 1959, Turkey applied for association with the EEC. The association agreement, signed in Ankara on 12 September 1963, came into effect on 1 December 1964. For a preparatory period of five years, Turkey, with EEC help, would improve her economic and commercial position. Then would come a transitional stage of up to twelve years, during which a Customs union would gradually be established between Turkey and the Community. Thereafter, when a full Customs union had been achieved, Turkey could apply for full membership. Turkey passed out of the preparatory stage on 22 July 1970.

NOTE

[1] The source of this story was the diplomat concerned, who had no business to tell it and must therefore remain anonymous.

CHAPTER 20

Landscape with Figures

(*i*) *The Country and the People*

THE TERRITORY OF the Republic is situated between 36° and 43° North and 26° and 45° East, and covers an area of 301,664 square miles, which is getting on for four times the size of Great Britain and just over one-tenth that of the continental United States. Thrace (*Trakya*) occupies 9,179 square miles in the south-eastern tip of Europe; the larger portion of the country, in Asia Minor, is known as Anatolia (*Anadolu*). There are some 4,000 square miles of lakes. In shape Anatolia is roughly rectangular, a thousand miles from west to east and, at its widest, 400 from north to south. The total length of coastline is 3,440 miles, while land frontiers amount to 1,711 miles. North lies the Black Sea; south, the Mediterranean; west, the Aegean. The neighbouring countries are as follows, the figures in parentheses being the length of common frontier in miles: Thrace is bordered to the north and west by Bulgaria (167) and to the south and west by Greece (132). Eastern Anatolia is bordered to the north by the USSR (379), to the east by Persia (282), to the south by Iraq (206) and Syria (545).

The land is rugged, the average height being 3,626 feet, as against 1,083 for Europe and 3,445 for Asia. The greater part of Anatolia is a treeless plateau, broken up by stretches of marshland and almost completely surrounded by mountains. This plateau rises steadily towards the eastern highlands. The highest peak, Mount Ararat (*Ağrı dağı*; 16,945 feet), on the frontier with Soviet Armenia, is the meeting-point of three great ranges, one skirting the Black Sea, the other two, Taurus and Anti-Taurus, running south-west towards the Mediterranean. South of the Anti-Taurus range lies a smaller plateau, which falls away into the great plain of Syria and Iraq and is watered by the Tigris and Euphrates.

North of the Gulf of İskenderun is the small but immensely fertile plain of Adana, rich in soil brought down from the Anti-Taurus by the Seyhan and Ceyhan rivers. Apart from this, the coastal plains are narrow, except on the Aegean and the Sea of Marmara.

In climate, Turkey presents a wide range of extremes, touching the warm temperate Mediterranean, the cold rainy Caucasus, and the belt of desert and steppe which runs from the Sahara to Central Asia.

The Black Sea region has a generally mild climate, with a narrow range of winter and summer temperatures, though towards the east summers are hotter and rainfall greater, because the mountains shut off the cold dry north winds. In this warm damp climate the mountain-slopes are wooded, and lemons, oranges, and hazel-nuts grow in abundance. Bafra, where the Kızıl Irmak ('Red River', the Halys of antiquity) meets the sea, is a particularly fertile region, and the whole coastal strip eastward from Sinop is famous for its tobacco. The west of the Black Sea area receives most of its rain in winter, the east in autumn. The highest mean annual rainfall of the whole country is at Rize, with over 70 inches; here are the tea-plantations.

A geological fault runs east–west on the latitude of the Gulf of Gemlik and Lake İznik. Movements towards this of the land to the north are the cause of earthquakes in a belt extending from Gallipoli through the Gulk of İzmit to Erzurum.

The climate of the central plateau is extreme, with temperatures ranging from −15°F in winter to over 100°F in summer. The average rainfall is low, but violent rainstorms are common in spring and autumn. The mean annual rainfall varies between 8 and 12 inches, except in the neighbourhood of the great Salt Lake (*Tuz Gölü*), where it is considerably less. This is wonderful country for apples and apricots.

The southern coast has a Mediterranean climate, with hot summers and warm rainy winters, the thermometer hardly ever approaching freezing-point. Rain in July or August is practically unheard-of, and Antalya people boast that their year consists of three springs and a summer. All along the coast grow oranges, lemons, tangerines, bananas, and cotton.

The Aegean coast has a similar climate, but summer is slightly less hot, and in the north of the region the winter can be cold. Figs, which need a mild winter and a hot summer, grow in abundance, as does some of the best tobacco. Here too are peaches and grapes, including the seedless grapes which make raisins. Between Aydın and the sea, at Söke, is the world's principal source of licorice-root.

The south-east has milder winters than the plateau, and scorching summers, with shade temperatures reaching 115°F. Cotton grows on the plains.

The climate of Thrace is similar to that of the plateau but with more rainfall. This is a good wine-producing area, and rice is grown along the River Maritsa.

This remarkable diversity of climate is matched by that of the landscape: mountains and rivers, orchards, forests, waterfalls, endless sandy shores, and vast plains.

The ethnological history is of great complexity. For thousands of years Anatolia has been a seat of empires and a highway for conquering armies and hungry nomads and God-drunk mystics. Cimmerians, Hittites, Phrygians, Lydians, Thracians, Persians, Greeks, and a hundred forgotten peoples had all set their seal on the land before the coming of the Romans. After the Roman empire was divided, the Byzantines held sway over Asia Minor till the eleventh century of our era. But even in the comparatively settled conditions of the early Byzantine empire, the ethnic picture did not remain static; whether as peaceful wanderers or reckless invaders, there was an endless stream of newcomers out of southern Russia and Central Asia. In the seventh century came the first Muslim armies, adding still more to the mixture of peoples. These new arrivals were not Arabs alone, for when the followers of the Prophet erupted from the Peninsula their numbers were swollen by non-Arab converts whom they picked up in their triumphant progress. Other converts came out of Asia, so that when the Seljuks arrived they found many bands of Turks settled in the land before them. Christianized Turks there were too, transplanted from the Balkans to meet some requirement of Byzantine imperial policy. A striking symbol of the heterogeneity of the people of Asia Minor is to be seen at Ankara, where the fifteenth-century Mosque of Hacı Bayram encroaches on the site of the Temple of Augustus, which was built on the foundations of a Phrygian sanctuary and was converted to a place of Christian worship in the sixth century.

Turkey is a very ancient land, still full of wonder. No Turk has felt this more strongly than Sabahattin Eyüboğlu (1908–73), who in 1956 wrote an essay called 'Our Anatolia':

> Why is this country ours? Is it because we came out of Central Asia with four hundred horsemen and conquered it? Those who take this view don't really regard this country as their own, don't consider it their native land. They see themselves as strangers in the place they live in . . . This country is ours because it is ours,

> not because we conquered it . . . By now we are both the conquerors and the conquered . . . The history of our people is the history of Anatolia. Once we were pagan, then we became Christian, then Muslim. Our people built the temples and the churches as well as the mosques. It is we who filled the gleaming white theatres, as we filled the dark caravanserais . . .

But Eyüboğlu's attitude was shared by only a tiny minority, because most Turks prefer to believe that they are indeed of the pure breed of Ertuğrul and his Ghazis.

An anthropometric investigation, carried out in 1937 and 1938 on 64,000 Turks in all parts of the country, produced these results: the average height of Turkish men was 1.652 metres (5 feet 5 inches), of women 1.522 metres (5 feet), the tallest people being found in the east of the country. Roughly three-quarters of the population were brachycephalic, the average cranial index of men being 83.33, of women 83.78. The straight and leptorrhine (narrow-nostrilled) type of nose predominated. Concave noses were rare. Only 14 per cent of men and 17 per cent of women had dark eyes, blue eyes being not uncommon. The slanting Mongoloid eyes were found in barely 5 per cent of all those examined. The most common hair-colouring was medium to light brown. Only 30 per cent of the samples had dark hair. The general conclusion was that most Turks were of Alpine type, with a sprinkling of Dinaric.

Although this investigation is the most comprehensive yet carried out in Turkey, the numbers involved may not seem impressive to the layman. The results, however, square with one's subjective impressions. Certainly the amateur ethnographer will find his self-confidence shaken if he tries to identify the Turkish students among a crowd at the Sorbonne.

The following table, based on the 1965 census, shows the division of the population, including infants, by mother-tongue:

Abkhaz	4,563
Albanian	12,832
Arabic	365,340
Armenian	33,094
Bulgarian	4,088
Circassian	58,339
English	27,841
French	3,302
Georgian	34,330

German	4,901
Greek	48,096
Italian	2,926
Jewish	9,981
Kurdish	2,219,547
Laz	26,007
Serbo-Croat	17,627
Spanish	2,791
Turkish	28,289,680
Zaza	150,644

Abkhaz and Laz are Caucasian languages. Most of the speakers of the former live in the provinces of Bolu and Sakarya, while the Lazes, who are great seafarers, are mainly to be found in Artvin, Kocaeli, and Sakarya.

The Arabic-speakers are numerous in Adana (22,356), Hatay (148,072), Mardin (79,687), Siirt (38,273), and Urfa (51,090).

Adding to the number of those who gave their mother-tongue as Kurdish the 429,168 who gave it as their best spoken second language, we arrive at a total for Kurdish-speakers of 2,648,715. The total for Zaza, a distant relative of Kurdish, may be similarly brought up to 171,057.

In the 1945 census there were 4,463 people who gave Gipsy as their mother-tongue, but this language is no longer shown in the census-returns.

The term Jewish (*Yahudice*) does not mean Yiddish, because most of the Jews of Turkey are Sephardi. Presumably the mother-tongue of the majority of people under this heading was Ladino. This is, basically, the Spanish of the fifteenth century, brought with them by Jewish refugees after the expulsion from Spain in 1492, with numerous borrowings from the languages of the eastern Mediterranean and, more recently, from French. It was formerly written in Hebrew characters, but nowadays in the Latin letters of the new Turkish alphabet. Some of the 7,226 who gave Spanish as their mother-tongue or best second language may also have meant Ladino. Many of the older generation of Jews, especially members of the wealthier families, speak French at home, because they received their education at the schools of the Alliance Israélite. This organization was founded by French Jews in 1860, to establish schools for Jewish communities in French North Africa and the Middle East, and so to bring about their emancipation by bridging the gulf between medievalism and modern civilization.

The next table, also based on the 1965 census, shows the division of the population by religion:

Muslims		31,129,854
Christians:		
Orthodox	73,725	
Gregorian	69,526	
Roman Catholic	25,833	
Protestant	22,983	
Other denominations	14,758	
Total of Christians		206,825
Jews		38,267
Other faiths		14,661
Atheists		1,212
Unknown		602

The figure given for Muslims, who constitute 99.17 per cent of the population, includes both Sunnites and Shi'ites (*Alevîs*). The claim of the latter to number over 12 million must be taken with a grain of salt, but no statistics exist whereby it might be refuted. It is greatly to be hoped that future censuses will do something about this. Failing that, a possible base for assessing their numbers is that Alevî men tend to wear walrus moustaches; this suggests a useful occupation for a team of energetic sociologists.

The number of Protestants in 1945 was only 5,213; the big increase probably reflects the American presence. The Jews in 1945 numbered 76,965; the decline in their numbers is due to emigration to Israel.

Turkish has two distinct words for Greeks who are citizens of Greece and for Turkish subjects of Greek ethnic origin, respectively *Yunanlı* and *Rum*. In 1965, the largest concentration of the latter was in Istanbul (47,207). In İzmir there were only 262. The only sizeable Jewish community, apart from Istanbul (30,831), was in İzmir (4,067). The Armenian centres were Istanbul (61,215) and Kastamonu (1,224).

The head of the Orthodox Church is the Ecumenical Patriarch, whose seat is at Istanbul, as are those of the Gregorian (Armenian) Patriarch and the Chief Rabbi. There is an Apostolic Delegate in Istanbul and a Roman Catholic archbishop of İzmir. The Roman Catholic dignitary known as the Patriarch of Istanbul does not reside in Turkey.

The 'other denominations' include the Nestorian Uniates (Chaldaeans), who have a bishop at Mardin, and the Armenian Uniates, under the Patriarch of Cilicia.

In the mid-nineteenth century there were Greeks and Armenians who wrote Turkish in their own alphabets. In 1841 the Imprimerie de Castro issued a broadsheet in Hebrew, Turkish, and Ladino, by command of Sultan Abdülmecid, urging the Jews of Istanbul to learn to speak Turkish, and in 1867 the Ottoman Ministry of Education accepted the principle that non-Muslim children should be admitted to state secondary schools. But two years later new regulations for public instruction were put into force by the ministry, and these included the following clauses:

> In every city-ward and village, or, if the circumstances warrant it, in every two wards or villages, there shall be at least one boys' school. In mixed wards or villages, there shall be separate Muslim and non-Muslim schools. The period of instruction shall be four years. The syllabus for the Muslim schools shall be as follows: the alphabet, Koran-recitation, elements of religion and ethics, with the rudiments of Ottoman history and geography, and useful knowledge. The three last subjects shall be taught to non-Muslims also, in their own languages.
>
> The syllabus for non-Muslim schools is as follows: religious instruction under the direction of their spiritual heads, writing, and outlines of arithmetic.
>
> In towns of mixed population, there shall be one grammar school for Muslims and one for Christians, if their community numbers more than a hundred families. The same applies to other non-Muslim communities . . .
>
> Lessons are to be given to every *millet* in its own language, from books written in that language. In the final year of the four, those who wish may learn French.

With minor modifications, these provisions remained in force until the proclamation of the Republic, when it was decreed that Turkish should be taught in all schools and should be the medium of instruction in history and geography. In other words, non-Muslims born before, say, 1915 did not, as a general rule, speak Turkish at home or in school. In the special case of Jewish children whose parents spoke Ladino but who went to one of the schools of the Alliance Israélite, Turkish was learned, if at all, as a third language.

Till well into the nineteenth century, a Christian or Jew was usually identifiable by his dress. The fact that this had ceased to be the case by 1922 was not generally known abroad, which is why not a few *Rum* were killed at İzmir by the Greek Army of Occupation, who took to shooting at anyone they saw wearing a fez. More recently, the 'infallible' criterion was pronunciation. Exactly like the man of Ephraim in Judges 12:6 – 'Then said they unto him, Say now Shibboleth: and he said Sibboleth: for he could not frame to pronounce it right' – Greeks were thought to be incapable of pronouncing the *sh*-sound. If a man told you he lived at Nisantas, instead of Nişantaş, you knew at once he was a *Rum*. Now that criterion too has begun to lose its value. The first generation of Christians and Jews to grow up under the Republic differed from their parents in speaking Turkish well. Their children and grandchildren speak it perfectly. So integration has begun to be possible for those who want it. The better newspapers play a commendable part by running articles whose message is our common humanity. The daily *Milliyet*, among the most liberal of all Turkish publications, printed, without comment, these two consecutive news-items from Edirne on 23 May 1965:

A Rum *Arrested On The Frontier*

A *Rum* named Oedipus Konstantinides, in business as an estate-agent at Kadıköy in Istanbul, has been arrested by our frontier-guards while trying to escape to Greece past Pazarkule. Oedipus, who has been charged with attempting to leave the country without a passport, said that he was trying to escape to Greece because he owed money to the Inland Revenue.

One of Our Race Finds Refuge

A member of our race named Ahmet escaped from Greece during the night and found refuge in Turkey. Ahmet, a resident of western Thrace, states that he fled to Turkey because he could no longer endure Greek oppression, and would make his home with relatives in the Motherland.

These two stories, taken in conjunction, are surely enough to make the angels weep; they must have given to think every reader capable of thought.

It may be that the experience the many hundreds of thousands of Turkish migrant workers in Germany are having, of being part of a minority in a strange land, will help to speed the collapse of the barriers, though to say this is perhaps to display too rosy a view of human nature.

The increase in the population is shown in the following table:

Year	
1927	13,648,000
1940	17,821,000
1945	18,790,000
1950	20,947,000
1955	24,065,000
1960	27,755,000
1965	31,391,000
1970	35,230,000
1972	37,538,000

In 1965 a birth-control campaign began. By 1969 there were 482 clinics, as well as mobile units touring country districts, but efforts to popularize the intra-uterine device were frustrated by persistent rumours that it caused cancer. The birth-rate in fact rose slightly, from 2.6 per cent at the start of the campaign to 2.7 per cent in 1972, against an average for western Europe of one per cent. If there were no radical change, the population was expected to be 54.5 million by 1987 and 64.9 million by 1995. The campaign continues; thus at some restaurants the customers are given paper napkins advertising such-and-such a 'harmless protection' which 'prevents unwanted pregnancy'. It may be that the section of the population which is responsible for the increased birth-rate does not go to that sort of restaurant or does not read. But the active opposition to the campaign does not come from the poor and illiterate. Colonel Türkeş thinks there should be no birth-control until the population of Turkey equals that of the USSR. In April 1969 his Grey Wolves broke up an international seminar on birth-control arranged in Ankara by the World Health Organization; they shouted such slogans as 'The great Turkish nation shall not be made impotent!' There is little fear of that at the moment; there are well over 13 million Turks below the age of fifteen.

In 1972, 38 per cent of the population lived in towns and cities, of which the biggest were Istanbul with approximately 2,225,000 inhabitants, Ankara with over a million, and İzmir with half a million. In the same year, of the total labour force of 14.3 million, 8.8 million were employed in agriculture, 1.5 million in industry, and 3.2 million in services. Those unemployed or engaged in unproductive jobs in cities totalled 750,000.

The steady rise in the population, with a consequent increase in the competition for good jobs and housing, has led to a growing emigration of skilled and semi-skilled workers to western Europe, mainly to Germany. By the beginning of 1973 there were well over half a million such, with a million on the waiting-list. Their remittances home now form an important part of the country's foreign earnings, totalling $740 million in 1972.

(*ii*) *Agriculture*

Agriculture provides over a quarter of the national income and some 68 per cent of exports. In 1967 the total acreage was divided up as follows:

	Percentage
Arable	30.6
Meadows and pastures	33.8
Vineyards, vegetable-gardens, orchards	3.0
Forest	16.1
Wasteland, lakes, marshes	16.1

Total cereal production in 1972 was upwards of 17 million tons, of which wheat accounted for 62 per cent, but this was insufficient for domestic needs. The yield is not high: France produces more wheat from 4 million hectares than Turkey does from 8.7 million. New strains, however, are now being tried.

Cotton, both for textile manufacture and for fodder, is grown mainly on the Mediterranean plains, especially of the south-east and of Hatay, and inland from the Aegean. The 1969 crop was 400,000 tons.

Olives grow all round the coast, except in the extreme north-east. There are some 70 million olive-trees, producing over 300,000 tons of olives and 150,000 tons of oil annually.

Tobacco is grown all over Turkey, the main areas being centred on İzmir and Samsun. Annual production in recent years has fluctuated between 88,000 and 190,000 tons.

Turkey used to be, after India, the world's chief producer of opium, mostly in the provinces of Afyonkarahisar (the name means Opium Black Fortress), Denizli, and Isparta. But on 30 June 1971, a decree was issued banning the cultivation of poppies and the production of opium from mid-1972; the opium harvest of 1972 was the last. This had happened at the request of the American government, which claimed that Turkish opium was the source of some

80 per cent of the heroin used by addicts in the United States. The Americans agreed to pay compensation to Turkish farmers, but the Turks maintained that the amount envisaged would cover only one-twelfth of the loss, which was estimated at over TL97 million a year to producers in Afyonkarahisar alone. The livelihood of 80,000 workers and their families would be imperilled, for finding alternative crops for the areas of poppy-cultivation would not be as easy as outsiders might think. The total loss to the country, including the return from the processing and transportation of the crop, was estimated at TL6,416,132,751 (about £200 million). Despite that suspicious lone lira, which seems designed to lend verisimilitude to this vast figure, there was no doubt that the loss would be very severe, and there was much bitterness against the Americans, who, it was felt, were bringing to bear on Turkey pressure which they could not or would not bring on other producing countries.

Milliyet (1 December 1972) gave the following table, ascribed to the US Bureau of Narcotics, showing the number of tons of opium coming on the legal and illegal markets from various countries in 1971:

	legal	*illegal*
Turkey	150	35–50
India	1,200	250
Pakistan	6	175–200
Persia	150	?
China	100	?
USSR	115	?
Yugoslavia	0.83	1.7
Japan	5	—
Thailand, Burma, Laos	—	750
Afghanistan	—	100–150
Mexico	—	5–15

Turkish sultanas have always been famous, but recent years have seen a great increase in viticulture for the purpose of wine-making, notably in the Marmara region and the İzmir plain, and the results are eminently drinkable. Almost 17 million litres of wine were produced in 1967, in addition to 8 million litres of *rakı*, the potent national drink, which is distilled from the juice of grapes and is flavoured with aniseed. When mixed with water it turns white and is therefore known as *aslan sütü*, 'lion's milk'. In the last year or two the habit has spread of taking it neat, with water as a chaser.

Visitors occasionally evince surprise that Turks, being Muslims, should drink at all, but it is wiser not to become involved in debate on this matter, as one may be faced in retaliation with such difficult questions as why the plastic arts have always flourished in Christian Europe despite what the Decalogue says about graven images, and why Christians expect Muslims to be more observant of the laws of God than they are themselves. A parliamentary question in May 1972 elicited from the Minister of Customs and Monopolies the information that Turks drank close on 9 million litres of *rakı* a year and that the total of all intoxicants drunk over the previous forty years was 1,333,608,244 litres. An incidental note which may interest tourists is that the city of Gaziantep prides itself on having the highest *per capita* consumption of alcohol in the country. As for the wine, much of it goes to France, where it joins the Algerian in the carafes of *vin ordinaire*. Some Turkish cynics suggested in the late 1950s that their country's support for the Algerian independence movement was based on the hope that an independent Muslim Algeria would end the production of wine, thus increasing the sales to France of the Turkish product. This is worth recording only as a reply to any who doubt whether the Turkish mind is capable of subtlety.

An idea of the importance of pastoralism in the economy is given by the following figures (in thousands) of domesticated animals existing in 1969:

Sheep	36,351
Goats	20,267
Cattle	13,189
Water-buffalo	1,178
Horses	1,110
Donkeys	1,938
Mules	291
Camels	39

As one would expect in a Muslim country, comparatively few pigs are kept; there are fewer than 5,000 pigs among the 8.2 million animals slaughtered for meat in each year.

Deforestation is a grave problem, which is taken so seriously by the authorities that the constitution (Article 131) excludes offenders against the Forestry Law from general amnesties. A great deal of unlicensed felling goes on; as the alternative fuel is dung, which the peasant is equally exhorted not to waste, he is in a cleft stick. In fact, over much of the eastern half of the country, dung is the usual fuel for cooking and for warming the house in winter. Still, the area devoted to forests is being steadily enlarged and the number of goats is being reduced (by 1.8 million between 1962 and 1969).

In 1966, 79.7 per cent of the area under cultivation was worked by draft animals and 20.3 per cent by tractors. By 1968 these figures had altered to 73.4 and 26.6 respectively. In the latter year there were 85,475 tractors in use, but also 1,983,000 wooden ploughs.

Rather than weary the reader with an account of the various attempts at land-reform which have been and are being made, it may be said simply that the size of the average landholding in 1952 was 19 acres and that the much-publicized distribution in the Menderes era did little more than increase the number of unworkably tiny holdings, so that in 1961, out of more than 2 million farms in private hands, there were only 3,358 exceeding 25 acres in area. The distributions had been mainly of uncultivated state land; the aghas (*ağa*), the big landowners, had not suffered. Over half the national income from agriculture still went to one-tenth of the farmers.

Not long after the 1960 revolution, the NUC exiled fifty-six aghas of the east and south-east, but in August 1962 they were allowed to return, because in fact fifty of them had turned out to be not particularly big landowners; they had been chosen more or less at random, while many richer and more grasping aghas had escaped. But instead of setting about the job properly the government let the matter drop, because aghas control votes as effectively as any pre-Reform Bill English squire. Here is a news-item of 20 April 1963, which is not unique:

> An agha called İsa Rejo, who bought the village of Sirbe, in the Açkale department of Urfa province, sent his men to demolish the 41 houses of the village while the villagers were away in the summer-pasture and to plough over the site with a tractor, thus leaving 300 people homeless.

In September 1972 there were still 743 villages belonging to individual landowners.

(*iii*) *Minerals*

Turkey has vast subterranean riches. The proclamation of the Republic found 90 per cent of the mining industry in foreign hands, but three-quarters of it is now owned by the state.

Great deposits of high-grade bituminous coal lie along the Black Sea coast, between Ereğli and Cide, with Zonguldak as the chief mining centre. The Zonguldak coalfields were not nationalized until 1940, when wartime difficulties prevented the importation of the equipment needed for modernization. The annual pithead production is about 7.7 million tons.

Lignite is found in Thrace and round Kütahya, 8.5 million tons being mined annually. For many years the government has been trying to popularize its use for domestic purposes, unfortunately with great success; the disastrous result of this policy is particularly evident at Ankara, which now has a severe smog problem.

Iron is mined at Divriği, in the mountains south-east of Sivas, and smelted at Karabük near Zonguldak, 600 miles away. Criticism has been levelled at the Turks by foreign economists for their shortsightedness in putting their only blast-furnaces so far from their only source of ore, which has to be carried all those miles by rail. But this criticism is unfair; or rather it is on the wrong plane. In 1937, when it was decided to build an iron-works at Karabük, in proximity to the coal-workings, mining had not yet started at Divriği, although it had long been known that iron ore existed in the neighbourhood. The original intention was to import ore from abroad to feed the furnaces of Karabük, which had a major place in Mustafa Kemal's plan to industrialize Turkey. One feels that the same critics would have been no less scathing if the blast-furnaces had been erected near Divriği, when it would have been necessary to bring coal all the way from Zonguldak and to transport the smelted iron some 250 miles to the nearest port, Samsun. Mustafa Kemal would no doubt have pleased the economists better by not building an iron-works at all, but he did not base his actions solely on economic grounds. The pithead production of iron is around 2 million tons a year.

Chrome is one of Turkey's most lucrative exports. It is mined at Güleman, north-west of Diyarbakır, and at Kütahya, Eskişehir, Denizli, and Marmaris. Production in 1969 was 665,122 tons.

Copper comes from Ergani, near Güleman, and from Hopa, in the extreme north-east. Production (refined) in 1969 was 19,274 tons. Hopa is also the centre of manganese-mining, which is in private hands. Production in 1969 was 25,258 tons.

Bauxite, the ore of aluminium, is found, among other places, at Akseki in the Devil's Mountains, north of the Gulf of Antalya. Production in 1969 was 1,900 tons.

Oil is well known to be Allah's gift to the Arabs and Persians; the Turks have not been so generously treated. Khanzadian's *Atlas de géographie économique de la Turquie*, published in 1924, marks two deposits immediately to the east of Lake Van and mentions another in the province of Erzurum. Some desultory test-borings had been made before the First World War, round the Sea of Marmara and the Gulf of İskenderun, but the results were not encouraging. In the 1930s, however, a systematic exploration was begun, because the industrialization programme was calling for more and more oil, which the shortage of foreign exchange made it difficult to buy abroad. The proximity of the Mosul oilfields gave grounds for hoping that workable deposits might be found within Turkey's eastern borders.

The original exploration was entrusted to a Turkish government agency, the Mineral Research and Exploration Institute (*Maden Tetkik ve Arama Enstitüsü*). Drilling began at Basbirin, some 25 miles north-west of Nusaybin, in 1934 and was continued in that region for several years. After the annexation of Hatay, drilling was also started at two sites there.

The first strike worth mentioning was made in 1940, at Ramandağ, 60 miles due east of Diyarbakır. The oil was found at a depth of 1,060 metres and had to be pumped to the surface for want of natural gas-pressure; still, the results were sufficiently promising for work to continue. Development was understandably slow during the war-years, as at Zonguldak, but as the end of 1947 approached with little to show for so much labour and expense, the Turks wisely brought in expert American help. Within a matter of months several strikes of commercial importance were made, and by mid-1953 nineteen wells were operating there. In 1952 oil was also found at Garzan, 10 miles north-east of Ramandağ.

In November 1952 the Council of Ministers, in accordance with the Democrat policy of denationalization, and profiting by recent experience, decided that the state should not attempt to compete with those better qualified to establish and run an oil industry. A contract was signed with an American firm to build a refinery and operate it for a year, after which time it would be handed over to the Turkish government, who would entrust it to a corporation in which private capital would be encouraged to participate. The site chosen was at Batman, within a few miles of Ramandağ and

Garzan, where a small experimental refinery had already been operating for several years.

In March 1954 a law was enacted allowing foreign firms to prospect for and exploit oil, a right previously reserved to the state. A national petroleum company (TPAO; *Türk Petrolleri Anonim Ortaklığı*) was set up at the same time. In 1960 Mobil made an encouraging strike at Bulgurdağ, 40 miles from Mersin, and the next year Shell found oil near Diyarbakır. But by 1967 Mobil had decided to discontinue their exploration. By the end of 1970 close on 300 test wells had been drilled, 55 by Shell and 122 by TPAO, but few wells were producing as much as 18,000 barrels a day, while in Persia the average daily production is 20,000 and a well there that produces only 10,000 is closed down. Turkish production in 1970 was just below 39 per cent of the country's needs, but this figure was falling, because of a decline in production as well as a rise in consumption. The fact that Shell were still interested, however, offered grounds for optimism. The production of crude oil in 1972 was 3.5 million tons.

(*iv*) *Communications*

The progressive-minded Pasha in Kinglake's *Eothen*, who was so preoccupied with wheels, would have been overjoyed to see the revolution which has come over Turkish transport since his day. The War of Independence showed up the disastrous paucity of roads and railways in Anatolia; when village women had walked over the mountains of the Black Sea coast, humping shells on their backs for the Nationalist guns in the interior.

The establishment of the Republic found the following railways in existence. Istanbul was linked to Europe by the Oriental Railway through Edirne and Sofia. From Haydarpaşa, on the Asian side of the Bosphorus, a line ran south-east, forking at Eskişehir; one line straggling eastward across the plateau to Ankara, the other running through Alayunt (whence a short spur led to Kütahya), then Afyon, Konya, and Adana to Fevzipaşa, throwing out short branches to the ports of Mersin and İskenderun. At Fevzipaşa it turned to cross the present Syrian border for Aleppo. At Muslimiya, between the border and Aleppo, was a junction from which a line came back to Mardin, Nusaybin, and eventually Baghdad.

From Bandırma, on the southern shore of the Sea of Marmara, a line ran to İzmir, sending out a branch from Manisa to Afyon, where, however, it did not connect with the main Istanbul–Baghdad line. From İzmir went the old British-built line to Aydın, Sarayköy, and Eğridir. Bursa was linked by a short line (now disused) to the Marmara port of Mudanya. And that was all, except for a line eastward from Erzurum, built by the Russians during the First World War, of narrow gauge as far as Sarıkamış and Russian broad gauge thereafter.

One of the Republican government's first concerns was to improve rail communications, an obvious prerequisite of any scheme for agrarian or industrial development. A further consideration was that the existing skeletal railway system radiated from Istanbul, whereas in the new Turkey all roads must lead to Ankara. As early as March 1924, funds were voted to construct a line joining the new capital to Kayseri, Sivas, and Samsun, and work began at once. A rail link between Fevzipaşa and Diyarbakır was then decided on, with the avowed purpose of improving access to the copper-mines at Ergani, though the difficulties experienced in moving troops during the Kurdish revolt may have been an additional incentive.

From Irmak, on the Kayseri line 30 miles east of Ankara, a branch was driven north to Karabük and Zonguldak (the mountains close the direct northward route from Ankara itself). This branch, of immense importance for mineral traffic, is called the Filyos line, after the stream in whose valley it runs from Karabük to the sea. A government publication recording the achievements of the first ten years of the Republic was able to say with pride:

> By means of the railways, we are reaching the coal and the copper, we have joined the Mediterranean to the Black Sea, we have reached Balıkesir [by the line built westward from Kütahya], we have passed Sivas. Tomorrow we shall be in Erzurum.

The government was determined not only to build new railways, but also to bring the existing ones under state ownership. At the beginning of the First World War, the German-owned stock in the Baghdad railway had been made over to a Swiss bank, and was therefore beyond the reach of the Reparations Commission. In 1922 a group of British banks came to an understanding with the Swiss and formed a new organization to resume control of the railway. It was when this organization made its purpose known that the Turks resolved to buy the foreigners out. In spite of all the difficulties confronting the young Republic, this aim was eventually achieved; the Istanbul–Konya section became Turkish on 1 January 1928, and the portion from Konya to the Syrian frontier in 1937. Meanwhile, the French-owned Bandırma–İzmir and İzmir–Afyon lines had been purchased in 1934, and in the following year the British-owned İzmir–Eğridir line. By the end of 1947, the last few kilometres of foreign-owned railway had been brought under state ownership.

To find the money (some £15 million sterling) for these purchases, while continuing to build new lines, was no mean feat. But it was done, with Turkish capital and by Turkish engineers, and the State Railways are a credit to the country. The railway reached Erzurum and passed it. The old narrow and broad sections to the Soviet frontier were replaced by standard gauge. By 1970 there were 5,000 miles of track, carrying over a hundred million passengers and close on 14 million tons of freight a year.

On 24 July 1958, the Economic Committee of the Baghdad Pact, now CENTO, announced that work had begun on joining the Turkish and Persian road and rail systems. The rail link was officially opened on 27 September 1971. The work had involved the construction of a dry dock at Tatvan, on the west of Lake Van, to build two ferries to carry the trains across the lake.

The CENTO road was to link south-eastern Turkey to Persia. The section crossing the frontier, from Şivelan (about 30 miles north-east of Hakkâri) to Rezaiye, was opened on 19 June 1966, and the last portion was due to be completed by the end of 1973.

One Turkish invention in the field of transport which other nations might usefully adopt is the *dolmuş*. A *dolmuş* is a taxi, distinctively marked, which plies on a regular route and starts as soon as it has its complement of passengers (the name literally means 'filled'). At busy centres of traffic in the cities there are *dolmuş*-stands, with a sign showing the authorized fares for each run; *dolmuş*-drivers, unlike ordinary cabbies, never haggle about the fare and do not expect tips. During rush-hours there is never a delay of more than a few minutes before the *dolmuş* fills up and moves off.

This mode of travel is cheap and speedy; and even though no driver considers his car full, however small its seating capacity, until it has at least five passengers on board, the occasional discomfort is well worth while. The system operates between towns too; for such long journeys one may book a place in advance.

Part of the city of Istanbul lies in Asia, and the little ferry-steamers of the City Lines carry over a hundred million passengers and about 4.5 million vehicles a year. The monstrous queues of lorries waiting to cross the Bosphorus – some had to wait as much as 24 hours – had always represented a huge loss both to the vehicle-owners and to the general public, because of the traffic problem they created in the busiest part of the city, near the main railway station at Sirkeci. The only solution was to build a bridge over the Bosphorus. Despite the obvious economic and social advantages, the prospect was one which saddened all who loved that most beautiful of waterways, a category including the present author and everyone else who had ever been privileged to see it. After his first sight of the new structure, however, he underwent a total conversion, because the bridge is a beautiful thing in its own right and does not disfigure its setting. Begun on 20 February 1970, it was opened on 30 October 1973.

The chief ports are Istanbul, İzmir, Samsun, Trabzon, İskenderun, and Mersin. Extensive programmes of modernization have been carried out at all of them. Turkey has acquired a considerable share of the Aegean and Mediterranean trade. Well over half the ships putting in at Turkish ports are Turkish-owned, though that is partly because the coasting-trade has been closed to foreign vessels since 1926.

A State Airways organization (*Devlet Hava Yolları*, abbreviated to DHY) was established in 1935 and, through the deficiencies then obtaining in road and rail transport, acquired an immediate popularity. An Englishwoman, nervous of flying, remarked after her first air-trip in Turkey that whereas a Western airliner, full of smart women and elegant men with brief-cases, must be temping to the Fates and is obviously potential headline material, there is something that inspires confidence about the unglamorous sight of a Turkish plane-load of rough-and-ready Anatolian peasant-farmers, who clearly have every intention of reaching intact the place for which they have bought their tickets. In 1956 DHY became a corporation with capital subscribed publicly, and was renamed *Türk Hava Yolları A.O.*, abbreviated THY. In 1971 its fleet comprised nine DC-9 and three Boeing 707 jets and seven Fokker F-27 turbo-props. In addition to the two international airports at Ankara and Istanbul (Esenboğa and Yeşilköy), there are sixteen airports in the country.

(*v*) *The Economy*

The roots of the perennial crisis in the Turkish economy in the 1950s and early 1960s were threefold: the enormous expenditure on defence, the virtual exemption of farmers from taxation, and the irresponsible extravagance of the Democrat Party regime. Inflation was the inevitable consequence.

In July 1962, the OECD set up a consortium to provide aid to

Turkey, the members being the Benelux countries, Canada, France, West Germany, the United States, and the United Kingdom. Meanwhile the Turks had been preparing a Five-Year Plan, under the guidance of Professor Jan Tinbergen of Holland, which began operating at the beginning of 1963. It was to be the first of three plans. It aimed to raise the rate of increase in the Gross National Product from under 5 per cent to 7 per cent, and in fact achieved 6.5 per cent. The private sector leaped ahead, though the state industries, which included some 40 per cent of manufacture and 80 per cent of mining, were not doing so well. The author, whose ignorance of economics is total, will content himself with reporting those few facts and the consensus of his economist friends, namely that the economic situation in 1974 looked reasonably cheerful. The reader who would like to know more than that is referred to the Bibliography.

(*vi*) *Education*

The Law of Unification of Instruction, of 3 March 1924, did not add only the *medreses* to the responsibilities of the Ministry of Education. The Ministry of *Evkaf* had controlled the religious schools created by private Muslim benefactors. The minorities had their own 'non-provided' schools. There were also schools established and controlled by foreign organizations: the admirable American institution, Robert College, for example, and the excellent schools of the Alliance Israélite, which played a great part in spreading French cultural influence throughout the Middle East. Finally, there were private schools, which were subject to no sort of control; some of these performed a useful service, but many followed the educational pattern set by Mr Wackford Squeers.

By bringing all these institutions under a unified control, the Nationalists were in a position to mould the new generation to the shape they wished. Even in the foreign schools, certain subjects, notably history, must be taught by Turkish-born teachers.

Education has always had, after defence, the highest financial priority. Thus in the 1973 budget, which totalled TL61,967 million, defence was given TL11,100 million, education TL10,776 million. Good intentions and hard work have achieved much: in 1935 there were 6,275 primary schools; in 1965 there were 30,466; in 1970 there were 37,243. But the position is not yet satisfactory. On 10 May 1967, the Minister of Education told a Press conference that in 1972 there would be no village without its school and that after that year literacy would be 100 per cent. On 28 April 1973, his successor announced that of the country's 60,000 villages 3,500 had no school. In 1972 the percentage of illiterates in the population aged seven and over was 55. In addition to the difficulties common to all countries with a rapidly increasing population, Turkey is involved in a vicious circle : the villages will never be fit for educated people to live and work in until more educated people go to live and work in the villages. The Village Institutes once seemed capable of breaking the circle. If the authorities genuinely fear that to restore them to existence would mean flooding the countryside with rabid leftists, the remedy is in their own hands, for the Ministry of Education has to approve the curricula of all educational establishments and there are inspectors whose job is to see that the curricula are being taught. It may also be pointed out that there has been no shortage of leftists during recent years, despite the absence of the Village Institutes.

Primary school (*ilkokul*) is compulsory for five years from the age of seven. A leaving-certificate entitles the child to go on to the three-year middle school (*ortaokul*); about 10 per cent of primary-school leavers do this.

About 20 per cent of middle-school leavers go on to high school (*lise*), which is normally for three years, with a choice between arts and sciences after the first year.

Parallel with these there is a range of technical and vocational schools. Primary-teacher training schools take graduates of primary schools for a six-year course, or of middle schools for three. The schools for prayer-leaders and preachers (*imam-hatip*) take primary-school graduates for four years and middle-school graduates for three. The State Conservatoires and the Istanbul Municipal Conservatoire are very much a law unto themselves; if you find yourself with a seven-year-old musical genius on your hands there is no point in making him or her wait five years to begin professional training.

Advanced education is provided by universities and schools of higher education (*yüksek okul*, literally 'high school,' not to be confused with the British and American term for what in Turkish is called *lise*). The capital has three universities : Ankara (founded 1946), Middle East Technical (METU, founded 1956), and Hacettepe (1967). The great gate of Istanbul University bears the proud date 1453, but this is to be taken as a compliment to the love of learning displayed by Mehmed the Conqueror, rather than as the authentic date of the university's foundation. Its oldest faculty can claim unbroken descent from the medical school founded in March 1827 on the initiative of Mahmud II's chief physician, Mustafa Behçet Efendi. Istanbul also has the Technical University (1944) and Bosphorus University (1971). At Erzurum is Atatürk University (1958), at İzmir the Aegean University (1955), and at Trabzon the Black Sea Technical University (1963). For want of teachers the bulk of the lecturing at the last-named has been done by professors from other institutions, mostly Istanbul Technical University, who commute the 700 miles to Trabzon every week, give as many as eighteen lectures in three days, then fly back to Istanbul to do their stint there. Some have been doing this ever since 1963. In the summer term of 1972 they numbered seventy-five, and a scheme was being elaborated whereby these peripatetics would be seconded for a year at a time. It is not surprising that proposals to establish universities at Diyarbakır, Bursa, and Konya have been greeted by Turkish university teachers with something less than enthusiasm.

The shortage of teachers and the pressure on available university places is aggravated by the excessively humane practice of allowing virtually any number of attempts at the final examinations. Thus in the academic year 1966–67 the universities admitted a total of 12,200 freshmen but graduated only 5,867.

(vii) *Administration*

Turkey has a highly professional Civil Service whose members do not change with changes of government. There is a considerable degree of centralization as far as political decisions are concerned, but many non-political matters are dealt with by elected local bodies.

The country is divided into sixty-seven provinces (*vilâyet* or *il*), each under a *Vali* appointed by the Ministry of the Interior. He presides over the General Provincial Assembly, elections to which are held every four years, and over its Standing Committee, which examines the provincial budget; it also approves plans for public works and may take decisions on urgent administrative matters, subject to subsequent ratification by the Assembly. The latter, with the *Vali*'s approval, may raise loans for public works, health, and education within the province.

The divisions (*kaza* or *ilçe*) and subdivisions (*nahiye* or *bucak*) of each province also have their centrally appointed administrators (*Kaymakam* and *Müdür* respectively) and their elected local councils.

The smallest administrative unit is the village. The Village Council is made up of all residents of six months' standing and at least eighteen years of age. It elects the headman (*Muhtar*), the prayer-leader (*İmam*), and the Council of Elders. The latter body decides the amount of tax each villager is to pay for local expenses, and also has juridical powers: it settles disputes among villagers and may impose small fines.

(*viii*) *Justice*

The jury system does not exist in Turkey. The 'Basic' Courts consist, in principle, of a presiding judge and two assessors, but minor cases may be settled by one judge sitting alone. Petty cases, civil and criminal, are decided by Peace Courts, with one judge. In many places the Basic Court is combined with the Peace Court. Free legal aid is given to those who need it.

Labour Courts settle disputes between employers and employed and between the Workers' Insurance Association and the workman or his next-of-kin. They consist of a Basic Court judge and an elected representative of each of the two sides of industry.

The Court of Appeal automatically reviews decisions involving fifteen years' imprisonment or the death penalty. It does not reverse the decisions of lower courts; it either confirms them or sends them back for retrial.

There is a separate system of administrative courts with jurisdiction over appeals against tax-assessments and over disciplinary measures against government servants. Administrative suits are initiated before the Council of State. This also acts as a court of appeal for the lower administrative courts and has jurisdiction in suits alleging government liability or seeking restitution of rights violated by administrative action.

Reference has already been made to ill-treatment by the police of people in custody, usually for the purpose of eliciting information about accomplices. Leaving aside the question whether everyone who is in prison deserves to be, it may be said that the treatment of convicts in prison is generally humane and that amnesties are not infrequent. Experiments are being made with open prisons, and unskilled prisoners can be taught a trade. The Public Prosecutor's office and the labour exchanges co-operate to find jobs for discharged prisoners.

As a conclusion to this section there may be mentioned an ex-bandit of the author's acquaintance. His parents persuaded him to give himself up and they petitioned the governor of his native province on his behalf, pleading that he was a good boy who had been led astray by bad companions. The governor pardoned him and found him a job as a building foreman in another part of the country. When last seen by the author, late in 1972, he was working hard and well at his new trade.

CHAPTER 21

Summing up

TURKEY IS A going concern. The reader will understand the force of this remark if he has ever felt the naïve wonder one sometimes experiences when visiting certain foreign countries, about whether the policemen ever get paid and whether anyone cares if the ten o'clock train starts before noon or starts at all. Turkish policemen are paid and Turkish trains run on time.

But, given that nearly two-thirds of the people live in villages and that the average population of the village is under 600, it is not surprising that visitors from more heavily industrialized countries sometimes go away with the impression of two nations. There is the urban Turkey of the theatres, the smart cafés, and the literary reviews, and there is the rural Turkey with its primitive housing, its brutalizing toil, and its still fairly appalling illiteracy. The importance of this duality, which can be matched in every country with a largely peasant population, should not be exaggerated. Moreover, the Turks, who are as ready to criticize themselves as they are to resent criticism from outsiders (though they heed it), are fully aware of the shortcomings of the villages and are doing something about it; witness the fact that whereas in 1965 there were 30,000 miles of roads linking villages to main highways, in 1968 there were 103,780 miles. Where the 'two nations' idea falls down is that children of peasant families can and do have access to higher education. If one talks to businessmen or civil servants or university teachers and asks them where they come from, the answers are liable to be place-names from anywhere on the map of Turkey. Fifty years ago the answers would have been very different; most of the important people would have been born either in Istanbul or in whatever corner of the empire their fathers happened to be governing. It is worth remembering that Turkey has no tradition of class-prejudice. After all, many of the great men of the Ottoman empire in the days of its glory were slaves. The first Grand Vizier of the Köprülü family started life as a scullion. An earlier Grand

Vizier, İbrahim Pasha, who held office under Süleyman the Magnificent for thirteen years, had been brought to Turkey as a boy, a captive of the Barbary corsairs. Although his enemies might criticize him for his arrogance, none thought to blame him for being the son of a common Italian sailor. So nowadays the children of villagers can and do rise to high positions in the Republic, and nobody cares who their fathers were. The professor does not think of himself as belonging to a different order of creation from the janitor; the professor has his duties and the janitor has his duties, and each is entitled to respect from the other in the measure of his performance of those duties.

Political observers abroad, when dealing with Turkey, may mislead themselves and others when they talk about the importance of the peasant vote. What is important about it is that it exists; that in the last twenty years the peasant has come to understand that once every four years his mark on a piece of paper can unseat the mighty, if the mighty have not done the job he sent them to Ankara to do. But anyone who thinks that the peasant vote is a uniform entity, and that the peasants all over the country will vote for the same party, is not going to be a very accurate political prophet.

Nor is it correct to suppose that the peasants are the embodiment of religious reaction. One is more likely to meet fanaticism in the cities, among the small shopkeepers and tradesmen, but it is everywhere the exception and nowhere the rule. Here is an instructive story that came out of Hayrabolu, a tiny town in Thrace, 40 miles south-east of Edirne. The Muslim clerics of the region decided, in June 1968, that they would no longer officiate at the funerals of people who drank alcohol, nor would they attend the religious ceremonies preceding a civil marriage (the only sort the law recognizes) if alcohol was to be given to the guests. The local taxi-drivers thereupon declared a counter-boycott: they would no longer accept these clerics as passengers, but would provide free transport for any cleric who ignored the ban. This action received a good deal of popular support and was endorsed by fourteen local organizations, including the Women's Union, the Anti-Tuberculosis League, the Young People's Sports Club, and the Oil-seed Co-operative, who staged a silent protest march and distributed a manifesto. The four clerics who had been primarily responsible were publicly denounced for 'outraging national and religious sentiment'. After two weeks of this, the ban was called off.

There is a surprising consistency about the attitude to religion of each successive Turkish government, whatever its complexion. In the first place, they all make more concessions to religious opinion than the out-and-out secularists would like. The Ankara correspondent of *The Times* wrote (27 May 1966):

> For all Turkish political parties the abuse of religion in order to win votes is like some sort of secret vice: it is fatally easy. A pious look, a promise to build a new mosque in a village, the ostentatious use of the word 'Allah', or the keeping of the Ramazan fast, all these are worth thousands of votes at election time. In this deadly sin the Justice Party, like its predecessor the Democratic Party, is generally considered to be the worst offender.

Even the National Unity Committee was not guiltless: it donated to two religious training-schools the proceeds of the sale of official photographs and films of the trials of the fallen Democrats. But there is another side to the picture. Every government, even that of the Democrat Party, has taken care to restrain any manifestation of religious extremism that might damage the foundations of the secular state. The occasional fanatics who proclaimed that only a restoration of the Caliphate could solve Turkey's problems got as short shrift from Menderes as they got from İnönü (though perhaps not so short as they would have got from Atatürk). Every politician knows that only so long as the dichotomy of religion and state is preserved can the Republic endure as its founder conceived it and as the majority of its thinking people, literate or otherwise, wish it to be.

The position of women has vastly changed in the Republican period. Legally they suffer from fewer disabilities than do their sisters in some democracies far older than Turkey. There is one rate of pay for the job, regardless of the sex of the person doing it. Women have the vote and can be elected to public office, including the Presidency of the Republic. The building of Atatürk's mausoleum was supervised by a woman engineer, and a woman architect was responsible for the restoration of Mehmed the Conqueror's fortress of Rumeli Hisar on the Bosphorus. In March 1971 Dr Türkân Akyol became Turkey's first woman cabinet minister; she was Minister of Health, but lost her place in a cabinet reshuffle that December and went back to being a professor in the Medical Faculty at Ankara. In January 1973 for the first time a woman became head of a Turkish university: Saffet Rıza Alpar, the sixty-nine-year-old Professor of Industrial Chemistry at Trabzon, was appointed Rector. In May 1973 Nermin Neftçi became the first woman Deputy Speaker of the National Assembly. But to prolong the list of such eminent women is to miss the point, which is that any ordinary girl who wants a job can get one. That is the test of emancipation, not the fact that a highly-talented or highly-placed woman may manage to gatecrash some masculine preserve. Two exceptions should be noted : there are virtually no waitresses and there are few women in the diplomatic career. But that, as a wise old journalist named Burhan Felek once said, is perhaps as it should be, 'because women are more sensitive and sincere than men, and so much openheartedness is no qualification for diplomacy'.

It would be conveying a false impression to suggest that all Turkish males accept the emancipation of women, any more than all West European males. Volkan Şölen, who teaches soil science in the Istanbul Faculty of Forestry, tells how for a brief period in 1967 she was a practising forester. The first day, she noticed that the labourers seemed rather unhappy and were clearly not putting their backs into their work. On the second day they would not work at all. When she asked what was wrong, they hung their heads and would not answer. She persisted and eventually one of them replied : 'Don't be vexed with us, Ma'am, but it comes hard to take orders from a woman'. The third day none of them turned up for work, and Dr Şölen decided to switch to teaching.

Nor would it be right to imply that all Turkish women are equally emancipated. In rural areas it is still the regular practice for an intending husband to pay brideprice to the girl's father. It was reported from Sivas in 1964 that a villager had been trying for two years to find a girl or widow to marry at a brideprice he could afford. In Sivas province not even a widow was available for less than TL3,000. So he had abandoned hope of finding what he wanted at Sivas and was moving on to Tokat. On the other hand, in the next year three hundred villagers, representing one hundred villages in Kayseri province, attended a meeting to discuss brideprice; they agreed that they could not find husbands for their daughters because the prevailing level of brideprice was too high. They then swore to abide by the decision taken at the meeting, which was to freeze the price at TL3,000 for a previously unmarried girl. Information is lacking about how the situation has changed since then.

There is still some polygamy, which cannot be quantified. The census of 1945, when few Turks were working abroad, showed 97,357 more married women than married men, and one could reasonably use that as a guide to the sort of numbers involved. The 1965 census showed 138,109 more married women than married men, but in view of the mass emigration of workers in the 1960s and 1970s, it would be unscientific to use this figure as the basis for any conclusion about the existence of polygamy. What is sure is that although the law recognizes only civil marriage and civil divorce, in country districts, particularly in the east, marriages are still contracted in front of the imam in accordance with Islamic practice, which allows a man up to four wives at a time, while divorce is still in the old Islamic form of repudiation. The following table[1] shows the number of marriages and divorces and the number of marriages per thousand of population for nine provinces in 1968. The first three are those which contain the three principal cities. The second three are situated in the west of Anatolia, the last three in the east.

Province	*Population*	*Marriages*	*Marriages per 1,000*	*Divorces*
Ankara	1,852,000	8,993	4.8	630
Istanbul	2,551,000	19,406	7.6	2,011
İzmir	1,338,000	8,035	6.0	694
Afyon	526,700	1,774	3.4	233
Aydın	559,200	2,098	3.8	382
Burdur	203,400	648	3.1	146
Ağrı	266,000	114	0.43	12
Bingöl	163,900	73	0.45	5
Hakkâri	94,240	33	0.35	4

Lest it be thought that by some odd chance people in the east just don't marry, a rough calculation of the percentages of married people in the population aged fourteen and over in one province within each group gave the following result: İzmir 63.1; Burdur 73.1; Hakkâri 67.7.

It is sometimes said that Turkish authorities tend to do everything strictly by the book, so one example of their flexibility and humanity deserves to be noted in this context: every few years the Assembly quietly passes a law to legitimize illegitimate children, the majority of the beneficiaries being the offspring of 'imam-marriages'. But it is known that some bigamists contract a civil marriage with one wife and have her registered as the mother of all their children, thus achieving a do-it-yourself legitimization.

And what are the Turks like? Their manner is reserved. It is possible to travel by train right across Anatolia with no more risk of being spoken to by the other occupants of the compartment than there would be in England; hence, perhaps the old appraisal of the Turk as 'the Englishman of the East'. When they are having a party, at the stage in the evening where even the English would be singing, Turks recite poetry. They do not generally present so broadly-smiling a face to the world as do some of their neighbours; they have a steadiness and a dignity, that *gravitas* on which the Romans prided themselves and which is not at all the same as gravity. It is a product of 600 years of empire, 600 years of knowing that if they made the wrong move the barbarians might break through and the world collapse. Hospitality and courtesy to the stranger are part of one's duty as a human being. If a tourist's car is surrounded by a swarm of laughing and pushing children, it takes only one fourteen-year-old boy or girl to say *Ayip!* ('Shame!' and send them scurrying. Turkey is the only country in the author's experience where the proprietor of a small hotel utterly refused to present his bill to a departing traveller, whom he had never seen before or was likely to see again, saying 'Please! You are our guest'.

Because Turks do not laugh much in public, 'dour' is an adjective that is often applied to them, as to the Scots; and like the Scots they are said to have no sense of humour. Shades of Nasreddin Hoja and Compton Mackenzie! One cannot help mentioning at least an informal gathering of civil servants in Ankara at which there was some discussion of a proposed American expedition to Mount Ararat, with equipment for melting the ice and snow off the timbers of Noah's Ark. Most of those present expressed more or less ribald scepticism, though one pointed out that if by any mad chance the Ark really were there, it would make Ararat the biggest tourist attraction in the world. A senior official shook his head gravely and observed: 'I'm worried that it will lead to a spate of offences against the Forestry Law. Once the locals start up their souvenir-shops, we won't have a tree left standing'.

Another obvious characteristic is over-sensitivity. In the Turkish translation of *Macbeth* the witches' cauldron contains neither nose of Turk nor Tartar's lips. 'Turk-disparagement' is an offence in Turkish law. On the other hand, any word of praise for Turks or Turkish institutions, however ill-informed, is sure of the widest publicity. 'How will this look to the foreigner?' is a question they constantly ask themselves. Despite President Johnson's unpopularity with Turks after the incident of his letter, Demirel circulated at the conference where he successfully competed with Bilgiç for the chairmanship of the Justice Party a photograph of himself taken with LBJ. There are still some people who believe that it favourably affected his chances; even if they are wrong, Demirel at least must have thought it would help.

By way of corollary to this attitude is the indignation Turks tend to feel when the foreigner does not live up to the high standard of civilized behaviour they expect of him. In 1965 a columnist wrote about 'the new breed of beggars who play guitars to collect money and who exhibit signs reading "Help an artist to see the world" '. What infuriated the writer most was that these people were called tourists. 'They're not what I understand by "tourist". I call a tourist a person who arrives in our country by air, and hires a Cadillac during his stay at the Hilton'. The indignation can go a little too far. In 1967 a newspaper published, under the heading 'This too is a tourist!', a photograph of an amiable-looking policeman with arm outstretched, obviously giving directions to a neat and short-haired though bearded young man. The caption ran:

> With the coming of spring the tourist invasion has begun. Besides the tourists of quality, who reserve accommodation in hotels and leave a good deal of currency in the country, the flea-bitten adventurous desperadoes have also started to put in an appearance. Our picture shows one of the flea-bitten tourists being cautioned by a policeman.

Since then, however, the realization has dawned that 'tourist' is not synonymous with 'millionaire', and reasonably-priced hotels are springing up all over Turkey. So why multiply words? The reader interested enough to follow the author thus far should consider going and seeing for himself what the Turks are like. He will find not the Terrible Turk, not the Lazy Turk, but a friendly decent soul trying, like the rest of us, to make an honest living in this troubled and confusing world. And he will find a country beautiful beyond all description.

NOTE

[1] Extracted from *Marriage Statistics 1968* and *Divorce Statistics 1968*, both published by the State Institute of Statistics, Ankara, 1969.

Bibliography

(The place of publication is London unless otherwise indicated.)

On the earliest history: René Giraud, *L'Empire des Turcs célestes* (Paris, 1960) and Sir Gerard Clauson, 'The early history of the Turkish-speaking tribes', in his *Turkish and Mongolian Studies* (1962).

For the origin and nature of the Ottoman dynasty: Paul Wittek, *The Rise of the Ottoman Empire* (1938). Though the author is a little too kind to Tamerlain, this is an outstanding work which shows that historical research can be as exciting as any detective story. Then comes Halil Inalcik, *The Ottoman Empire: The Classical Age 1300–1600* (1973). Thereafter there is not much to recommend except the antiquated Stanley Lane-Poole, *Turkey* (1888) and Edward S. Creasy, *History of the Ottoman Turks* (1878; reprinted Beirut, 1963), until we get to the nineteenth century: Şerif Mardin, *The Genesis of Young Ottoman Thought* (Princeton, 1962), Roderic H. Davison, *Reform in the Ottoman Empire 1856–1876* (Princeton, 1963), and, invaluable for the early twentieth century too, Bernard Lewis, *The Emergence of Modern Turkey* (Oxford, 1968). The long article 'Turkey; history' in *Encylopaedia Britannica*, which is the work of a succession of contributors over the centuries, is useful for facts and dates. To put flesh on the bare bones: Raphaela Lewis, *Everyday Life in the Ottoman Empire* (1971).

The titles of the following works sufficiently indicate their nature: Feroz Ahmad, *The Young Turks; the Committee of Union and Progress in Turkish politics 1908–1914* (Oxford, 1969); George S. Harris, *The Origins of Communism in Turkey* (Stanford, 1967); Allan Cunningham, 'The Wrong Horse? – A study of Anglo-Turkish relations before the First World War', in Albert Hourani (ed.), *Middle Eastern Affairs* (St Antony's Papers No. 17,

Oxford, 1965); Edward Weisband, *Turkish Foreign Policy 1943–1945* (Princeton, 1973). All of these are warmly recommended, as are the following.

Clement H. Dodd, *Politics and Government in Turkey* (Manchester, 1969). Suna Kili, *Turkish Constitutional Developments and Assembly Debates on the Constitutions of 1924 and 1961* (Istanbul, 1971).

H. C. Armstrong, *Grey Wolf* (1945), is to be taken with a grain of salt, entertaining though it is; Mustafa Kemal was not the snarling schizophrene the author would have us think. Incomparably superior is Lord Kinross, *Atatürk: The Rebirth of a Nation* (1964).

For the geography: J. C. Dewdney, *Turkey* (1971) and W. C. Brice, *South-West Asia* (1966). For the economy: Z. Y. Hershlag, *Turkey, the Challenge of Growth* (Leiden, 1968); J. P. C. Carey and A. G. Carey, 'Turkish agriculture and the five-year development plans', in *International Journal of Middle East Studies* III (1972); Peter Mansfield (ed.), *The Middle East: A Political and Economic Survey* (1973).

SOME TURKISH PLACE-NAMES

(In the left-hand column of the following table are the modern equivalents of the older names, shown in the right-hand column.)

Ankara	Angora
Antakya	Antioch
Antalya	Adalia
Bergama	Pergamum
Beyoğlu	Pera
Bodrum	Halicarnassus
Bursa	Brusa
Edirne	Adrianople
Elâzığ	Mamuret-el-Aziz
Gaziantep	Aintab, Antep
Hatay	Alexandretta
İstanbul	Constantinople
İzmir	Smyrna
İzmit	Ismid, Nicomedia
İznik	Nicaea
Kadıköy	Chalcedon
Kayseri	Kaisarieh, Caesarea
Kırklareli	Kirk Kilisseh
Malazgirt	Manzikert
Selânik	Salonica
Tekirdağ	Rodosto
Trabzon	Trebizond
Üsküdar	Scutari
Yeşilköy	San Stefano

Map of TURKEY showing principal places mentioned in the text.

Boundary of the Republic

Vilayet boundaries

Railways

●...... Chief town of Vilayet

o....... Other places

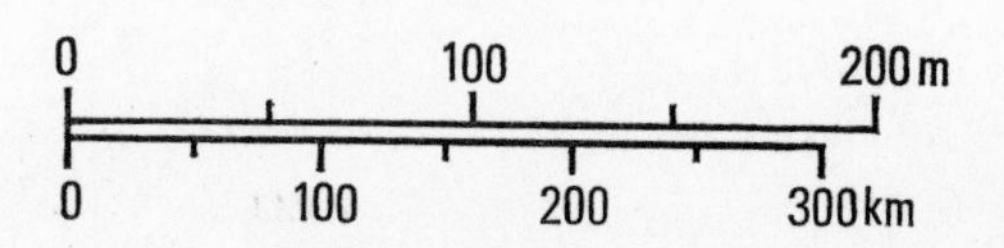

Turkey and her neighbours

ZONGULDAK
Filyos
Cide
İnebolu
SİNOP
Azdavay
Bafra
SAMSUN
Karabük
KASTAMONU
Ereğli
BOLU
ÇANKIRI
Yeşil Irmak
AMASYA
Kızıl Irmak
ÇORUM
TOKAT
R. Sakarya
ANKARA
Boğazköy
SİVAS
YOZGAT
Gordium
Polatlı
KIRŞEHİR
Tuz Gölü
NEVŞEHİR
Ürgüp
KAYSERİ
Akşehir
Aksaray
NİĞDE
KONYA
MARAŞ
Ulukişla
R. Seyhan
R. Ceyhan
Ereğli
GAZİ
Akseki
Karaman
ADANA
Fevzipaşa
Tarsus
Manavgat
Mersin
İskenderun
İÇEL
HATAY
Alanya
Antakya
Anamur

Turkey and her neighbours

Index

English alphabetical order has been followed, without regard to accents and diacritical marks. For political parties in the Republican period, see under parties, political. *Treaties, Pacts, etc., are listed chronologically under* treaties and international agreements, *except for Lausanne, which is indexed separately.*

Printed in Great Britain by
The Garden City Press Limited, Letchworth, Hertfordshire, SG6 1JS